The Behavioral Development
of Free-Living
Chimpanzee Babies and Infants

MONOGRAPHS ON INFANCY

Lewis P. Lipsitt, Editor

The Behavioral Development of Free-Living Chimpanzee Babies and Infants

By Frans X. Plooij

Department of Developmental Psychology
University of Nijmegen, The Netherlands

with:
Drawings by David Bygott
Foreword by Gene P. Sackett

ABLEX PUBLISHING CORPORATION
Norwood, New Jersey 07648

Printed in the United States of America.

Library of Congress Cataloging in Publication Data

Plooij, Frans X.
    The behavioral development of free-living chimpanzee babies and
infants.

    (Monographs on infancy)
    Bibliography: p
    Includes indexes.
    1. Chimpanzees-Behavior.   2. Animals—Infancy of.
3. Mammals—Behavior.   I. Title.   II. Series.
QL737.P96P57   1982   599.88'440451   83-25804
ISBN 0-89391-115-1

ABLEX PUBLISHING CORPORATION
355 Chestnut Street
Norwood, New Jersey 07648

Contents

Preface

Lewis P. Lipsitt

With the appearance of this volume on the free-ranging behavior of chimpanzee infants, our eagerness to publish scholarly monographs on animal infant behavior and development, as well as human infancy, is evident. We are delighted that Frans X. Plooij has chosen to publish his important work, with its elegant observations and measurements of chimpanzee behavior in the field, as our first offering on animal infancy in the *Monographs on Infancy*. It is a special pleasure, too, to produce a volume with such handsome visual displays as those provided by Dr. Plooij's colleague, Dr. David Bygott. As Professor Gene P. Sackett suggests in his Foreword, this is pioneering, exciting work. The painstakingly gathered data provide us with a richer understanding of the behavioral repertoire and developmental characteristics of the chimpanzee, and at the same time increase our comprehension of human development. It has been a great pleasure to cooperate with Dr. Plooij in bringing his work to fruition.

The *Monographs* constitute one component of a tripartite publishing program on infancy begun in 1978 by Ablex Publishing Corporation under my editorial direction. Another part is the journal, *Infant Behavior and Development,* in its sixth volume as this monograph appears, and under the Editorship of Carolyn Rovee-Collier. The third part is the *Advances in Infancy Research,* the first annual volume of which appeared in 1981.

The relatively brief research articles appearing in the journal are nicely complemented, we hope, by the two other styles of publication. The *Advances* are intended for intermediate size manuscripts which are critical syntheses of specialized research areas, usually capitalizing upon, but not limited to, the results of the authors' own programmatic research. The *Advances* are intended as collations of data and inferences, not principally as repositories of primary data which are best submitted to journals. The *Monographs,* on the other hand, are for longer manuscripts and usually will report original data. They are also for reports of extended research programs and collaborations. All three publication styles involve editorial scrutiny, including judgments of research experts other than the Editor. In the *Monographs* series, comments by other experts in the area circumscribed by the Monographs are solicited to provide the basis of a Foreword or of a concluding Commentary or both.

We welcome and will provide a serious review of good innovative ideas that report or promote progress in the scientific study of infant behavior and development. We will not be bound by any traditions that do not yet exist. Our policy is to attract and publish high quality manuscripts.

Lewis P. Lipsitt, Editor
Department of Psychology, and
Child Study Center
Brown University
Providence, R. I. 02912

Foreword

Gene P. Sackett
University of Washington

The study of behavioral development is probably the most complex and difficult research in biobehavioral and social science. Understanding development involves an understanding of evolutionary-genetic, physiological-anatomical, and social-ecological processes which interact on variable time schedules to produce changes in motor behavior and adaptive competence. For primate species, steady progress has been made in describing normative developmental courses of specific motor behaviors, as well as perceptual, cognitive, and social skills and abilities. However, less progress has occurred in integrating knowledge about genetic, structural, and behavioral mechanisms through testable theories that can be modified by new data and better experiments and research methods. I found the data, research methods, and thought in this monograph exciting because it does present the skeleton for just such an operationalized theory of human and nonhuman primate development.

Plooij's study began with quantitative observation of motor response development and its social-ecological context in six chimpanzee babies. Using comparative-ethological methods in a natural African environment, Plooij describes the induction (initial appearance) and facilitation (subsequent change or lack of change) of motor acts in the repertoire of each individual animal, observed for periods of several months to several years. Using these case study descriptions, Plooij addresses the basic question of what organizational processes determined the observed course of development in these babies. Comparisons presented between human and chimpanzee babies identify compelling similarities in development, which suggests that the theory offered to explain the descriptive findings should be useful for both human and nonhuman primates.

Plooij's theory is based on a hierarchical systems control feedback model originally proposed by Powers. Although hierarchical systems do seem to fit many facts of development, I must admit to finding them often rather incomprehensible and always ad hoc when applied to prediction of specific aspects of development. However, in Plooij's hands I have been presented for perhaps the first time with clear behavioral operational definitions identifying hierarchical levels of perceptual-cognitive-motor competence. Most importantly, these definitions lead to empirical tests for the induction and facilitation of new levels of control. This is accomplished by postulating a deceptively simple perceptual control system involving the regulation and processing of sensory stimuli through either perceptually undifferentiated or differentiated mechanisms. Which type of mechanism operates developmentally depends on maturation level interacting with situational-social contexts. The result of all this is a testable theory whose validity will depend on both behavioral and neuroanatomical-physiological evidence.

The utility of the theory can be seen at even its simplest proposed level of hierarchical organization. In newborns, it is assumed that only two levels of control determine variability in motor responses. The first, and lower, order of control involves intensity discrimination with no ability to differentiate sensations from different modalities. Thus, all receptor sources feed into a summed intensity value with no qualitative distinctions in sensation. In essence, this first order of control concerns intermodal equivalence. The second order of control—the only higher order available to newborns— involves behaviors serving to adjust intensity changes about "ideal" perceptual set values serving to regulate basic physiological processes such as temperature, feeding, and arousal as reflected in sleep-wakefulness cyclicity. Although these ideas are not unique, their integration into a predictive theory may be.

Let us consider two findings concerning human newborns. First, until about 2–3 months of age babies generally fail to prefer novel over familiar patterned visual stimuli, although a preference for stimuli differing in intensity can be demonstrated. This is exactly what should happen if intensity changes are the only dimension affecting the regulation of input by motor behaviors. Second, consider the controversial recent findings that very young human babies show differential looking directed at 3-dimensional visual stimuli based on the correspondence between the shape of the visual stimuli and the shape of oral-tactual stimulation from sucking on a pacifier. This could occur by at least two mechanisms. The baby could process the sensory information from a round-smooth pacifier or one with raised nubs in terms of form; and when presented with a round-smooth versus nubbed visual stimulus, it could match the tactual and visual form information. In this case, the baby would be performing true intermodal matching on a higher level dimension independent of modality. On the other hand, and as predicted from Plooij's theory, the different oral-tactually experienced shapes could elicit different stimulus intensities, which are matched or approximated by the intensities elicited from the visual shapes. In this case, behavior is being determined by intermodal intensity equivalence—a primary attribute of any sensory modality. This interpretation seems preferable, as there is little or no evidence for true intermodal matching in either human or nonhuman primate newborns.

Anyway, enough said about my own reasons for excitement over this work. My hope is that readers with either evolutionary, biological, or psychological interests in development will also see some things worthwhile here; and that these ideas will lead to a more constructive attack on fundamental problems of development concerning continuities and discontinuities produced by processes at all levels of analysis.

Gene P. Sackett
Seattle, Washington

Acknowledgments

The data on which this publication is based were collected in the Gombe National Park, Tanzania, at the Gombe Stream Research Center. I am grateful to the Ministry of Natural Resources in Dar es Salaam and to the Director of National Parks for allowing me to work in the Gombe National Park. I am also grateful to Dr. Jane Goodall for allowing me to use the facilities of the Gombe Stream Research Center which enabled me to carry out my project.

This research would have been impossible without the initial encouragement of Dr. H. Albrecht. Invaluable help and support throughout the project were given by Dr. H.C.J. Oomen, professor of Animal Ecology at the Catholic University of Nijmegen, and Dr. G.P. Baerends, professor of Ethology and Ecology at the University of Groningen. I would like to express appreciation to Drs. H.W. Lissmann and P.P.G. Bateson, and to Dr. R.A. Hinde for welcoming me as a guest to the Sub-Department of Animal Behaviour, University of Cambridge, England. I should like to thank Dr. G.P. Baerends, Dr. R.A. Hinde, Dr. H.H.C. van de Rijt-Plooij, and Dr. M.J.A. Simpson for their tireless and imaginative advice, suggestions, and criticism throughout the analysis and writing of this work. I am indebted to Dr. J.D. Bygott, Dr. A.R. Cools, Dr. J. Hanby, Dr. A. Kortlandt, Mr. F. Marcelissen, Dr. M. Riksen-Walraven, Dr. D. Shapiro, Dr. A. Smitsman, Dr. C. Snow, and Mr. F. Veldman for many stimulating and constructive discussions.

I would especially like to thank Dr. J.D. Bygott for making the line-drawings with which this publication is illustrated. I am grateful to Dr. E.E. Shillito of the A.R.C. Institute of Animal Physiology at Babraham, Cambridge, and to Dr. C. Clarke of the Veterinarian School of Cambridge for kindly permitting me the use of their Sonographs. Furthermore, I am also grateful to Dr. W.H. Thorpe and Dr. J. Hall-Graggs for kindly allowing me the use of their melograph, as well as their Nagra-recorder at various times.

The facilities of the Psychological Laboratory, University of Nijmegen, Netherlands,* were made available to me in the final stages of writing this work through the good will of Dr. F.J. Mönks, Professor of Developmental Psychology. I would like to thank all people of the audio-visual service department of this laboratory, and in particular Mr. G. Bes, Mr. Th. van Haaren, Mr. F. Mooren, and Mrs. I. ten Brink for their help in editing audio-tapes and their production of the graphs and figures. I am also grateful to Mrs. C. Kerbusch-McKelly for typing parts of the manuscript.

This research was financially supported by the Netherlands Foundation for the Advancement of Tropical Research (WOTRO grant no. W84-66), and the Dr. J.L. Dobberke Stichting voor Vergelijkende Psychologie.

---

* The author's present address is: Gemeentelijk Pedotherapeutisch Inst., Amsterdams Pedologisch Centrum, Ijsbaanpad 9, 1076 CV Amsterdam, The Netherlands.
Manuscript received October 1980; accepted December 1981 ■

1

Introduction and Study Aims

THE PROBLEM

My ultimate interest was and is the development of human babies. I believe, however, that the study of the development of behavior in nonhuman species is of great help in understanding the development of human behavior. Knowledge of a wide variety of other species in general, and of living primates in particular, enables one to place the knowledge of our own species in a much wider, evolutionary framework. This leads to recognition of aspects of human behavior which otherwise would have remained unnoticed. I know this from my own experience, since after studying chimpanzee babies and infants I began studying human babies in interaction with their mothers (Plooij, 1978b). Several of these aspects will be discussed in the various chapters of this book. They also appear from a study of contact between mother and offspring in a wide variety of mammal species by Blurton Jones (1972a).

In his study Blurton Jones (1972a) thoroughly discussed the essentials of the comparative method. Among other things he stressed that it may be dangerous to start comparing the behavior of two or more species before it has been shown that these species belong to the same taxonomic group on other than behavioral grounds. Chimpanzee and man have been shown to be very closely related on anatomical, biochemical, and immunological grounds (see King & Wilson, 1975 and Zihlman et al., 1978).

After it has been shown that two species are closely related, not only the behavioral similarities should be established, but also the differences and the species-specific characteristics should be appreciated. The latter are all the more important, since it has been shown, recently, that chimpanzees and man share similarities in many more aspects than were hitherto suspected. Attributes such as consciousness (Griffin, 1976; Shafton, 1976) and language (Fouts, 1973; Gardner & Gardner, 1969, 1978; Laidler, 1978; Patterson, 1978 a, b; Plooij, 1978a; Premack, 1971; Rumbaugh et al., 1973)

1

may not be so uniquely human after all. Or, in Bruner's (1978, p. viii) words, many gaps are bridged

> that before were not so much empty as they were filled with corrosive dog-matism. The gaps between prelinguistic communication and language proper as the child develops, the gap between gesture and word, between holo-phrases and sentences, between chimps signing and man talking, between sign languages and spoken ones, between the structure of action and the structure of language.

Therefore, more specifically speaking, studying the early development of behavior in chimpanzees and making comparisons with research on human infancy can make a real contribution to the knowledge of the onto-genetic development of our own species.

The subject of the ontogenetic development of the organization under-lying behavior is very old indeed. Kortlandt (1955) has given a review of the major opinions on the subject, going as far back as Aristotle. Limiting my-self to this century, there seem to be two opposing lines of thought:

1. Ascending development proceeds through the emergence of isolated units followed by an ascending integration into a hierarchy.
2. Differentiation development proceeds from the beginning through the progressive expansion of a perfectly integrated unity and the in-dividuation within it of parts which acquire various degrees of dis-creteness.

As examples of differentation the works of Coghill (1929), Humphrey (1969), Condon (1979), Koffka (1924), Bower (1974, 1978), and Bower and Wishart (1979) may be mentioned. Coghill's (1929) study of the embryology of behavior in the newt Amblystoma showed that movement patterns of various body parts develop in accordance with the differentiation concept. This is true for the human fetus as well: Humphrey (1969) showed that the very first response observed in fetuses of 8.5 weeks menstrual age (26 mm long) is the so-called "total pattern reflex" (the beginning of which is ob-served one week earlier in the bending of the head to one side). The response involves the organism as a whole (neck, trunk, pelvis, arms, mouth). For in-stance, movements of the mouth and the arms are dominated by the trunk musculature and form an integral part of the total pattern. Only later do they more or less acquire discreteness. A further increase in discreteness was found in the facial musculature (innervated by the seventh cranial nerve). As soon as there is reflex action of these muscles, some of the background movements of smiling and laughing may appear in the human fetus, but the movements are very crude because the muscles themselves are not well dif-ferentiated (Humphrey, 1969). In fetuses of 18 to 29 weeks the muscles and the nerves innervating them are so developed and differentiated that the facial movements observed can be related to the same discrete muscle actions as in adults (Oster, 1978; Oster & Ekman, 1978). The fact that mouth- and arm-musculature initially form an integral part of a total pattern is still evident, early postnatally, in the synchronized sucking- and hand-movements. In my study of newborn human babies which was mentioned earlier (Plooij, 1978b, in preparation) many examples of this total unity are observed. For instance, the movements of one arm mirror the movements of the other arm. Even a blink of the eyes is mirrored in a movement of the feet. These observations are in line with Condon's (1979) finding of self-synchrony in human newborns. The perfectly integrated unity does not only apply to behavior patterns. As Coghill (1929) has pointed out, according to the "Gestalt" school of psychology (Koffka, 1924, pp. 131 ff.) perception is also a total unity from the beginning. The recent "unitary theory of development" by Bower and Wishart (1979) also stresses this aspect.

As an example of the ascending type of development the work of Kortlandt (1940 a, b, 1955) on the development of behavior in cormorants should be mentioned. In the period of 2–7 weeks after hatching (and after the leg movements have become integrated into simple locomotory patterns enabling the bird to creep on its belly) a number of isolated behavior units emerge such as twig-quivering, munching fish, walking, and flying. After a period of relative rest (7–8 weeks), these isolated behavior units become integrated into functional sequences. For instance, while walking and climbing, the birds collect twigs in order to insert them in their own nest (nest-building behavior). Or, the birds perform hunting and capturing behavior followed by eating.

In the domain of animal behavior Hinde (1970) reviewed the development of motor patterns and the integration of discrete types of behavior into functional sequences. Very little detailed, analytical research has been done (Klopfer, 1974, p. 269), except for the studies of Kortlandt (1955), Kruijt (1964), and Hailman (1967) concerning different species of birds. Rosenblatt (1976) reviews the studies on altricial, non-primate mammals. More recently, a detailed study of the morphogenesis of behavior in cats was reported (Baerends-van Roon & Baerends, 1979). Also the development of play in cats has been described (Barrett & Bateson, 1978; Egan, 1976). The determinants of the ontogeny of communicative behavior in stumptail macaques were studied by Chevalier-Skolnikoff (1974).

All of these studies find support for the idea that in the course of ontogeny a hierarchical organization emerges which becomes increasingly complex.

Yet, Welker (1971) argues that such a classification into hierarchies has not been validated by systematic or thorough attempts to use ontogenetic criteria. Welker (1971) is of the opinion that too little attention has been paid to accurate descriptions of overt behavioral sequences themselves and to a delineation of their ontogenetic development. He continues to note that criteria for classification of behavior "are derived primarily from observations of already organized behavior patterns of mature, experienced animals, and consequently are not applicable to the developing patterns characteristic of neonatal and inexperienced animals". Condon (1977, 1979) reaches the same conclusion from his frame-to-frame analysis of human neonates.

Moreover, all examples of differentiation come from neonatal (and embryological) development. The unity of all behavior still predominates and the individuation within this unity of parts has not yet progressed so far as to result in isolated units followed by an ascending integration into a hierarchy. The neonatal "reflexes" could be considered to contradict this statement. However, Touwen (1978) argues that "reflexes", in the sense of stereotyped stimulus-response relationships, do not exist in healthy human newborns. He observed that in repeated palmar-grasp reflex trials the sequence of finger flexion around the stimulus varied three out of five times. Therefore, he concludes that there is a difference between the "reaction" of a healthy newborn and the "reflex" of a brain damaged patient.

In contrast, ascending development seems to predominate at an older age in chimpanzee babies. From the age of 5 months onwards, one could not help observing isolated behavior units. Chapter 4 will describe how the behavior repertoire expanded thereafter. Further evidence presented in Chapter 6 indicates that these isolated behavior units only become integrated into functional sequences at a much later age.

Therefore, in line with Werner's (1948) ideas on development, it should be concluded that neither type of development fits all facts. Rather, one type of development (ascending development) seems to replace the other (differentiation) during ontogeny. This is not surprising if one considers that, after a number of parts have differentiated from the total unity, this unity would be lost if these parts were not held together, or integrated, by a system which was hierarchically superior to these parts.

The question to be discussed, then, is at exactly what age the change-over takes place between differentiation and ascending development. It is not yet clear what type of development predominates during the age span between the neonatal period and the age of 5 months. More specifically, the question arises whether differentiation development predominates up till the age of 5 months, or whether the changeover takes place earlier.

Towards the age of 2 months, major changes in neonatal behavior and perception have been reported in the human literature. For instance, McCall et al. (1977) examined the principal components of the "California first year" and the "California preschool" tests at various ages and discovered periods in which the character of the components stays more or less the same, and periods in which the components alter considerably. Simultaneously with these changes in the composition of the first principal components, they also found changes in the stability of individual differences. A first dip in the cross age rank-order correlations was found at the age of 2 months. Another example is the finding that beyond 1 to 2 months a baby is capable of focussing on qualitatively distinct features, figures, or patterns (Salapatek, 1975, p. 194).

Even if one accepts the idea that the changeover between differentiation and ascending development takes place around the age of 2 months instead of 5 months, it is still difficult to specify what the supposed system (integrating the differentiated parts) would be like, how many levels of integration would develop between the ages of 2 and 5 months, and how the overt behavior as observed in the baby could have resulted from them.

This difficulty may arise from the fact that until now research, looking for evidence in favor of the idea of systems integrating discrete parts, concerned only older individuals. In these studies the behavior repertoire was supposed to be composed of a number of discrete patterns of behavior (among which were the patterns usually called "fixed action patterns"). Systems were envisaged to control a group of functionaly related activities (McFarland, 1971, pp. 205–206) and the discrete patterns of behavior were used in the search for the existence of the integrating systems (Baerends, 1956, 1976; Hinde, 1953). The difficulty in finding what systems control the behavior of babies younger than 5 months, therefore, is that these discrete patterns of behavior do not yet exist.

There may be another way, however, to establish the existence of such systems. If the hierarchical integration of parts which differentiated from the total unity starts before the age at which discrete behavior patterns emerge, it is only logical that such a hierarchical integration concerns, among other things, the ontogeny of movement-regulation leading up to the ability to execute discrete behavior patterns. In such regulation, feedback through proprioception as well as other perception (of the results of movement outside the body) has been found to play an important role in primates (Marsden et al., 1978; Polit & Bizzi, 1979) in mice (Fentress, 1976a), and some bird species (Baerends, 1956, 1970; Bastock et al., 1953). In such feedback, a deviation from set-values plays a crucial role (Baerends, 1976). As soon as the perceived stimuli conform to the set-values, all activity aimed at restoring those values stops. Such stimuli have been called "consummatory stimuli" (Bastock et al., 1953). Thus, systems may also be thought of as controlling set-values in the perception, effectuated by the behavior, as a result of which consummatory stimuli can be observed. Consequently, these consummatory stimuli can be of help in finding the systems.

There are two early studies in which this idea is expressed. Kortlandt (1940a; 1955, pp. 171–172) speaks of "hierarchically organized appetites" where an appetite is defined as "either the performance of a specific activity or the presence of a specific external object or situation (consummatory situation) which causes the ending of a variable sequence or series of activities leading to this particular activity situation''. The appetites are arranged in levels that successively mature and integrate during ontogeny. Baerends (1941, p. 206), in an analysis of the causal factors controlling the provisioning behavior of a digger wasp, speaks of a hierarchy of different types of appetitive behavior (''Hierarchie dieser verschiedenen Formen des Appetenzverhalten'').

A search for consummatory stimuli may, therefore, be a fruitful approach in an attempt to detect existing systems. Then the next task would be to find how far these systems could be considered to be part of different levels in a hierarchical structure causing the consummatory stimuli to function as ''hierarchically nested stopping rules'' (Dawkins, 1976). Finally, we want to know how such a structure develops.

SEARCH FOR CONSUMMATORY STIMULI

I shall first illustrate what is meant by ''a search for consummatory stimuli''. It is known from the literature that thermoregulation plays an important role in neonatal behavior: e.g., Prechtl and Schleidt (1950, 1951) showed that hamsters turn their ventral body surface toward an optimal heat-source and follow this source with their belly if it moves sideways. In a similar vein, Peiper (1951) reports work by Schendel which shows that rooting in human neonates can be elicited by a warm object approaching the mouth without touching.

Control through this simple consummatory stimulus (optimal temperature) may also apply to other overt behavior of neonates. For instance, rooting in the direction of the nipple may be guided by a temperature gradient. It is well known from several studies on mammalian species (Jeddi, 1970, 1971; Rosenblatt, 1976) including man (Peiper, 1951) that the snout region is very temperature sensitive and that temperature, besides touch, plays a role in finding a nipple or the home region (in kittens; see Freeman & Rosenblatt, 1978). Welker (1959) showed for neonate puppies that the responses of advancing or turning the head to light contact are especially predictable under conditions of nonoptimal temperature.

Babies of 2 months and older, however, show overt behavior which can no longer be directed at obtaining such simple consummatory stimuli. For instance, finding a nipple through rooting (via a temperature gradient) disappeared (Prechtl, 1958). From this age onwards, babies showed the so-called ''directed head turning response'' and go straight to the nipple if they are constantly on the body of the mother. In the latter case, they must find their way over the body of the mother in a different manner. Other characteristics must have become important as beacons for finding the nipple.

Thus, the question arises what new consummatory stimuli started to rule the behavior of babies of 2 months and older? This question is not readily answerable. These stimuli are, so to speak, hidden. Similar ideas have been expressed by Hofer (1978, "hidden, regulatory processes") and Golani (1976). The latter showed that chaos seemed present in the observed behavior as long as one did not know what was controlled. As soon as one did know, order appeared in the same overt behavior.

Even if this question is answered, the second and third question remain: Do the new and the old consummatory stimuli function in hierarchically nested stopping rules and how does this develop?

When my thoughts had developed thus far, my colleague A.R. Cools noted that Powers' (1973) hypothetical construct might be very useful as a lead to detect the consummatory stimuli which control the behavior at different hierarchical levels. Cools' suggestion turned out to be true. Therefore, I shall now state briefly the essential features of Powers' hypothetical construct. Next, I shall present the principal characteristics of the successive, hierarchically nested consummatory stimuli.

HIERARCHY OF CONSUMMATORY STIMULI

Generally speaking, Powers' (1973) hypothetical construct stands for the way in which the organization of the human nervous system functions. It provides a functional block diagram of how overt behavior is regulated. This regulation of overt behavior is thought to result from the control of perception; it is continuously aimed at reaching or maintaining certain perceptual set-values. These set-values can belong to different levels in a nonlinear hierarchical organization and higher-order set-values are able to adjust lower-order ones.

Speaking more specifically, the hypothetical construct consists of a hierarchy of negative feedback control systems in which each higher-order system controls a number of lower-order systems. The principles of each control system are depicted schematically in Figure 1. It first shows two kinds of elements basic to the hypothetical construct: neural signals (perceptual signal, reference signal, and error signal) and neural functions (input function, comparator function, and output function). The Input Function (Fi) causes the one signal leaving it (perceptual signal) to be a function of the many signals feeding into it. In the Comparator Function (C) the perceptual signal resulting from the input function is compared with a reference signal. As long as a discrepancy is measured between the two signals, the comparator function produces an error signal. When receiving an error signal, the Output Function (Fo) exerts control by adjusting reference signals for lower-order systems. Thus, a control system ultimately controls its own perception. This perception will be changed continuously until the dis-

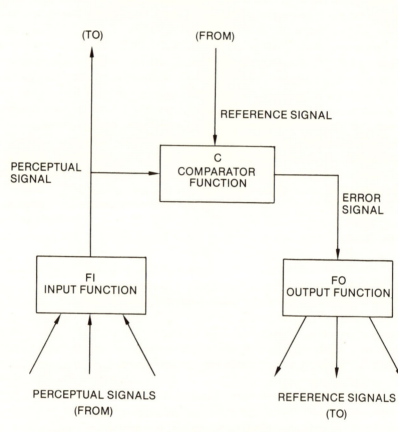

Figure 1. Negative feedback control system.

crepancy between the incoming reference signal and the resultant perceptual signal is zero. Then the error signal becomes zero as well and all activity directed at adjustment ceases.

Since the perceptual signal that equals the reference signal stops all adjusting activity, it has to result from what we have called a consummatory stimulus. Therefore, knowledge of the perceptual signals belonging to the hierarchically nested control systems can help us in our search for the hierarchically nested consummatory stimuli. In Powers' model each level has its own type of perceptual signals which thus should correspond to a particular type of consummatory stimuli.

To understand this we now have to look at the way the hierarchy of control systems in Powers' model is built up. It is schematically represented in Figure 2. Seven orders (levels) of control are depicted. The pyramidal structure of the hierarchy resulting from the bottom to the top is omitted for the sake of simplicity.

The lowest order subserves the interaction with the environment. A first-order input function can be defined as a set of sensory receptors which always respond at the same time ("the most likely tie being physical proximity"; Powers, 1973, p. 147). First-order input functions can only encode intensity. This is because neural currents only vary in the units of impulses per second and first-order perceptual signals do not carry extra information to identify the kind of stimulation. Consequently, first-order input functions cannot make any distinction between the type of stimulation caused by physical phenomena just outside the nervous system. Thus, after having been transformed to neural phenomena ("first-order transformation"), all stimuli (coming from pressure, light, sound, vibration, deep touch, surface touch, balance organs, taste buds, olfactory organs, muscle spindles, tendon receptors, etc.) are qualitatively alike. There is also no distinction between proprioceptive and exteroceptive stimuli. Therefore, in Figure 3, all first-order input functions are placed on one line at the boundary between system and environment, irrespective of whether they are situated in the muscles (muscle spindles and tendon receptors, producing first-order perceptual signals marked "1") or elsewhere (producing first-order perceptual signals marked "2" and "3"). As illustrated in Figure 3, not all first-order input functions send their intensity signals towards a first-order comparator function. Only a limited number of the total collection of first-order input functions is under direct control via the muscles. The other first-order input functions send their intensity signals directly to second-order input functions.

The process by which these second-order input functions create one second-order perceptual signal out of a set of intensity signals is called a second-order transformation. According to Powers (1973, p. 100, ff.), the second-order input functions are probably located in the sensory nuclei in the brain stem and upper spine. These nuclei have been associated with various modalities of sensation. One sensory nucleus contains many second-order input functions. Each of them receives a different set of first-order perceptual signals and combines them (for instance by weighted summation) to produce a single second-order perceptual signal (see Figure 3), which stands for a quality of sensation. Although each nucleus tends to receive signals from particular kinds of first-order input functions, there is much overlap and first-order perceptual signals from many different sources (eyes, ears, proprioception, balance organs, etc.) may all feed into a single second-order input function. This is the reason why it is not always possible to classify a sensation under one of the labels such as taste, smell, temperature, etc. Sensations can be much more difficult to imagine than these straightforward examples. It also implies that at this level of control, information coming in from all sources and directions is integrated.

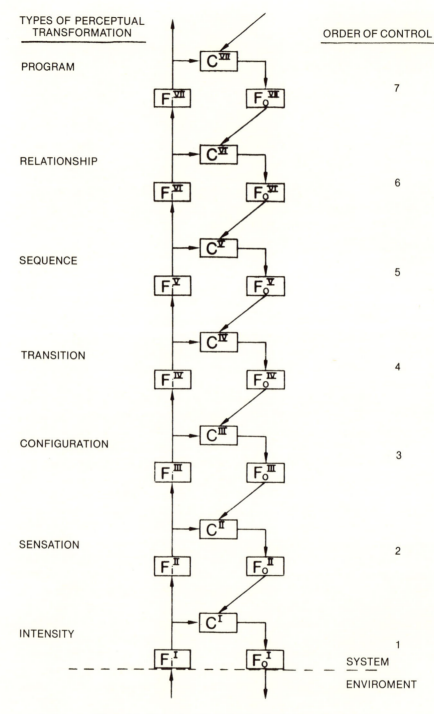

Figure 2.   Hierarchy of negative feedback control systems.

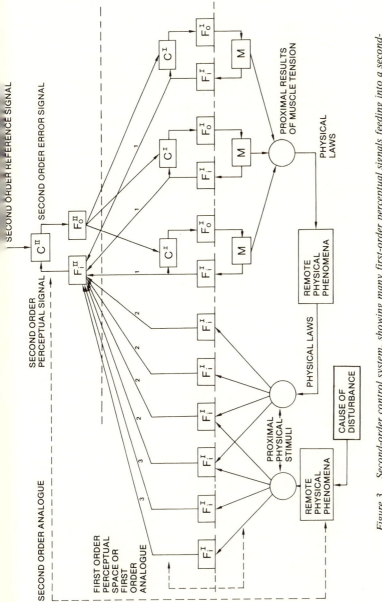

Figure 3. Second-order control system, showing many first-order perceptual signals feeding into a second-order input function. Examples of directly (1), indirectly (2), and uncontrolled components (3) of the sensation vector are illustrated as well.

Fi = Input function   I = First-order
Fo = Output function   II = Second-order
C = Comparator function   M = Muscle

11

In order to appreciate the difference between these second- (and higher-) order transformations and the first-order transformations, the following is pertinent. Whereas each first-order perceptual signal corresponds to a local physical phenomenon just outside the nervous system (such as a light intensity, a chemical concentration, an influx or outflow of heat, a mechanical deformation), each second-order perceptual signal is dependent on a set of many first-order perceptual signals. If the second-order transformation is performed through summation, the sum of this set of signals may remain the same notwithstanding great variation in the single signals of this set. This is called an "invariance" and the second-order perceptual signs is said to be an invariant function of a set of first-order perceptual signals. Because each first-order perceptual signal corresponds with one local physical effect, and each second-order perceptual signal depends on many first-order perceptual signals, a second-order perceptual signal cannot correspond in magnitude to any single local physical effect. It has to correspond to some more general variable or derived quantity.

In the same way as a second-order perceptual signal is an invariant function of a set of first-order perceptual signals, so is a third-order perceptual signal (called a "configuration") an invariant function of a set of second-order perceptual signals. A third-order input function is designed to perceive an invariance in a set of second-order perceptual signals. Powers (1973) gives the following examples. A certain arm-hand configuration is perceived as the same despite varying levels of effort and despite changes in orientation of the arm relative to the body. Visually, third-order control might mean perceiving a pattern as constant regardless of the amount of illumination or the orientation in (three dimensional, Euclidian) space. Phonemes in humans are auditory configurations.

Fourth-order input functions perceive transitions (see Figure 2) from one state of the third-order perceptual space (set of third-order perceputal signals) to another. Restricting oneself to proprioception, this implies that a system with no more than four levels of control should be able to make smooth transitions between one body configuration and another and thus execute a controlled movement. Powers (1973) argues that not only the change of one (static) state of the third-order perceptual space into another may be considered a transition. A more general concept of transitions is that of partial derivatives which may be seen as the proportion of change in one variable with respect to a change in another. One example of this is that not only changes in the momentary value of a discrepancy are detectable, but also changes in the rate at which it changes (when being reduced to zero). If the capacity to perceive and control such transitions would not be present, the detecting and correcting entity would tend to overshoot or to undershoot or to oscillate about its mark.

Fifth-order input functions are designed to perceive sequences in which lower-order perceptions occur, such as sequences of transitions in posture (proprioception). According to Powers, (1973, p. 139), a short and familiar sequence of such transitions in posture is walking. Generally speaking, I think that all movement patterns which are usually listed when the behavioral repertoire of a particular species is described are such short and familiar sequences of transitions in posture.

Sixth-order input functions are designed to perceive relationships (see Figure 2). Relationships are defined as those invariants that appear in collections of independent events (= short, familiar sequences = fifth-order perceptions) and lower-order perceptions. Examples given by Powers (1973, pp. 155–159) are space-time relationships, cause-effect relationships, but also the logical concept "and" as a relationship, to name a few.

Seventh-order input functions perceive programs. Such programs are defined to involve a definite list of relationships brought about one after the other. Powers (1973, pp. 160–168) gives the example of "eating porridge with a spoon": first put spoon *into* the porridge, shovel some porridge *onto* the spoon, put the spoon *into* your mouth (and not *against* your eye), etc. The program is not a list. It is a *structure,* and at the nodes of this structure are tests or decision points (if-statements): a point where the list of operations being carried out is interrupted and some state of affairs is perceived and compared to a reference state of affairs. Sometimes such choice points may form a "tree". In this tree, the *network,* not the particular path followed, is the organization in question. Programs can be organized to obey any imaginable rules: not only deduction, but superstition, grammatical rules, expectations about the consequences of behavior in the physical world, experimental procedures, mathematical algorithms, recipes for cooking and chemistry, and the strategies of business, games, conversation, and love-making. "Plans and the structure of behaviour" by Miller et al. (1960) is a good textbook of seventh-order behaviour, according to Powers (1973, pp. 160–168).

Higher-order input functions do exist, according to Powers, but the seven orders, described above suffice for our purpose, as we shall see later.

Thus, the nervous system can be envisaged as consisting of a number of concentric "shells". The collection of first-order control systems forms the outer shell. These control systems are the only ones which interact directly with the external world (see Figure 2). Higher-order control systems do not and cannot respond directly to physical stimuli. "They depend on it, but the form of that dependence is determined in the brain, by the neural computers which create perceptual signals layer by layer through transformations of one set of neural currents into another" (Powers, 1973, p. 37). Each layer (order of control) contains a certain type of perceptual signals.

These types of perceptual signals correspond with the classes of consummatory stimuli we are looking for.

THREE PROCEDURES TO FIND THE CONSUMMATORY STIMULI

Before starting the search for different classes of consummatory stimuli with the help of this information about types of perceptual transformation, it is necessary to discuss how it can be decided that a particular type of perception is under control. After all, the information about types of perception obtained so far is derived from a hypothetical construct and the observer only has a recording of overt behavior available. What overt behavior should be observed before one can conclude that a particular type of perception is under control? I have used three methods in making this decision.

One way to decide whether a particular type of perception (and thus a certain class of consummatory stimuli) is controlled is to study reactions to disturbances.'' An organism can be said to control a variable with respect to a reference condition (consummatory stimulus) if every disturbance tending to cause a deviation from the reference condition calls forth a behavior which results in opposition to the disturbance'' (Powers, 1973, p. 47). In the type of field study which I have conducted it is impossible to apply disturbances and look for the countering behavior. What can be done, however, is to look for naturally occurring disturbances (everyday life is full of them) and to observe the behavior following such disturbances. For this task it is helpful to be aware of three distinct ways in which the organism can counter a disturbance of its perception. Perception can be directly controlled, indirectly controlled, and uncontrolled. The feedback which is involved in direct control of perception has also been called ''action feedback'' (Annett, 1969) or ''kinesthetic feedback'' (Wiener, 1948). This feedback occurs entirely within the behaving organism and starts as soon as a response begins. This feedback can alter the response while it is happening. The feedback which is involved in indirect control of perception has also been called ''learning feedback'' or ''knowledge of results'' (Annett, 1969). This feedback is delayed in the sense that it does not alter the response while it is happening, but only later. It has been called ''knowledge of results,'' because the feedback loop runs partly outside the organism. Uncontrolled perception arises through disturbances from external sources in the environment which cannot be counteracted by the organism's own effects. The three ways in which disturbances can be counteracted are illustrated in Figure 3. The action-feedback loop is closed inside the organism in the muscles (M). The learning-feedback loop is closed outside the organism. It runs from muscle (M) to proximal results of muscle tensions to remote physical phenomena. These, in turn, cause proximal physical stimuli which stimulate first-order input functions. And finally, feedback is absent in those first-order perceptual signals (marked "3") which arise through an external cause of disturbance that cannot be counteracted by the consequences of muscle tensions.

A second way to decide what class of consummatory stimuli is under control concerns the speed of control systems. First-order control systems are very fast. About 0.1 sec or even less (a few tenths of a millisecond) will be the least significant time interval. The higher the order of control, the slower the system. This allows all orders of control to work simultaneously. Furthermore, all control systems can oscillate when they become unstable. The higher the order of control the lower its frequency of oscillation must be (see Powers, 1973, p. 116). Thus, the frequency of this oscillation provides information about the order of control involved. Powers gives several examples. "Clonus" oscillations result from unstable first-order control systems when muscles exert too much effort. They oscillate at roughly 10 Hz. Several types of "tremors", such as the ones of Parkisonianism, oscillate at approximately 3 Hz and witness second-order instability. Finally, "overt-correction" such as over- and undershooting the target while reaching out for something results from an unstable third-order control system.

A third way to decide what class of consummatory stimuli is controlled is concerned with the degree of variability of overt behavior. A change during development from rigidity to variability in the control of a certain variable indicates that the order of control involved has changed from being highest to being one but highest. This follows logically from Powers' (1973) hypothetical construct: As long as a certain control system is the highest in the hierarchy there are no higher-order control systems which adjust the reference signal and variation is absent. As soon as these higher-order control systems become operative, the reference signal starts being adjusted and the variability in behavior is observed. This was found to be true for the behavioral development of cormorants. Kortlandt (1955, pp. 190–192) showed that normal variability of behavior proceeds mainly at a level just below the highest order of control which is operational. Furthermore, he concluded that this "zone of variability in behavior ascends in the same degree as does the progress in maturation". Kortlandt (1955) suggested from Bingham's (1928) descriptions of ontogeny in the chimpanzee that the same principle applies to behavioral development in this ape.

ORGANIZATION OF THE MONOGRAPH

Although the questions raised in this introduction are presented in a way which suggests this study was designed beforehand to answer them, this is only part of the truth. Undeniably, I started this study to find out more about the ontogenetic development of the organization underlying the behavior of free-living babies and infants. But in the field I merely observed the behavior sequences of these babies and infants in a way described in Chapter 2. I read Powers (1973) after my return from the field, and formulated the assumptions and operalizations in which to interpret the observational data.

In this book this sequence of events (first observation, then interpretation) is preserved in each chapter for the following reasons. Although I intend to show that the Powers model supplies a convenient framework which integrates the data I obtained as well as a variety of data from the literature, I want to be careful and keep distinguishing facts from hypothetical construct. Otherwise the danger is real that I may start thinking as though the model really exists. My data only "prove" the existence of particular orders of control insofar as I assume the model.

Therefore, Chapters 3–6 of this book are divided according to age. In each chapter a description of the overt behavior typical for the age range shall be given. Chapter 3 concerns the perinatal period, ending at 2 months of age. Chapter 4 covers the age period of 2–6 months. Chapter 5 describes behaviors emerging between 6–12 months. And, finally, Chapter 6 touches on the changes which were observed beyond the age of 1 year.

In the discussion of Chapter 3 attention is paid to the sleep-waking cycles, to the helplessness of the newborn baby, and to individual differences. Comparisons are made with our own species.

The main question which dominates the discussions of the remaining chapters is whether it is possible to find evidence for the ontogenetic development of an increasingly complex, hierarchical organization underlying overt behavior. In these discussions the descriptions of overt behavior shall be interpreted in the light of the assumptions and operalizations formulated above.

Furthermore, comparisons are made between the results of this study and the human literature. Striking resemblances will be shown.

2

General Methods

STUDY AREA

The study was carried out in the Gombe Stream National Park, Tanzania. This park lies on the eastern shores of Lake Tanganyika (Figure 4A). In 1960, Jane Goodall initiated research here and free-ranging chimpanzees (Pan troglodytus schweinfurthii) have been studied since.

The general structure of the park, the climate, flora, and fauna have been described by van Lawick-Goodall (1968), Clutton-Brock (1972, 1975), and Wrangham (1975). The research center has been described by van La-wick-Goodall (1967a, 1968, 1973).

An artificial feeding area was set up in 1962. The disadvantages of the feeding methods used at that time and the change in the manner of feeding after 1968 have been described by Wrangham (1974). In 1975, Wrangham concluded that size and form of the community range and the importance of natural food sources were not greatly influenced by the artificial feeding schedule in the years 1971–1973. I conducted my study from May 1971 until March 1973.

In a similar vein, my data suggest that the influence of the artificial feeding on the associations between mothers with offspring was minimal if not absent. I found that mothers with babies were alone most of the time (Table 6, p. 72). Furthermore, I saw that all mothers were perfectly able to decide whether to meet or to avoid others. Moreover, if other individuals were already too close, mothers could be observed to hide behind large trees and in dense vegetation until the others had left.

Chimpanzees also make use of the structure of the environment for their social lives to heighten the chances of meeting or avoiding other individuals. In order to illustrate how they did so, I will briefly describe the environment. The general structure of the park is indicated in the park-map through symbols (Figure 4B). An escarpment, which runs parallel to the lake-shore, forms the inland boundary of the park. Rivers run down the

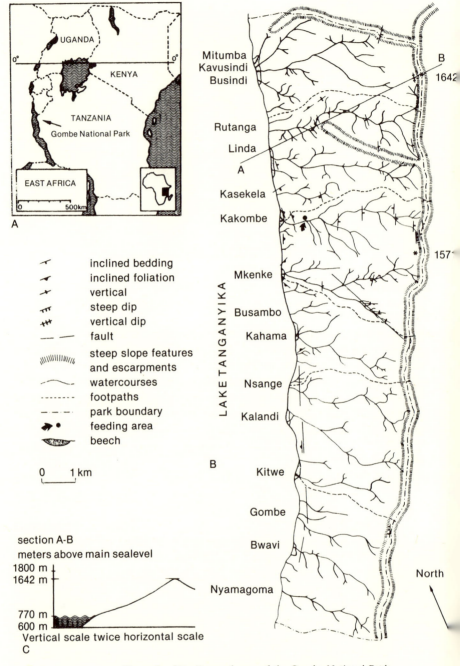

Figure 4. Situation and map of the Gombe National Park.
A) Map of East Africa indicating the location of the Gombe National Park in Tanzania
B) The general structure of the Gome National Park.
C) West-east profile of the park (along the line A-B in Figure 4B).

escarpment and into the lake. The river valleys are often narrow and V-shaped and are, consequently, separated by ridges. These ridges isolate the valleys visually and acoustically, and chimpanzees are observed to make use of these characteristics. On the one hand, chimpanzees who tried to avoid others were seen to climb over a ridge and down into the next valley. On the other hand, chimpanzees who intended to join others were observed to climb the top of a ridge, either to survey the next valley visually and auditorily, or to vocalize themselves and, thus, attract the attention of others. The others, in turn, might decide to draw no attention to themselves or might decide to respond by vocalizing and/or approaching the chimpanzee on top of the ridge.

STUDY POPULATION AND SUBJECTS

Individuals

All the individuals of the study population are listed in Table 1. Name, initial, date and/or year of birth, and kin are given. A human observer can easily learn to recognize each individual within a few weeks, by the face, the voice, the gait, the profile and sometimes even the smell. All individuals listed were fully or partially habituated to human observers.

Babies and infants associate with their mothers all the time and depend on them. I studied six mother-offspring pairs (see underscored names in Table 1).

TABLE 1
Demographic Data of the Study Population

NORTHERN COMMUNITY

INDEPENDENT MALES

Name	Initial	Date and/or Year of Birth	Kin
HUGO	HG	(1938)	unknown
MIKE	MK	(1943)	unknown
HUMPHREY	HM	(1948)	(sibling of ML)
FABEN	FB	(1953)	son of FL, sibling of FG FF FT, uncle of FD
EVERED	EV	(1955)	sibling of GK
FIGAN	FG	(1956)	son of FL, sibling of FB FF FT, uncle of FD
JOMEO-GIN	JJ	(1957)	sibling of SH
SATAN	ST	(1959)	unknown
SHERRY	SH	(1961)	sibling of JJ

TABLE 1 (Cont.)

INDEPENDENT FEMALES

Name	Initial	Date and/or Year of Birth	Kin
FLO††	FL	(1922)	mother of FB FG FF FT, grandmother of FD
PASSION	PS	(1945)	mother of PM PF
MELISSA	ML	(1950)	mother of GB GM, sibling of HM
NOPE	NP	(1951)	mother of MU
ATHENA	AT	(1954)	mother of AL
NOVA	NV	(1954)	mother of SS
PALLAS	PL	(1955)	mother of PT
GIGI	GG	(1956)	no infant, siblings unknown
MIFF	MF	(1958)	mother of MZ
FIFI	FF	(1959)	mother of FD, daughter of FL, sibling of FB FG FT
WINKLE	WK	(1960)	mother of WL
SPARROW*	SW	(1962)	unknown
PATTI*	PI	(1962)	unknown

DEPENDENT MALE OFFSPRING

Name	Initial	Date and/or Year of Birth	Kin
FLINT††	FT	01-03-1964	son of FL, sibling of FB FG FF, uncle of FD
GOBLIN	GB	06-09/07-09-1964	son of ML, sibling of GM
MUSTARD	MU	29-10/22-11-1965	son of NP
ATLAS	AL	19-09/02-10-1967	son of AT
PLATO	PT	07-09-1970	son of PL
FREUD	FD	21-05/24-05-1971	son of FF, grandson of FL, nephew of FB FG FT
PROF	PF	25-10/28-10-1971	son of PS, sibling of PM
WILKY	WL	21-10-1972	son of WK

DEPENDENT FEMALE OFFSPRING

Name	Initial	Date and/or Year of Birth	Kin
POM	PM	13-07-1965	daughter of PS, sibling of PF
MOEZA	MZ	19-01/22-01-1969	daughter of MF
SKOSHA	SS	24-03/29-03-1970	daughter of NV
GREMLIN	GM	14-11/23-11-1970	daughter of ML, sibling of GB

*	Largely unhabituated individuals who were seldom observed.
††	Florence died in Aug. 1972 and her juvenile son Flint in Sept. 1972.
parenthesis	Parenthetical information is suspected, but not certain
underlined names	Subjects in the present study.

Age Classes

The terms baby, infant, juvenile, adolescent, and adult are used throughout the text. They refer to the following age-classes:

baby	0–6 months
infant	1/2–5 years
juvenile	5–9 years
adolescent	9–14 years
adult	>14 years

Except for the terms baby and infant, use of the terms is the same as van
Lawick-Goodall's (1973). The age-classes "baby" and "infant" were distinguished on the basis of major behavioral changes that I observed.

OBSERVATION METHODS

Pilot Study and Main Study

"Familiarity with an animal's behavior will tend to require years of experience if the animal is a mammal or a bird with a complex repertory" (Fagan
& Goldman, 1977). In the Gombe Research Center years of experience were
already present and transferred from one researcher to the next. Therefore,
I only needed six months to become familiar with the chimpanzees and their
environment (pilot study). During this period I spent 407 hours in the field,
collecting data as follows.

The first three weeks I stayed in camp (feeding area) in order to learn to
recognize the chimpanzees individually.

Thereafter, I began following the chimpanzees on foot when they left
camp. "It is necessary intellectually to soak in the environmental complex
of the animal to be studied until we have a facility with it which keeps us as
it were, one move ahead" (Schneirla, 1972). During 4 weeks, chimpanzees
from all age/sex classes were followed indiscriminately and an overall picture was gained.

From then onwards, I restricted following to the six mother-infant
pairs included in this study. During observations, a running commentary
(see Hutt & Hutt, 1970) was dictated into a portable cassette-tape recorder
strapped to my chest. Out of these observations *grew* a list of environmental
events which I considered important (pp. 24–25) and a list of behavior
categories (elements) which I observed repeatedly (pp. 22–23 and Appendix
A).

The main study ran from January 1972 until March 1973. During this
period a further 975 hours were spent collecting data.

My study is essentially a series of case studies. This is not to say that it is impossible to gain an integrated view about early development from these separate cases. Figure 5 shows that there was enough overlap in the ages of the babies and infants to allow for verification of observations on one individual through comparison with another individual.

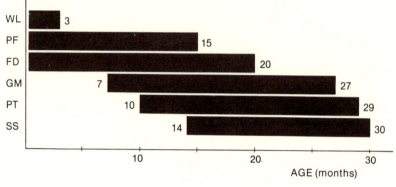

Figure 5.   Age spans of the subjects.

A further argument in favor of building up an integrated view about early development by comparing individual case studies is the fact that it is difficult to use individuals as their own controls in order to verify observations. Babies grow so fast that it is not allowed to assume that during any period the organization underlying overt behavior remains constant.

Defining the Behavior Categories

Whenever a behavior category is mentioned in the text below, a three-letter code is added between brackets to enable the reader to find the defintion of this category. The three-letter codes are alphabetically ordered and illustrated by line-drawings in Appendix A.

Three criteria were used for defining behavior categories. First, as I mentioned in the introduction, before the age of 5 months it was very difficult to observe motor-patterns which were sufficiently stereotyped to enable definition and quantification. As a result, the number of behavior categories which were finally defined is not only very limited, but hardly any one of these categories concerns *patterns* of motor-activity. Only the categories mountaineering (MON), rooting (ROT), and sucking (SUC) consist of regularly recurring, patterned movements. And even these categories could not be recognized anymore when the baby was out of the usual context of ventro-ventral contact with the mother's body. For instance, when the baby was lying in the supine position on the ground in between the legs of the mother, the patterning in the movements of the extremities as described in the definition of the category mountaineering had disappeared. Instead, the category "moving" (MOV) was used to discriminate mobility of the extremities from immobility. The definition of most other categories was based on the consequence of motor-activity itself, such as eyes-closed (EYC), sitting (SIT), and playface (PFH). Composite motor-sequences such as walking quadrupedally (WAQ) or climbing (CLI) could first be recognized after the fifth month. Only relatively simple movements such as grasping (TAK) could be distinguished from the age of 3 months onwards. Between the ages of 5–12 months the order in which these composite motor-sequences occurred was so erratic that they could not be defined in accordance with consequence. Only after 12 months did a definition of categories according to consequence (e.g., nestbuilding = NES) become possible.

Except for this age-dependency criterion a second factor played a role in defining the behavior categories. I found it impossible to conform to Altmann's (1965), Struhsaker's (1971), and Welker's (1971) demand that the description of the behavior of the whole organism should be in terms of mutually exclusive categories. This finding is supported by later literature. Brannigan and Humphries (1972, p. 44) concluded that "Grant's (1968) method of summarizing stochastically the non-verbal behavior in interviews by treating it as a simple sequence of 30 or so units can now be seen to be an oversimplification. The units have different durations and may *overlap* in complex ways in sequence". Additionally, Powers (1973, p. 127) argued that "configurations" (e.g., body posture, vocalization, facial expression) can be perceived and controlled simultaneously by an organism and that exclusive pairs of configurations are rare. Furthermore, Parker (1974) showed that the great apes as a group demonstrate a higher degree of behavioral diversity than monkeys and other mammals as indexed, among other things, by the number of different combinations of body-part used and action performed. In harmony with these findings, the majority of the behavior categories listed in Appendix A concern body-parts. The categories are divided into 11 groups in such a way that in each group only one body-part is involved (i.e., face, torso, right arm, etc.). The intra-group units *are* mutually exclusive (see Appendix B). Units from different groups may combine. In the field, I described the continuous stream of behavior of the whole organism in terms of a sequence of combinations of these units. These combinations themselves are not named here; this would have produced an enormous list. It is important to realize that the demand for mutual exclusiveness of all behavior categories partly resulted from statistical constraints and, after all, "statistical methods do not tell biologists how to define behavior-units" (Fagan & Goldman, 1977, p. 269).

Thirdly, I rejected the "priority-rule-observation-system" of Struhsaker (1967). This author presented priority rules in case more than one behavior-unit occurs. I found it impossible to decide what behavior-unit should be selected, for example, if a chimpanzee infant walks quadrupedally (WAQ) while stamping on the ground (STA), looking at another individual (LAT), having its hair out (HAI), and showing an erection (PEN).

Defining the Environmental Categories

All stimuli an infant overtly reacted to were recorded without exception. In addition, I recorded a number of environmental categories which exerted influence on the infant every time they occurred, whether the infant reacted overtly to them or not. These categories were:

Presence of other chimpanzees.   The distance from any individual to the infant was recorded. The distance categories, following those used in Hinde and Spencer-Booth's (1976) observation system, were:

1. *Ventral:* the infant is ventral to another individual if most of its weight is supported by that individual and encompassed by arms and thighs of the other individual. "Ventral" includes sitting on the ground between the thighs and facing the other individual.
2. *Not-ventral:* this includes any other position of the infant on the body of another individual (when most of its weight is supported by that individual), when it is not ventral; e.g., on the other individual's back, head, lower-arms and lower-legs, and outer surface of the upper-arms and legs.
3. *In contact:* most of the infant's weight is supported by the ground or vegetation, but the infant's body is touching the other individual's body. Excluded are the times when the infant is sitting in between the thighs of another individual and facing that other individual (then the infant is said to be ventral).
4. *Within arm's reach:* the infant is within arm's reach of another individual if it is out of contact of that other individual and if the other can touch the infant by extending his or her arm. This distance varies a little with the circumstances, but usually it is approximately 1.5 meters.
5. *Within 5 meters:* the infant is within 5 meters but out of arm's reach of another individual.
6. *Within 15 meters:* another individual is over 5 meters but less than 15 meters away from the infant.
7. *Visible:* another individual is visible but over 15 meters away from the infant.
8. *Out of visibility:* another individual is out of visibility but closely around the infant. For instance, behind a bush from the point of view of the infant.

A mother was associated all the time with her infant and any change from one distance-category to another was reported. Furthermore, every 5 minutes the distance from the infant of every individual was checked. Arrival and departure of other individuals were recorded. Chimpanzees not visibly present around the infant may vocalize, thereby signalling, at least, their locations. Therefore, any chimpanzee vocalizations were recorded whenever they occurred. A code for their loudness, which is a measure of the distance of the vocalizing individual(s) to the infant, was added. The codes were: 1. very loud; 2. normal; 3. faint.

Presence of other species. Two humans were always present: the observer and a field-assistant. Whenever the distance between the observer and the infant was less than 5 meters, this was noted. The field-assistant always stayed 20 meters or more behind.

The following species that became visible or audible were recorded: baboon (Papio papio), red colobus (Colobus badius), blue monkeys (Cercopithecus mitis), redtail monkeys (C. ascanius), buffalo (Syncerus caffer), bushbuck, bushpig, snakes, lizards, humans.

Vegetation-noise. The Gombe chimpanzees reacted to vegetation-noise very strongly. For instance, the rustling of living leaves or the crunching of dead leaves indicate movement and movement may be danger caused by other animals being around such as the buffalo. Furthermore, falling branches are a real danger. Sometimes the chimpanzees jumped up when the wind suddenly rustled the leaves, only to find out they were mistaken.

Weather variations. The weather conditions were of influence on the chimpanzee infants. When it started raining the infant would stop playing and return to its mother. Even if the rain had stopped, the soil could still be wet, which might prevent the infant from leaving its mother if she was on the ground. Furthermore, newborn babies reacted in a special way to thunder (see pp. 49–50). The following weather variations were recorded:

> sun versus no-sun
> blue sky versus cloudy
> dry versus rain
> dry versus wet soil
> thunder

Location. I always recorded whether the mother-infant pair was in camp or out of camp and whether it was on the ground or in a tree. I had the strong impression after my pilot-study that when out of camp and high in trees the infants went further away from their mothers.

Sampling

During the main study, I followed each mother-offspring pair (listed in Table 1) on foot around the day when the baby or infant was 0.5, 1.5, 2.5, etc. months old. A newborn baby was followed daily for the first week of life. I dictated my observations onto a cassette-recorder (Sony 110A).

My focus of interest was the chimpanzee baby or infant. I *continuously* recorded the behavior of the baby or infant in terms of combinations of the behavior categories listed in Appendix A. This way of recording was based on two arguments. First was the notion that "data on animals not engaged in specified activities are as essential as data on animals that are" (Hinde, 1971, p. 4). Therefore, the behavior of an infant that was just sitting and looking around, for example, was recorded as such and not lumped into an element called "other behaviors". Second, during the first year of life the behavior could not yet be described according to consequence. As a result, it was not yet possible to limit my observations to certain periods of time containing, for instance, feeding behavior. It was even impossible to limit my observations to periods containing "social" as opposed to "non-social" behavior for similar reasons to those expressed by Watzlawick et al. (1967): If two individuals are so close together as a chimpanzee mother-baby (infant) pair, it is impossible *not* to behave (socially).

Furthermore, I recorded every activity of the mother or another individual which could be relevant in inducing off-spring behavior, such as:

1. All the behavior the baby or infant reacted to together with the distance of the other individual.
2. If the infant did not react overtly, then all the behavior that was directed towards the baby or infant more than by mere locomotion (normal speed), together with the distance of the other individual.
3. If the behavior was not directed towards the infant:
   a. All the behavior of the mother (indicated where not possible) together with the distance from the mother.
   b. The activities of individuals that come within arm's reach of the infant.
   c. the non-vocal signals from individuals residing within 5 meters of the infant, such as: hair out, erection, swelling, bipedal swagger, branching, drumming, head tip, rocking, slapping, stamping, throwing, and/or charging display.

I ranked the priorities of the observation to be recorded roughly in the same order as they are presented here. If, for instance, the infant and its mother were in camp and three males would enter camp, one bipedally swaggering, another slapstamping, the third drumming, all having their hair out, I recorded: "males one, two, and three charge into camp" and focused my observation on the infant and its mother. Further, if an infant was out of arm's reach of its mother and interacting with another individual I could not possibly record the behavior of the mother as well and, therefore, recorded: "mother out of arm's reach". Thus, the continuous recording of the behavior of the infant and the individual it was interacting with had top priority.

Bad observation periods, however, occurred and started when I could not see everything that was done by the infant or the individual it was interacting with, usually when foliage separated me from either or both individuals. The frequency and the duration of such periods varied with the location and seasons. During the wet season all trees had their leaves and the grass was high, resulting in frequent and long-lasting bad observation periods. However, it was often possible to continue recording the group structure during such periods.

The decision when to stop observing a mother-infant or -baby pair altogether was made in advance so that there could be no bias in the recordings caused by continuing observation when something "interesting" was going on. I would follow each mother-infant or -baby pair as long as was necessary to collect 300 minutes of good observation (this was called a "follow"). This usually took 1–2 days constantly in the field, because roughly two-thirds of the following time is made up of bad observation.

It sometimes happened that I did not manage to keep up with the mother-infant pair, especially when they were "traveling" through very dense undergrowth. Consequently I "lost" them and when my guesses about their whereabouts failed, I returned to camp and waited there for them to come in. Thereafter I would follow them again and complete my 300 minutes of good observation.

Transcription

Back in camp, the observations on the cassette-tape were transcribed onto stencilled forms (see Figure 6). This was done in the following manner. In the upper right hand corner is written:

MA/INF the initials of the mother-infant pair under observation

DATE day, month, and year

BOTTOM condition of the genital region of the mother with a scale from 0 to 1 (see "swelling" in Appendix A)

OBS surname of the observer

The upper left corner will be discussed later.

Columns from left to right:

C every minute the mother-infant pair is in camp (feeding area) a tick is placed in this column.

B when there is bad observation during the complete minute a tick is placed in this column.

5 when the observer is more than 5 meters away from the infant during the minute or part of that minute a tick is placed here.

vine	1		
fig	1		

MA/INF __FF-FD__   DATE __09-05-1972__
BOTTOM __0__   OBS __Plooy__

C	B	5	T	N	Behaviour Sequences	DEP	ARR	Structure	W
v			1507	FD	sab OB(vine)|ste-pff|15| pul FT-pff |pwr FT-pff |————				
			00	FF	4 gro FT ———— 4scr-sit-lar|4 lve FD-waq				
				FT	4 sit-lar ———— 3 pwr FD-Fx|				
				FD	lve FT-waq-fol FF|30|app FF-cli |cln FF-lar|45|————				
				FF	4 avo FD-waq |2 waq-lve FT|2 waq				
				FT	4 grs |5				
v	v		1508	FD	cln FF-lar|15|——|lve FF-cli |fol FF-waq ||	WK			
			00	FF	2 waq |B |—|4 waq-lve FD|4 avo FD-waq|				
	v		1510	FD	cli FF-lar|lve FF-cli|avo FF-waq |15|——|30|| cln FF-lar|45|——			FF 2	S
			00B	FF	2 waq |4 waq |4 fol FD-waq|B |—||B |2 cli |——			FLO,FT 6	D
				FD	————lve FF-cli|dan-lar|				C
				FF	2 sit-lar|3 sit-lar|				
	v		1511	FD	dan-lar |lve FF-cli-app FT|app FT-cli|bit-FT|15|——|gym				
				FF	3 sit-lar|4 lve FD-cli |5 sit-lar |————				
				FT	4 lie-lar |3 lie-lar |——|—3 lve FD-cli				
				FD	dan-lar |30|—|gym|————|45|sit-lar |gym				
				FF					
				FT	4 cli-lve FD| |4 sit-lar|4 cli-lve FD|5				
	v		1512	FD	gym |15|—|app FF-cli|dan-lar|lve FF-cli|gym|30|—|45|—————				
				FF	5 sit-lar |—|4 |5 |—— |—| |—5 sit-lar-F				
v	v		1513	FD	gym |app FF-cli||				
			00-B	FF	5 sit-lar-F|4 ————||				
	v		1515	FD	|| 30|tak FF-sit-lar|45|—			FF 3	S
			00	FF	|| 3 grs-F			FLO,FT 5	D
	v		1516	FD	tak FF-sit-lar|tak FF-plu-oB(fig)|15|—tak FF-bit-oB(fig)|30|—————				C
			00	FF	3 grs F |————|——|—3 bit oB(fig)-F				
				FD	45|— etc.				
				FF					

Figure 6.   Transcription form. For explanation see text.

T   the minute during which there is good observation is written down in the 24-hour system (for instance 1507). On the line under these four figures is written 00 indicating the beginning of the first 15 seconds of that minute and -B if there is bad observation during that period. If a minute is not mentioned at all this means there is bad observation and the observer is more than 5 meters away from the infant.

N   the initial of the infant or baby that is observed is written on the same line as where the minute (1507) is indicated. Under the initial of the infant or the baby the initial of the mother is indicated. Under that, initials of other individuals may be written whose behavior is of relevance in indicating infant behavior. If there is stimulation that is of relevance to the infant it is indicated in this column with the letter S. If there are chimpanzee vocalizations in the distance and if it is impossible to determine the name of the vocalizing chimpanzee, then the directions N(orth), E(ast), So(uth), or W(est) are written in these columns.

Behavior sequences: The sequence of infant- or baby-behavior is written on the same line as the infant's initial and runs from the left to the right. The behavior categories are encoded with a three letter system (see

Appendix A). The three letter code reflects the name of the behavior unit it stands for. This makes it easy to remember them (for instance "pul" stands for "pulling"). The code of any behavior category which is directed towards an object is followed by the captial letters OB and the name of the object between parentheses (for instance: sab OB(vine); see first line of Figure 6). The name of that object is written in the upper-left-hand corner of the form as well. This is a preliminary analysis to know the kind of objects an infant interacts with most. The code of any behavior category which is directed towards another individual is followed by the initial of that individual (for instance: pul FT; see first line of Figure 6). If two or more behavior categories occur simultaneously, these form a combination of behavior units. The three letter codes of the behavior units involved are written one after the other, separated by hyphens (for instance: ste-pff; see first line of Figure 6). A vertical line separates one combination of behavior categories from the next. A time scale of 15 seconds was applied. The 15th, 30th, and 45th second of a minute are indicated by the figures 15, 30, and 45 written in between two vertical lines. The 00th second of a minute is written in column T. The behavior category combinations of the mother and other individual(s) following any behavior category combination of the infant are written under the latter combination, each on its own line indicated by the initial in column N.

DEP   whenever one or more individuals leave the group (= individuals visible to the observer), their initial is indicated in this column on the line of the particular minute.

ARR   whenever one or more individuals arrive in the group, their initial is written in this column on the line of the particular minute.

Structure: Every 5 minutes individuals visible to the observer are checked.

W   the weather is checked every 5 minutes. The letters s, d, and c stand for sun, dry, and cloudy respectively.

Observer Reliability

It was impossible to test inter-observer reliability in the field, because it was difficult for two observers to be both in the best observing spot. For a short period during my study there was a portable video-recorder available in Gombe, together with a monitor. One of my infants was taped during an episode which was as "difficult" as possible: A number of other individuals were present and my infant was playing with another infant. The result was 13 minutes of video-recording. If my intra-observer reliability was reasonable over repeated observations and transcriptions of this video-tape, all my intra-observer reliabilities over other episodes would be as good or better.

The intra-observer reliability test was done on two successive evenings. The transcriptions of the audio cassette-tapes were done with an interval of one week between successive transcriptions.

The analysis was done as follows:

First, an overall measure of reliability was calculated. The total number of behavior category combinations was counted. This number depends not only on the behavior-sequence of the infant but also on the behavior changes in the other individuals. Therefore, it is quite a sensitive measure. According to this measure, intra-observer reliability is high: the first transcription had 215 combinations versus 217 for the second. This gives a reliability of .99.

Second, the infant-behavior-sequence of the first test was compared with the one of the second test. For every 15-second period the frequency of *newly started* behavior categories was established. Thereafter, the behavior categories of the two corresponding 15-second periods were compared and the number of behavior categories that were the same were counted. Numbers of all the 15-second periods were added together and the total was called S. The total number of behavior categories (S + the other categories that were dissimilar) was taken as the sum of those 15-second period frequencies which had the highest number of units (T). The intra-observer reliability (R) was calculated according to the formula:

$$R = 100 \times \frac{S}{T} = 76\%$$

and the result is shown. I consider this result acceptable, as the test had been made as difficult as possible. Nevertheless, it is instructive to look into the mistakes made.

The cause for the dissimilarities was roughly threefold. First, in many cases the sequence was the same, except that in one test a behavior category combination was transcribed just before a 15-second time marker and just after the same maker in the second test. This implies that the accuracy of the time-markers was plus or minus a few seconds. The way the 15-second time scale was obtained needs explaining in order to understand this. My wrist-watch contained a proper stop-watch. I dictated time every 15 seconds onto my cassette-tape together with all the other observations, while following chimpanzees. The time marker was sometimes forgotten, especially when a lot of interaction between the infant and other individuals was going on. During transcription, I corrected this omission by measuring the time from the last time-marker mentioned, with the help of a stop-watch. Since the tape recorder was replayed at the original recording speed, and since this speed was very constant (only a fraction of a second difference per minute, under various conditions) the inaccuracy of a few seconds could not possibly be explained by time dictation and/or transcription. The only possible reason left then, is that my dictation of the behavior observations lagged behind a little when a lot happened at once and, furthermore, that this lagging behind varied from test to test.

Second, there are some examples where the categories in Test I were dissimilar *but related* to the categories recorded in Test II. For instance, "looks at" (LAT) versus "glimpse" (GLI). Here a judgment of the duration is crucial and it is understandable that mistakes are made in marginal cases.

Third, behavior categories were recorded in one test and missed in the other. Mostly, these were short-lasting categories such as glimpse, yawning, self-scratching, shaking. Taking these kinds of mistakes into consideration I feel confident that the intra-observer reliability is high enough to use the data for further analysis.

3

Perinatal Period

The way in which a chimpanzee baby is treated by its mother has been described by van Lawick-Goodall (1968, pp. 222–257) in the sections on mother-offspring and sibling-relationships. The behavioral development of babies and infants was considered only briefly (van Lawick-Goodall, 1968, pp. 285–291, and p. 221) and a note was added stressing the desirability of further work in this field. In this book the focus will be on the developmental processes.

This chapter is concerned with the perinatal period. It will be divided in two parts: the prenatal period (including parturition) and the neonatal period. For the prenatal period only those maternal behaviors will be described which may influence the development of the baby. The neonatal period is defined here as lasting from birth to the age of 2 months. The limited behavior repertoire of the baby during this period is described.

PRENATAL PERIOD

Self-protective behavior by expectant chimpanzee mothers is not obvious in the wild, according to van Lawick-Goodall (1968, p. 223), although she suggests that females sometimes go off by themselves during the final days of pregnancy and thus avoid strenuous forms of social activity. Two females became pregnant during my study: Passion and Winkle. I managed to follow the latter during the last month of her pregnancy for 13 days from night-nest to night-nest. Figure 7 shows, separately for every day, how far Winkle traveled. It is clear that she restricted her movements only during the last day before parturition. Figure 8 illustrates that Winkle did not avoid social activity until that same last day before parturition. I do not believe that the low percentage of time Winkle spent in a group on the 19th, two days before parturition, has anything to do with her pregnancy. A similar day was recorded 22 days before parturition (September 24) and on both

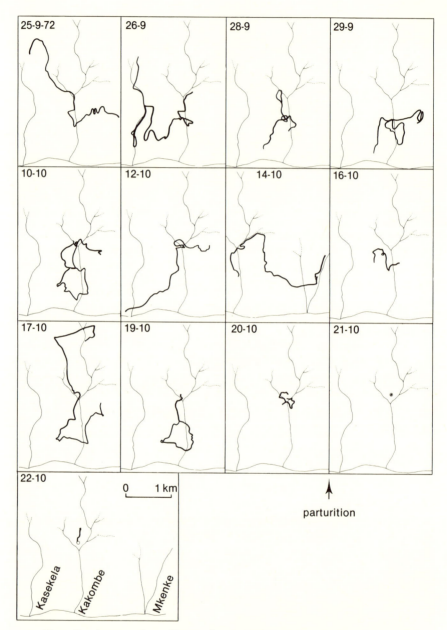

Figure 7. Amount of travel by one female (WK) during the last month before parturition. The eleven maps indicate the amount of travel on eleven separate days from dawn to dusk.

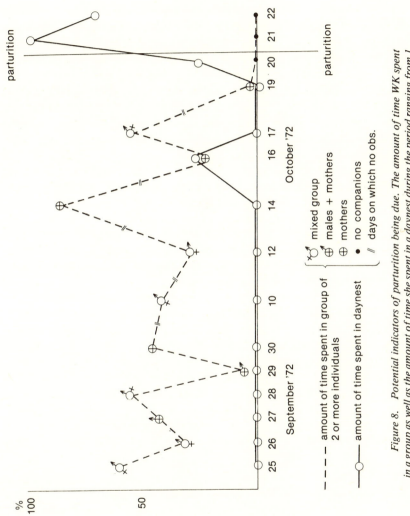

Figure 8. *Potential indicators of parturition being due. The amount of time WK spent in a group as well as the amount of time she spent in a daynest during the period ranging from 1 month before until 2 days after parturition.*

35

days Winkle was "termite fishing" nearly all day. Wrangham (1975) argued that the party size correlates with the amount of competition for food; when termites are not abundant, which was the case at that time, termite fishing is best done alone.

A better indicator of the parturition being due was the construction of a platform or "nest" in a tree during the daytime. This is unusual for a chimpanzee. Four days before parturition Winkle did this for the first time. When a mother and her infant passed under the tree, Winkle descended and joined them. The next day Winkle was very active again and traveled a great deal in a large, mixed group (males, oetrus females, mothers with their children). The last day before parturition Winkle made several nests during the day and rested in them. It may be that the first time she made a daynest, contractions had started but stopped again, whereas the second time contractions continued and parturition resulted.

Therefore, my observations confirm van Lawick-Goodall's observation that self-protective behavior is absent during the prenatal period. This also fits Pond's (1977) statement that this is true for all mammals. Van Lawick-Goodall's suggestion that females go off by themselves during the final days of pregnancy is supported by my data insofar as the last day before parturition is concerned. Whether the females do so in order to avoid strenuous social activities or because their physical condition (contractions) simply forces them to, remains an open question.

Birth has never been observed in the wild. Although Winkle was followed until parturition, I was unable to observe much because she made a nest high in a tree and gave birth there. However, from the first postnatal day on, I had spells of good observation on her baby Wilkie (WL). As for the other babies born during my study period (see Figure 5), Freud (FD) was over 1 week old upon my arrival at Gombe. The second baby, Prof (PF), was first seen when he was a few days old. His mother, Passion (PS), was so habituated to my presence that she sometimes sat down not more than 2 meters away from me, on her own accord. This permitted very detailed observations.

NEONATAL PERIOD

The newborn chimpanzee baby is half a "naked ape": the ventral side of the torso, neck, and head as well as the insides of arms and legs are relatively hairless. On the contrary, the dorsal side of the torso, neck, and head as well as the outsides of the extremities are thickly covered with hair. Furthermore, the skin of the "naked" body parts is yellowish brown whereas the skin that is covered with hair is dark.

There are two more anatomical aspects of the chimpanzee newborn which are very striking, although their functional significance escapes me. First, the Gombe chimpanzee newborns wear a "mask": as an exception to the rule that the skin of the ventral side of the torso and neck and the facial side of the head is light brown, the skin around the eyes is dark. Second, the skin of the bottom is hairless and its color is purplish red, as is the color of the palmar surface of the hands and the planar surface of the feet.

These anatomical aspects disappear soon. The mask has disappeared completely by the age of 5 weeks. The purplish red color of the skin of the bottom, the palmar surface of the hands, and the planar surface of the feet has disappeared by the age of 7 weeks and the white tailtuft starts to grow at that same age and is over 1 cm long by the age of 2 months. The growth of hair on the ventral side of the torso starts at the age of 2 months and 1 month later it is covered with hair. Teeth have not yet erupted during the neonatal period.

The behavioral repertoire of the chimpanzee neonate is very limited. In fact, the newborn baby is extremely helpless. It does not yet walk or even sit. When not sleeping, the neonate may show clinging (CLM), lying (LIE), mountaineering (MON), moving (MOV), erection of the penis (PEN), rooting (ROT), sucking (SUC), and/or a number of vocalizations: dreamscream (DSC), infant-grunt (GRU), infant-bark (IBA), infant-scream (ISC), infant-squeak (ISQ), staccato (STC), uh-grunt (UHH), effort-grunt (ZEG), whimper-ho (ZHO), and whimper (ZWH). Furthermore, it gives all the responses as elicited in the Brazelton neonatal behavioral assessment scale (Turney, 1978).

In this chapter, I elaborate on the waking recurrences, sucking, clinging, mountaineering, rooting, effort-grunt, staccato, uh-grunt, whimper-ho, and whimpering. The first section of this chapter will deal with the waking and sucking recurrences. The newborn babies spent all their time on the ventral side of their mother's body, supported, sleeping, and waking. When the babies were awake, one of the behavior categories to be observed (see foregoing paragraph) was sucking. Chimpanzee babies are demand-feeders: The feeds are short-spaced and short-lasting.

In a later section, it is shown that the neonate was not able to remain clinging to the body of its mother without any help. Thereafter, mountaineering and rooting as a means to reach a nipple are discussed.

Finally, the conditions in which a number of vocalizations occurred are described in detail. These vocalizations are the effort-grunt, the staccato, the uh-grunt, the whimper-ho, and the whimpering. The conditions in which these vocalizations were given reveal much about the way in which the chimpanzee babies perceived the world around them. The development of the vocal repertoire of the Gombe chimpanzees shall be described elsewhere (van de Rijt-Plooij & Plooij, in preparation).

Waking and Sucking

What do the waking and sucking recurrences (as defined in Young and Ziman, 1971) of a chimpanzee baby look like? Although a thorough study has been made of the ontogeny of sleep in captive chimpanzee babies (Balzamo et al., 1972 a, b), there is good reason to collect additional data about the sleep recurrences of babies in the wild. The authors mentioned stated that some differences existed between animals raised by the mother and those cared for in the nursery, but without elaborating any further on their observations. Also in the human literature differences have been reported between babies from different caretaking environments (Casaer, 1979; Sander et al., 1972). It seems interesting to me to compare these differences with the differences in sleep behavior between captive, nursery-raised and free-living, mother-raised chimpanzee babies. If these differences turn out to be similar, this may be helpful when placing human baby-caretaking into an evolutionary framework.

In the field it was impossible to collect measures such as EEG, ECG, EMG, reflecting the waking- or sleeping-states of the baby such as can be done for human babies (Prechtl, 1974) or chimpanzee babies in captivity (Balzamo et al., 1972 a, b). I only recorded whether the baby had its eyes open (EYO) or not (EYC). Nonetheless, this need not invalidate comparison, because Sander et al. (1972) have shown that these two types of measures (simply recording whether the eyes are open or closed versus recording motility in a more sophisticated way) correlate highly. Comparison may be restricted, however, by the fact that Sander et al. (1972) had periods of good observation which lasted all day long, whereas, in my study, these periods were at most no longer than 108 minutes (Table 2). Consequently, my records were fragmented. I have tried to overcome this difficulty by constructing a picture of sleep during a day through combining in the following way data from good observation periods of several days.

One of the babies (PF) was observed in its first week during 5 successive days. The available data were all collected continuously between 7.00 and 17.00. I divided each day into 10-minute periods (e.g., 07.10–07.19, 07.20–07.29, etc.) and recorded for every period on how many of the 5 days I had good observation during all of that period and whether the baby's eyes were open (EYO) or not. If during any minute of a 10-minute period the eyes had been recorded as open, the whole period was scored for EYO. Correspondingly, if good observation did not exist during the entire 10-minute period, but EYO could nevertheless be observed during part of it such a period was scored for EYO. This manner of scoring, which is very much biased towards EYO, was chosen on purpose to be sure that in any period scored for eyes closed (EYC) the baby was fast asleep during the whole period. Sucking and non-sucking were scored in the same way. In

TABLE 2

Frequency Distribution of the Durations of Periods
'Good Observation' for the Baby PF at Two Different
Ages (Week 1 versus Weeks 2-9)

Duration Good Obs. (mins.)	AGE BABY	
	Week 1	Weeks 2-9
1-5	54%	60%
6-10	23	14
11-15	9	5
16-20	4	7
21-25	4	5
26-30	1	1
31-35	2	3
36-40	0	0
41-45	0	1
46-50	0	0
51-55	0	1
56-60	1	2
61-65	1	0
66-70	1	0
> 70(108)	0	1
N	91	86
total duration (mins.)	822	875

Figure 9 these data have been plotted in accordance with the following rules: If, for a particular 10-minute period, the number of good observation days with EYO and EYC was equal, the end score was plotted as neutral. If the end score showed a difference between the number of days, only the eyelid position occurring on the greatest number of days was plotted for that number of days.

For two reasons these data are restricted to the first two months. First, at the age of 2 months the neonatal period was defined as finished. Second, Sander (1969) and Sander et al. (1972) also restricted their study to the first two months. The data of week 1 were presented separately from the data of weeks 2-9 because Sander et al. (1972) found a change in sleeping-pattern around the age of 1 week.

Figure 9a gives the results of week 1. This graph shows that the baby slept for at least 20 minutes around 9:00, shortly after 12:00, and around 15:00. This was true for all days on which I had "good observation" (two or more). The baby was much more awake during the morning than during

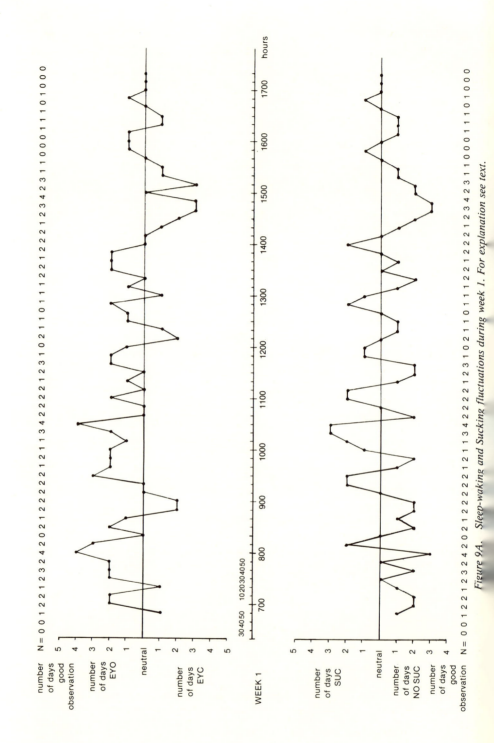

Figure 9A. Sleep-waking and Sucking fluctuations during week 1. For explanation see text.

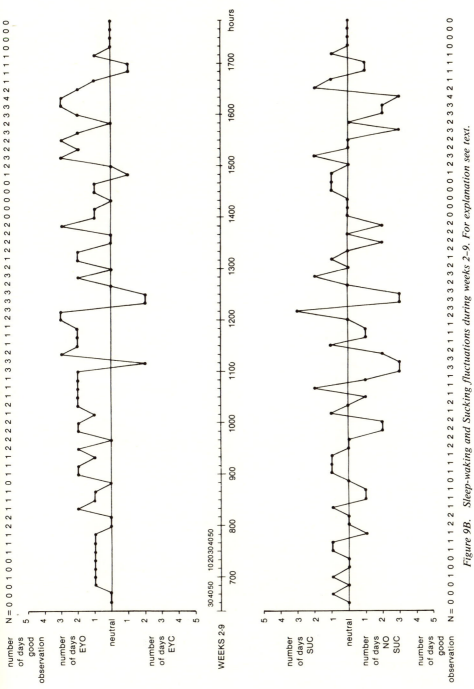

Figure 9B. Sleep-waking and Sucking fluctuations during weeks 2-9. For explanation see text.

41

the afternoon. The afternoon sleep period around 15:00 lasted much longer than 20 minutes and the baby was more frequently observed with EYO during the morning than during the afternoon. Between 7:00 and 8:50 and between 9:30 and 10:40 the baby was observed with EYO for up to 4 separate days. When looking at periods of EYC recorded on at least 2 days of good observation (data based on only 1 day were not considered) a recurrence of sleep of 2–3 hours seems to appear. In the intervals one can say that the baby was frequently awake; its eyes were not open continuously. Table 3 gives the frequency distribution of the durations of EYO-periods of which I saw both the start and the end. Mostly, the baby kept its eyes open for only a few minutes at a time. Only 5% of the EYO periods lasted 10 minutes or longer with a maximum of 22 minutes. Still, the baby had its eyes open for 30% of the time I could observe it well. This result is far from the notion that "the newborn sleeps almost all day" (Balzamo et al., 1972b).

TABLE 3
Frequency Distribution of the Durations of EYO-units
for the Baby PF at Two Different Ages
(Week 1 versus Weeks 2–9)

Duration EYO (mins.)	AGE BABY	
	Week 1	Weeks 2–9
0–1	40%	39%
1–2	9	16
2–3	11	6
3–4	17	10
4–5	4	2
5–6	4	5
6–7	4	2
7–8	4	4
8–9	0	5
9–10	1	1
> 10	4	9
N	70	99
total duration (mins.)	249	493
duration per 100 mins. good observation	30	56

Figure 9a also gives the incidence of sucking. Most surprising to me is that sucking is so regularly intermittent. With this way of plotting, one would not expect such regularity unless a rather constant sucking cycle exists. Furthermore, this figure suggests that the intervals between sucking are rather short (approximately 1 hour). Of course, such a conclusion cannot be drawn from these data alone. It is possible that the baby went on the nipple on the average of every 3 hours, whereas the times on the nipple were at random with respect to clock time. The intervals between sucking might well appear shorter in Figure 9a because of lumping data across days.

In order to settle this issue, I plotted the frequency distribution of the durations of sucking-intervals (which I observed from start to end; Figure 10). None of the intervals laster longer than 100 minutes. A few intervals during the afternoon sleep period lasted between 70-100 minutes. Most of the intervals lasted less than 70 minutes. Thus, it is safe to conclude that the intervals between sucking are rather short.

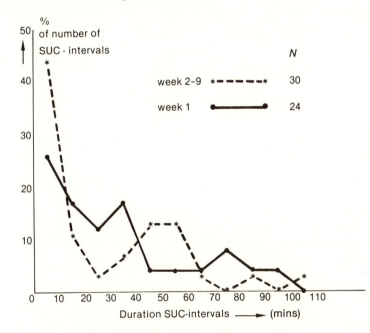

Figure 10. Frequency distributions of the durations of sucking-intervals (from the start of one SUC-unit to the start of the next SUC-unit).

Usually, the duration of one go on the nipple was short: only a few minutes (median = 3 minutes). However, the baby might stay on the nipple for up to 10 minutes (Figure 11).

During the remainder of the first 2 months I followed this baby, PF, for 6 days as compared with 5 days in the first week. This resulted in a roughly equal number of minutes good observation: 875 for weeks 2-9 versus 822 for week 1 (Table 2). I recorded and plotted EYO and SUC in the same way as I did for week 1 and the result is shown in Figure 9b.

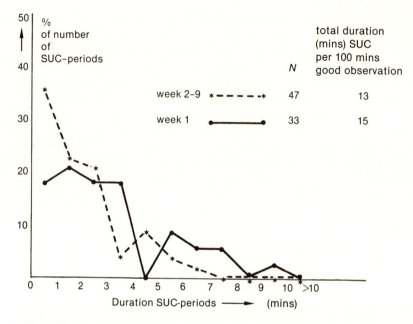

Figure 11.   Frequency distributions of the durations of sucking for two different ages of the baby, together with the total duration SUC per 100 minutes of good observation. The median duration decreases from 2–3 to 1–2 minutes whereas the quartile deviation stays 1 minute. The range decreases as well: from 10 to 7 minutes. The total duration of SUC does not change. Therefore, the baby sucks more frequently and for shorter periods with increasing age.

The sleep period around 9:00 had disappeared and the long sleep period in mid-afternoon had vanished almost completely. Only the midday sleep period remained and another one shortly after 11:00 had appeared. Furthermore, it is striking that EYO was scored for many 10-minutes periods in succession. This is in accord with the frequency distribution of the duration of the periods in which the baby was observed to keep its eyes open continuously (Table 3): Twice as many long periods (≥ 10 minutes) occurred and the maximum duration rose by a factor of 3 from 22 minutes to 63 minutes. Overall, the baby was awake twice as much (nearly 60% versus 30%). Again, this is in striking contrast with the observation of Balzamo et al. (1972b) that a captive chimpanzee newborn in the second month of life still sleeps during most of the day. Surely, by 1 month of age the free-living chimpanzee baby was already *awake* more than half the day. This decreasing trend in the time spent sleeping continued over the first months. From 4 months on only a short period of approximately half an hour to an hour remained. On this point I agree with Balzamo. This daytime napping slowly disappeared after the second year.

In weeks 2–9 the distribution of sucking over the day seems to have changed as well, if one compares Figure 9b with Figure 9a. Closer examina-

tion of the frequency distribution of the durations of sucking and of the duration of the intervals between sucking (of which I saw both the start and the
end) revealed that the time pattern of the organization of sucking changed.
The percentage of time spent sucking during weeks 2–9 was the same as in
week 1 (Figure 11). The baby sucked for shorter durations (median of 1–2
minutes versus 2–3 minutes before, while extremely long sucking of up to 10
minutes disappeared) but more frequently (Figure 11). Not only were there
more intervals of 41–60 minutes in weeks 2–9 versus more intervals of
61–100 minutes in week 1, but also the increase of very short intervals of
1–10 minutes in this second period was striking (Figure 10). These very short
intervals resulted from the fact that several sucking occurrences clustered in
time. One may call such clusters bouts. These bouts did not occur at any
time during the day but prevailed between 9:00–9:30 and 14:20–15:20, i.e.,
roughly the periods during which the baby slept in week 1. When comparing
Figures 9a and 9b for these times of the day, one notices sucking peaks during weeks 2–9 where there were sleep periods in week 1. I shall come back to
this phenomenon in the discussion.

Clinging (CLM)

A chimpanzee baby in the wild was not able to remain clinging to the body
of its mother with the help of its Moro-response, palmar grasp, and traction
response (for a definition of these terms see Prechtl and Beintema [1964,
pp. 45, 34, and 43]). Clearly, the mother could not rely on them and had to
support (SUP, CRA) and often even carry (CAR) her baby. The proportion
of time the mother supported or carried her baby differed greatly between
individual mothers. In all it decreased sharply after 2 months (van de Rijt-
Plooij, 1982). In other words, some mothers supported and carried their
babies almost continuously from shortly after birth whereas others restricted
themselves to the minimum necessary not to lose their baby. Consequently,
during locomotion over greater distances (= travel) babies from the first
group were safe; they rarely whimpered or screamed. Babies in the second
group, on the other hand, whimpered frequently when loosing their grip on
the mother's hair, dangling from only one or two of their four limbs. Baby
PF and mother PS belonged to this latter category. However, in this baby
whimpering had practically disappeared after three months (Table 4, pp.
60–61). The maternal support is of vital importance to the baby. Without it,
the baby would surely fall off and may die. I observed a natural experiment
demonstrating this. Madam Bee had raised two infants successfully when
one of her arms was paralyzed during a presumed polio-epidemic (van
Lawick-Goodall, 1971, p. 217–224). The two infants that were born afterwards died within a few months. I had the occasion to make observations
on the first of these two infants: Bee-hinde. Her body was full of wounds
and scratches, so she must have fallen repeatedly. Whenever her mother

moved about without supporting her, she whimpered and screamed continuously. Especially when support was needed most, such as during climbing, the mother failed to give it.

After 2 months the baby is able to support its own weight.

Mountaineering (MON) and Rooting (ROT)

Mountaineering and rooting subserve sucking. Through these behaviors a nipple is reached. Through mountaineering the baby progresses up the body of the mother and reaches the vicinity of the nipples with its mouth. Through rooting the baby zooms in on one nipple: as soon as a nipple touches the perioral region of its face the baby moves its head in that direction, opens its mouth, and takes that nipple into its mouth. The baby does not always reach a nipple. Sometimes it gets "lost" and starts whimpering (ZWH). This causes the mother to reposition it in the ventro-ventral position, head upwards, which gives the baby a new start. I have never observed a baby being actually "given the breast" by a mother.

From the end of the first month, struggling over (STR) was observed. It is a very inefficient way of locomoting, resembling crawling, and differing from mountaineering.

The Effort-grunt (ZEG)

In the field I had the impression that this vocalization was given whenever a baby was moving (MOV) or struggling over (STR) the body of its mother. I reasoned that if this were true, counting the effort-grunts would be a reliable measure of the activity-level of a baby.

In order to test this field impression, I took approximately 1,000 minutes during which I had good observation from the records on PF in between the ages of 1 and 6 weeks. Because effort-grunts can only be scored reliably if an observer is within a distance of 5 meters from the baby, I made a further restriction in that I only looked at the minutes which combined good observation with an observer within 5 meters and in this way I obtained a total of 978 minutes. For those minutes I recorded whether the baby was moving and/or emitting effort-grunts.

It turned out that in 90 out of 103 minutes (87%) the baby was moving, it emitted effort-grunts. On the other hand I recorded 72 minutes during which the baby produced effort-grunts without moving. On inspection, it turned out that during those minutes the baby was usually lying in the prone position over its mother's thigh, head outwards. One could speculate that in such a position the baby was keeping balance, which involves muscular effort not visible in gross movement.

Although much rarer, effort-grunts were also observed in other age classes and in both sexes, and again in combination with an increased effort.

For instance, a juvenile standing on its head and an adult male trying to break open a bee's or wasp's nest using a long thick branch as a lever and not succeeding.

On these grounds the frequency of effort-grunts per 100 minutes of good observation (together with observer within 5 meters) can be used as a measure of the level of that kind of activity of the baby, which is associated with muscular effort. In Figure 12 this frequency is plotted against age. During the first 2 months there was a rise in this frequency, due to the beginning of "struggling over" towards the end of the first month and "reaching for" (REF) things towards the end of the second month. Between the second and fifth month the frequency declined towards zero. During this time the babies became increasingly able to locomote: in the fifth month the babies left their mother for the first time and were able to stand and walk quadrupedally, stand bipedally while holding themselves, and climb.

Whimpering (ZWH) and Staccato (STC)

During the first days of life these two vocalizations frequently go together. Not only could each of them follow the other closely in time, but it could also happen that a mixture of the two vocalizations was given: For instance, whimper might merge into a staccato within one and the same exhalation. First I shall describe the causation of these two vocalizations separately. In the discussion of Chapter 4, I shall come back to the significance of their temporal linkage.

Whimpering (ZWH) and whimper-ho (ZHO). The following conditions elicited whimper-ho's or whimpering in the newborn baby.

1. Discrepancy from ventro-ventral contact with the mother. This could be caused in a number of situations.
   a) The mother sits and feeds or lies and rests, and the baby stops clinging and rests in the mother's lap. Because the mother does not cradle (CRA) enough the baby slides slowly out of her lap onto the substrate (the ground or a branch in between her legs). When the baby is not able to get back into the lap through clinging, it starts whimpering. Usually, a mother reacts to this by pushing her baby back against her belly (CRA or SUP), sometimes without even glancing at it. As soon as the ventro-ventral contact is restored the baby stops whimpering and clings to its mother.
   b) If the mother moves suddenly while sitting or resting the baby usually performs a Moro-response and whimpers thereafter.
   c) During locomotion over greater distances (travel) the baby is no longer able to support its own weight and loses its grip on the

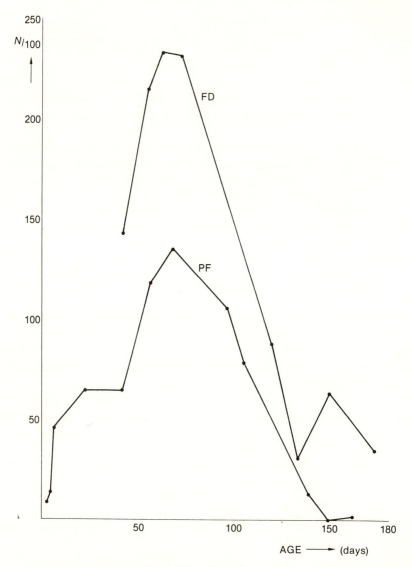

Figure 12.   The frequency of effort-grunts (ZEG) per 100 minutes of good observation over age for the two babies PF and FD.

mother's hair. Dangling from only one or two of its four limbs it utters a ho (ZHO), whimper (ZWH), or even scream (ISC). As a reaction, the mother supports (SUP) it. This enables the baby to cling to its mother's hair again with all fours. As soon as the ventro-ventral contact is restored, the baby stops vocalizing.

d) In 5 out of the 47 instances in the first month of life, baby PF gave ho's as a reaction to its sister pulling or grooming it. This vocalization did not start until the baby lost ventro-ventral contact with its mother, as a result of the actions of the sibling. Therefore, one may conclude that the baby reacted to the discrepant body position and not to its sibling as another individual.

2. Discrepancy from nipple in mouth. The following situations occurred.

   a) If a newborn baby while rooting failed to meet a nipple, it started whimpering as rooting continued. This whimpering continued until a nipple was reached and sucking started.

   b) When a baby was already sucking and, for whatever reason, lost the nipple it whimpered and rooted again until sucking was resumed.

3. Rough handling.

   a) When thorns of vines were scratching the back of the baby.

   b) When mothers roughly groomed or repositioned the baby it sometimes gave ho's or a whimper.

4. When, from the end of the first month, the babies were observed struggling over (STR) the body of their mothers when they were lying, whimpering often occurred.

5. At sudden and very intense stimulation such as loud sound.

Staccato (STC) and Uh-Grunt (UHH).   In the first 3 months of life these vocalizations were given in the following contexts:

1. At the occasion of sudden loud noise, such as thunder, breaking wind, metal slamming on metal, metal shoved over concrete, cracking or breaking of a big branch, the sound of scratching (by another chimpanzee closeby), human speech, the sound of a bird, chimpanzee vocalizations.

2. When a big object was moving within or into the field of vision of the baby. This occurred, for instance, in the following situation. A baby lying on its back in the lap of the mother was approached by another chimpanzee which came unseen from the back. From the baby's point of view, this chimpanzee came all of a sudden "around the corner". Another example was humans appearing in the baby's field of vision. Once I observed a baby giving a staccato when a cloud moved in front of the sun and its shadow, moving quickly over the ground, reached the baby.

3. A sudden movement of the mother transferred to the baby, such as when the mother was pantgrunting and her belly was rapidly going

up and down, or when the baby was pushed back against mother's ventral surface rather abruptly.

4. Lying prone on the belly over a thigh of the mother with the head outwards and looking down into the grass. This was observed frequently. Because I could not approach the baby close enough to see what may have elicited vocalizations (e.g., movement in the grass), I cannot relate this context to the ones mentioned above.

5. One loud staccato was given by baby PF when for the first time it stood bipedally. While holding its mother and upon reaching this body-position it gave a loud staccato (STC). In this odd context I observed the staccato only once; I found it difficult to understand and shall come back to it later in the discussion of Chapter 4.

Also in Chapter 4, it will be shown that in the first 3 months the chimpanzee babies uttered these vocalizations predominantly not as a reaction to the quality but to the intensity of the stimulus (see pp. 63–64 and pp. 77–79). Consequently, assuming that the intensity of the stimulation to which they are exposed is constant over age, the frequently of these vocalizations per unit of time is a useful measure of the babies' reactivity.

Something like post-stimulatory facilitation played a role at this age (neonatal period): As soon as one staccato was given, much less intensive stimulation was needed to produce a second one, and a third, etc.

DISCUSSION

In the following discussion a large number of references will be made to the human literature. There are two reasons for this: first, most of the relevant research has been done on humans and only very little on other primates. Second, comparisons will not only be made between captive chimpanzees and free-living ones, but also for differences between these and between human babies from different caretaking environments.

Individual Differences in Activity/Reactivity

From the work of Escalona (1968, 1973) it is known that individual differences in activity and perceptual sensitivity in human babies at or shortly after birth persist and have an influence on later development. Consequently, for a developmental study as the present one it seemed worthwhile to try and assess such early individual differences. Handling babies was out of the question. Examinations such as those used to assess individual differences in human newborns by Prechtl and Beintema (1964) and by Brazelton (1973) could not be done. Furthermore, good observation on a chimpanzee newborn was fragmented, because most of the time the baby was hidden behind the arms and/or legs of the mother while she was supporting or cradling it. However, hearing could be used in the assessment of individual differences. Within a distance of 5 meters from the baby, I was able to hear all the vocalizations used by the baby. Two different vocalizations have proved very useful to determine the individual differences in activity and reactivity: the effort-grunt (ZEG) and the staccato (STC) or uh-grunt (UHH).

In an earlier section, (pp. 46–47), it was shown that counting the effort-grunts was a reliable measure of the activity-level of a baby. The graphs in Figure 12 demonstrate that the two babies PF and FD showed statistically significant individual differences, FD being the most active baby (Wilcoxon matched-pairs signed-ranks test, two-tailed, $p = .01$).

The frequency of the staccato (STC) or the uh-grunt (UHH) per unit of time is a useful measure of the reactivity of the babies, as was mentioned on pp. 49–50). Figure 13a gives the number of these vocalizations per sample of 300 minutes good observation within 5 meters for the first four months and shows that FD consistently produced 2 to 3 times as many vocalizations. This happened in spite of the conditions being in favor of PF since there was much more group calling around PF than around FD (see Figure 13b). Not only did FD vocalize more frequently, but he also did so more loudly and strongly. One could hear his staccatos even when he was far away and out of sight!

The individual differences in activity/reactivity between the two newborn babies Freud and Prof as measured through the frequencies of effort-grunts and staccatos were striking. The chances that these differences were due to differences between the mothers are slim. Passion was much more brusque, active, and inconsiderate of her baby than was FF (van de Rijt-Plooij, 1982). This should have produced the opposite result.

One may ask whether several different measurements of reactivity or activity would have confirmed the present finding. If the answer is yes, the measurement of responsiveness in chimpanzee neonates as reported here is probably a very useful measure of general responsiveness. Escalona (1968, 1973) and Korner (1971) have argued that such individual differences in general responsiveness do exist in human neonates and that they "may be characterized either as predispositions for certain patterns of development and adaptation later on, or else as potentials for excellence or unusually strong development in particular areas" (Escalona, 1973, 145–148).

Turkewitz et al. (1971), on the other hand, found that a human neonate's relative responsiveness as defined by one response does not predict its relative responsiveness in other responses. however, the three response measures used by these authors (cardiac acceleration, lateral conjugate eye movements, and finger extension or flexion) may not have been well chosen. The authors assume that cardiac acceleration is the cardiac component of orientation and that the other two measures (eye movements and finger extensions) are musculo-skeletal components of orientation. The former

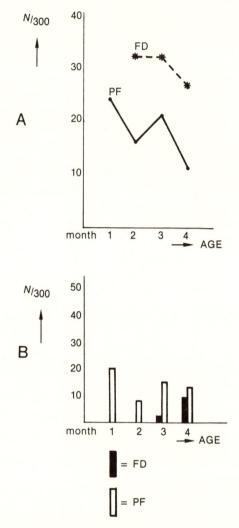

Figure 13.   Individual difference in reactivity.
A) Number of staccatos (STC) and uh-grunts (UHH) per 300 minutes of good observation
from birth to 4 months for the two babies PF and FD.
B) Number of times group calling around the babies.

assumption was refuted by more recent evidence, as reviewed by Berg and Berg (1979), which shows that cardiac acceleration in newborns fits the criteria for a defensive response. These criteria were the same as the ones used by Turkewitz et al. This could explain why Turkewitz et al. only found a significant, positive correlation between rank-orders as measured through lateral conjugate eye movements and finger extension (orientation) and not otherwise. It is interesting to note that the only rank-order which correlates reasonably positively (though not significantly) with the rank-order of cardiac acceleration is the rank-order of finger flexion (a defensive response).

Thus, Escalona's (1968, 1973) conclusion that individual differences in general responsiveness do exist seems not to be controverted by the available evidence. It is in line with the concept of a unitary orientating response (Anohkin, 1958; Sokolov, 1960). The few studies of concomitant autonomic (cardiac) and musculo-skeletal responses done during the last decade support this concept: Sustained cardiac deceleration is accompanied by increased eye-opening and decreased head movements (Berg & Berg, 1979).

Recently Turney (1978) announced the application of human neonatal and infant behavioral assessment scales to chimpanzee babies in captivity. I would recommend incorporation of the measure of reactivity reported here in their assessment procedures, because of the advantage of its being directly derived from chimpanzee research.

Waking and Sucking

One may safely conclude that chimpanzee babies in captivity sleep much more (almost all day) than their free-living cousins. In my opinion one of the main reasons is likely to be the caretaking environment. The captive chimpanzee babies were kept in a typical nursery environment as we know it so well from our own hospitals and from which it undoubtedly stemmed. This meant that they were in a horizontal position most of the time, be it prone or supine (see Balzamo, 1972a). The free-living babies, on the other hand, were on their mother's bodies all the time, and thus spent relatively little time in a horizontal position.

The idea that body position influences the waking cycle is not new. Gesell (1945) reported human babies to be more alert in a more upright position. This was confirmed by Korner and Thoman (1970). Bower (1974) considers the semi-upright position to be the ideal experimental situation. All the face-to-face preverbal communication studies are done with the baby in an especially designed baby-seat (e.g., Brazleton et al., 1974, 1975; Papousek & Papousek, 1977; Plooij, 1978b; Trevarthen, 1977). Finally, Casaer (1979) verified the idea experimentally: The semi-upright position does not influence the waking cycle in that the baby "remains in state 3 (alert and awake, see Prechtl & Beintema, 1964) for long epochs" at the expense of state 2 periods and without influencing the deep-sleep periods. Putting babies in a cradle in a horizontal position most of the day is a very recent phenomenon in our western society if we think in terms of an evolutionary time scale. It is a derivation from the natural pattern (Blurton Jones, 1972a): It influences the waking cycle of the babies and one can only speculate what influence this may have on further development.

A second reason that free-living chimpanzee babies sleep considerably less than chimpanzee babies in captivity may have to do with differences in another aspect of the caretaking environment, namely one single caretaker (the natural mother) and demand feeding for the former versus a number of different caretakers (changing every so many hours) and 4-hour schedule feeding for the latter. Sander et al. (1972) and Sander (1975) studied two groups of human babies for which the same difference was in effect and found among other things that day-night differentiation is reached earlier in the male babies with a single caretaker and demand feeding. These babies show a shift from being predominantly awake during the night towards being mostly awake during the day around the age of 1 week. Although nothing is known about how free-living chimpanzee babies sleep at night, the increase in the percentage of time that the baby had its eyes open during the day after week 1 (see Table 3) indicates that a similar differentation may have occurred.

As mentioned above, chimpanzee babies are demand feeders. As is witnessed by Figures 9a, 9b, 10, and 11, the feeds are short-spaced (5–105 minutes) and short-lasting (median of 1–3 minutes). This is in line with the quarter-hour to 2-hour feed-interval and the rapid cessation of sucking as suggested by comparative data on milk composition (Blurton Jones, 1972a). These data are also in line with independent findings on other chimpanzee babies from the Gombe (Clark, 1977; Nicolson, 1977; van Lawick-Goodall, 1968) as well as findings on human !Kung babies (Konner & Worthman, 1980). To give an example: Clark (1977) has found a mean of 2.7 occurrences of sucking per hour for babies not older than 6 months. Nicolson (1977) reports a mean of three times per hour for babies of 1 to 4 months. My data give a mean of two occurrences of sucking per hour over the first 2 months. However, it is my opinion that the nature of the data is such that they are not well represented by means. Both Figure 10 and 11 show the frequency distributions to be highly asymmetrical and to be positively skewed. Furthermore, after week 1, the frequency distribution of the sucking-intervals is bimodal (Figure 10). The first group of short intervals (<20 minutes is restricted to certain times of the day (I shall come back to this later). The mode of the second group of intervals is approximately 50 minutes. Interestingly enough, these data are in accord with Casaer's (1979, pp. 26–27) findings that in human babies "periods with a stable posture (state 1) and periods with unstable posture (state 2) neatly alternate; occasionally this cycle was interrupted by short awake periods with an overall increase in antigravity posture". From inspection of his graphs and figures for babies who were kept in the semi-upright position (60 degrees from the horizontal) this interruption appears to happen roughly every hour. This is in accord with Sander (1977) who reports REM/NREM cycles of 50–55 minutes.

These "short awake periods with an overall increase in antigravity posture" could possibly have resulted in the baby finding a nipple and sucking if only it had been on the body of its mother. This behavior reminds me of mountaineering and it would be interesting to verify whether this behavior actually leads to sucking in human cultures where the mothers do carry their babies on the body. Then it may turn out that the sucking of the wild chimpanzee babies and the waking-up of the human babies every hour may be part and parcel of the same process. Furthermore, this process may well be very old, evolutionarily speaking, since Grau et al. (1975) have demonstrated a reliable diurnal mobility cycle in young rhesus monkeys lasting for 67.5 ± 1.1 to 69.3 ± 0.8 minutes (plus a harmonic of 35.5 ± 0.5 minutes). Coincident with this cycle there was a sequence from sleep to self-grooming, picking, walking, climbing, and eating, returning progressively back to sleep. All these findings are in striking contrast with the study by Morath (1974) that reports a free running, endogenously regulated, 4-hour feeding rhythm in one human baby. However, although the author states that the baby was allowed to determine its own feeding rhythm (for the first 3 months of its life), the final decision to feed the baby was made by the caretaker: first of all the baby was left to cry for at least 5 minutes and even then the baby was often not fed when it was decided that other "causes" of crying (such as a wet diaper, wind, sweating, the pressure of a toy, restricted breathing) were present. Additionally, feeding was postponed during the so-called "crying hour". Before such studies are translated into guidelines for caregiving routines, they ought to be repeated on babies who are carried on the body of the mother and have the nipple available all the time. Finally, concepts such as "endogenously regulated" should be avoided since Casaer (1979) showed that rhythms in newborn babies are not altogether independent of environment.

The striking overlap of the eyes-closed-periods during week 1 and the sucking-periods during weeks 2–9 (Figures 9a and b) together with the finding that short sucking-intervals (<20 min, see Figure 10) are restricted to the same sucking periods (± 9.00, 13.00, 14.20–15.20, and 16.30) generated the hypothesis that with increasing age the diurnal rhythm may stay unaltered, although its appearance may change. Not only may eyes-closed-periods be replaced by long sucking-periods (many sucking-bouts separated by short intervals), but these sucking-periods, in turn, may be replaced by periods during which an infant is on the body of its mother much longer than during other parts of the day. Simpson and Simpson (1977) have shown that runs of long visits to the mother, or so-called "rest" periods, clearly exist in rhesus monkey infants. At an even older age, this "on the mother" may be replaced by proximity and grooming (GRO) or self-grooming (GRS) if no companion is available. Recently, some evidence in favor of the latter suggestion was presented by Nash (1978). She showed how in wild baboons (Papio anubis) the infant's sucking and riding were replaced by the infant grooming its mother or staying nearby. Further support for the hypothesis given above comes from the human literature on sleep-waking patterns: the cycle of 50 minutes which was discussed earlier is not only present in neonates but also apparent in the rest-activity pattern of the fetus (Sterman & Hoppenbrouwers, 1971) and furthermore in 8 month old children (Stern et al., 1973), albeit in different form (Parmelee, 1973).

The duration of the sucking-bouts changed drastically after week 1: The median duration shortened from 2-3 minutes during week 1 to 1-2 minutes during weeks 2-9. The median duration of 1-2 minutes is confirmed by Nicolson (1977) who reports a mean of 3.9 minute sucking-bouts. Since the median of frequency distributions with a considerable positive skewness is always less than the mean, this result and mine can be considered similar. The extra long sucking-bouts of more than 5 minutes disappear nearly completely after week 1. This was also reported by van Lawick-Goodall (1968, p. 227). The meaning of this phenomenon escapes me.

Helplessness

The chimpanzee newborn baby is primarily altricial: not able to cling properly, half naked, and helpless (but with the eyes open). Chimpanzees belong to the group of itinerant mammals. These give birth to relatively light offspring (below 4% of the maternal weight; see Pond, 1977). However, this need not necessarily go hand-in-hand with helplessness, because the young itinerant mammals tend to be well developed. Monkey-babies, for instance, are not so very naked on the ventral side of the body and are able to cling immediately after birth. Chimpanzee and man (and possibly the other apes as well) seem to stand apart from the remainder of the order of the primates in this respect. This has already been pointed out by Bolk (1926) in formulating his fetalization-hypothesis which states that hominization can be understood from a single, developmental principle, namely retardation. A high rate of retardation may lead to "retention": fetal, morphological characteristics become permanent. A maximum of retardation may even lead to "reduction": the loss of some characteristics. Our species shows a lot of retention and reduction. Over the last 50 years, Bolk's theory has been heavily criticized. This criticism was reviewed by Gould (1977). His end conclusion, however, was to reassert Bolk's claim: An essential characteristic of man as an organism is the slow progress of his life's course. The other apes share a number of fetal characteristics with our species, and strikingly more so than monkeys do. The nakedness is just one example. Although research since then has shown that accelerations for certain morphological characteristics may have occurred as well (Napier & Napier, 1967, pp. 38-39), something which Bolk (1926, p. 26) already mentioned, the initial stages in ontogeny are very similar. For instance Starck (1973) conducted a comparative study of the fetal development of the skull and reported that there is a striking resemblance between the chimpanzean and human stages of development and that the corresponding differences with a number of monkey-species (Cebidea and Cercopithecidae) are much greater. The consequence of this striking retardation in the apes is that their newborn babies are much more helpless and dependent on parental care than monkey babies.

As an aspect of helplessness I mentioned nakedness. It is part of the neonatal deficiency of thermal isolation: Classical neonatal nonshivering thermogenesis is insufficient to prevent hypothermia (which may be lethal if lasting long enough) of the neonate exposed to cold. Without the warmth of the mother's body the babies would die.

Another aspect of helplessness noted here was the lack of proper clinging. This finding is in sharp contrast with the finding of Riesen and Kinder (1952, p. 11) that the captive chimpanzee baby becomes a clinging infant promptly after birth. The "grasping reflex" was nearly as weakly developed in wild, newborn chimpanzees as in human newborns and it took weeks for the chimpanzee baby to be able to cling to its mother without any aid (see p. 45). The same was reported by Schenkel (1964) for captive gorilla babies. It has been said that the "grasping reflex" in human newborns is a rudiment of an earlier phylogenetic adaptation (Peiper, 1963). Because the grasping reflex in chimpanzee newborns was nearly as weakly developed, I oppose this view and argue rather that this newborn response is so weakly developed because its development is retarded. I venture to think that the early development of chimpanzee babies and human babies are almost equally retarded. If only the caretaking routines practiced on human babies in the western world would give the grasping reflex a chance, it would develop soon after birth. If a particular human type of baby care (i.e., nursery: babies not carried but lying in a cradle and schedule-fed) is given to chimpanzee babies, the grasping reflex deteriorates after 2-3 weeks (Balzamo, 1972a), just as with human babies! Carter (1973) similarly reports that the grasp and suspension reflex in newborn, captive gorillas is present only in the first few weeks and is valueless with regard to self-preservation. On the contrary, Konner (1972) describes how babies are carried by the "Zhun/ twasi" or !Kung Bushmen, (hunter-gatherer people living in South West Africa, Botswana, and Angola) and how this way of carrying enables them to grasp in the primate fashion. Blurton Jones (1972, p. 319) even concludes that there is nothing mysterious about the dying away of the grasping reflex in humans: it is not given a chance any more by the prevailing preconceptions about babies and baby-care."It is probably only through Freud's theories that sucking got the attention that grasping missed."

Therefore, on a par with Bolk's (1926) arguments against the notion of rudimentary organs one can argue that the weakly developed, newborn grasping refelx is not a rudiment of an earlier phylogenetic adaptation, but the result of developmental retardation which itself is submitted to selection pressures. The dying away of the grasping reflex in human newborns is not to be seen as a rudiment of a character no longer functional but as an example of the more general developmental phenomenon that any behavior deteriorates if it is deprived of experience. This hypothesis is supported, for instance, by experiments on kittens (Kovach & Kling, 1967) which have shown that the sucking "reflex" disappears after 3 weeks if not used before. Blakemore (1973) puts forward the theory that experience shapes connections in the brain by altering the strength of the inhibitory connections and so shaping the response of the brain-cells. That these connections are not lost forever but merely overridden by more powerful inhibitory ones if they are not kept in use over the early weeks of life was shown by Duffy et al. (1976). The striking phenomenon of developmental retardation in the apes will be discussed further in Chapter 4.

4

Early Life: Babies

In the foregoing chapter the behavior of chimpanzee neonates was described. In this chapter a description of the overt behaviors which are typical for the age range of 2–6 months is given. The upper age limit of 6 months is not chosen arbitrarily. Towards the end of the first half year, chimpanzees start to walk, to climb, to leave their mother, and to eat solid food regularly. Their behavior repertoire, which was very limited during the first half year, begins to expand. In general, the 6-month-olds are no longer so extremely helpless. In fact, the difference between the behavior of the neonates and the behavior of the 6-month-olds is enormous. Therefore, the changes in behavior during this age span require extra attention, with the question in mind whether it is possible to find evidence for the ontogenetic development of an increasingly complex, hierarchical organization underlying overt behavior.

First, the changes in the conditions which evoke the vocalizations whimpering and staccato shall be described. This is followed by a description of the waning of rooting and the emergence of biting together with the facial expression playface (PFH) and the vocalization laughing (LAC). Described next are early escape and the development of the phenomenon called "Fear of Strangers". Lastly, a rather miscellaneous group of changes concerning motor development is presented.

WHIMPERING (ZWH) AND STACCATO (STC)

The conditions in which these two types of vocalization are given change markedly after the neonatal period. These changes reveal a lot about the different ways in which chimpanzee babies perceive the world around them at different ages. The changing conditions will be described separately for each type of vocalization.

Whimpering (ZWH) and Whimper-ho (ZHO)

The frequency of whimpers and ho's which were uttered by the two babies FD and PF during the first 12 months are presented in Figure 14. The large individual differences are due to the differences in maternal support, as was explained in pp. 45–46). The changes over age of the conditions in which whimpers and ho's were given are only presented for the baby which vocalized frequently (PF).

Table 4 gives the frequency distributions over the first nine months for a number of conditions in which whimpers and ho's were given. From the right-hand side of this table one can conclude that three qualitatively different types of conditions eliciting whimpers and ho's predominate at successive ages. First of all, early post natally, only the contexts listed in pp. 47–49 (neonatal period) occur (discrepancy from ventro-ventral contact, discrepancy from nipple in mouth, rough handling, struggling over). After the first month of life, the frequencies of these contexts decreased markedly. Over the second, third, and fourth months they dropped practically to zero. Thereafter, the context named "discrepancy 3" scored the highest frequency during the fifth month: As soon as contact was broken and the mother was not within the field of vision, the baby whimpered. Finally, this context ceased to be effective in eliciting whimpers and ho's by the age of seven

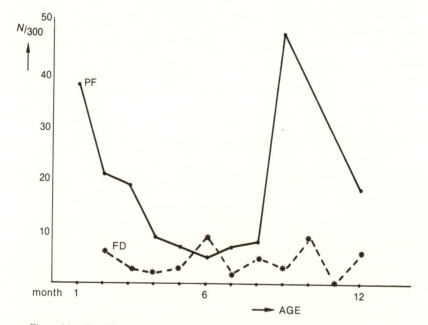

Figure 14.   Total frequency of whimpers (ZWH) and whimper-ho's (ZHO) per 300 minutes of good observation over the first year of life.

TABLE 4

Context Analysis of Whimpers (ZWH) and Whimper-hos (ZHO) Given By One Individual (PF) During the First 9 Months

AGE – Month 1	2	3	4	5	6	7	8	9	What Actually Happens	Common End Result	AGE – Month 1	2	3	4	5	6	7	8	9
6	3	3	3	1	0	0	0	2	Slides from body ma										
16	6	6	1	0	0	2	1	3	Sudden movement ma	⟩ discrepancy									
20	8	5	2	0	1	2	0	1	Travel	ventro-ventral contact	47	20	14	7	1	2	5	1	7
5	0	0	0	0	1	1	0	1	Other individual PUL										
0	3	0	1	0	1	0	0	0	Ma SCO + SCH										
31	5	1	1	1	0	0	0	0	Rooting	Unknown	45	6	3	1	1	0	0	0	0
7	1	1	0	0	0	0	0	0	Looses nipple from mouth	⟩ discrepancy	38	6	2	1	0	2	0	0	0
0	0	0	0	2	0	0	0	0	Ma CON, CUP	nipple in mouth										
3	0	0	0	0	0	0	1	0	Thorns of vines in back	⟩ rough	9	0	2	0	0	0	0	1	2
6	0	2	0	0	0	0	0	2	Firm handling by ma										
6	22	14	8	8	0	0	0	0	Off mother (4)	⟩ Struggles over	6	22	14	8	0	0	0	0	0
0	0	0	1	0	0	0	0	0	Baby leaves (LVE) ma	⟩ discrepancy 3	0	0	0	1	5	0	2	0	0
0	0	0	0	5	0	2	0	0	Ma LVE, baby FOL										
0	0	0	0	0	0	0	6	25	Baby LVE, APP ma	⟩ discrepancy 4	0	0	0	0	0	0	0	8	30
									Baby LAT others		0	0	0	0	1	0	1	0	0
									Baby FOL others		0	0	0	0	0	0	0	0	2
0	0	0	0	0	0	0	2	5	Intense Stimulation		0	1	0	0	0	1	0	0	0
									Total		145	55	35	18	8	5	8	10	41

months and was replaced by a context named "discrepancy 4": As soon as the mother went out of arm's reach or the infant itself had gone out of arm's reach, it started whimpering and followed or returned to its mother, respectively. As soon as the infant was back within arm's reach it stopped whimpering. It must have been changes in capacities of the baby which caused the changes in context eliciting whimpers and ho's. For instance, with respect to the decreased effectiveness of contexts which elicited these calls in the neonatal period, the changes in the mother's behavior occurring in the subsequent months would have caused more instead of less whimpering; she supported, carried and cradled less when the baby grew older. In the baby, on the other hand, rooting disappeared over the second month, together with whimpering (see left-hand side of Table 4). Apparently, the baby had learned where the nipples were. No longer did the baby root blindly but went directly for the nipple. Initially this was not easy because it had very limited means of locomotion at its disposal; consequently it struggled over its mother's body. This was mainly seen in the second and third month of life (Table 4). By the age of 3 months, the baby went straight for the nipple. Furthermore, it was able to cling to her fairly well without any support during travel (longer periods of locomotion of the mother). Also, by the time the baby had learned where the nipples were situated, it must also have learned features of other parts of the mother's body, since broken ventroventral contact no longer elicited ho's as long as the baby was in contact with the mother.

However, after the infant had outgrown the limitations of the neonatal period, a new issue became apparent in the context which was named "discrepancy 3". An example may illustrate this. When the individual Prof (PF) was 19-weeks-old, he was observed to walk for the first time. He used to walk around the mother and, consequently, contact with her was easily broken and restored again. Once he moved off in such a way that after breaking contact with mother she was right behind him and he started whimpering. He could easily have turned around and grasped his mother but he did not and continued walking, as far as 5 meters away from her, whimpering louder and louder. She watched him continuously and finally went over and gathered (GAT) him. Apparently, "out of sight" meant "out of mind" at this age and the baby was not able to represent its mother as being *behind* him. This limitation disappeared by the age of 7 months and was replaced by a limitation which showed up in the context named "discrepancy 4". The nature of this limitation and the way in which it disappeared during early infantile development will be discussed in Chapter 5.

A few contexts in Table 4 have not yet been described. They will be elaborated elsewhere and it is sufficient merely to mention them here. When the baby was 4 months and older it started whimpering while looking at other individuals. More about this will be presented in a later section (pp. 70–74).

Mother PS started nipple weaning at the age of 5 months. This occasionally caused PF to whimper as well. The subject of weaning will be covered by van de Rijt-Plooij (1982). As soon as the 8-month-old infant started following its mother while whimpering, it did the same towards other individuals who left it and with whom the baby interacted regularly. This observation will be further discussed in a later section.

Staccato (STC) and Uh-grunt (UHH)

The contexts in which these vocalizations were given during the neonatal period were described in Chapter 3. From the first three contexts one may conclude that the babies uttered these vocalizations not as a reaction to the quality but to the intensity of the stimulus: as long as the stimulation was abrupt and moderately intensive a staccato was given. In the field I had the impression that after the first months of life these vocalizations were rapidly restricted to interactions with other chimpanzees, either as a reaction to chimpanzee vocalizations or when seeing another chimpanzee approach in the distance.

To check this idea I did the following analysis. I defined "non-specific" stimulation as any member of the list of contexts given in Chapter 3 (pp. 49–50) not involving another chimpanzee[1]. Furthermore, I restricted the analysis to those minutes during which I had been within a distance of 5 meters from the baby all the time (see pp. 27–29), to make sure that I had not missed one single uh-grunt or staccato. All samples contained approximately 300 minutes.

In Figure 15 the percentage of the total number of staccato's and uh-grunts that was given as a reaction to "non-specific" stimulation is plotted against age for two different babies. Notwithstanding all the restrictions in favor of "specific" stimulation, both babies reacted predominantly to "non-specific" stimulation during the first 2–3 months and showed a marked shift towards "specific" stimulation thereafter.

If it is true that, from the age of 3 months onwards, a chimpanzee reacts primarily to "specific" stimulation when producing a staccato or uh-grunt, one would expect the frequency of these vocalizations to correlate highly with the amount of chimpanzee activity around the baby. I checked this expectation in the following way. I took the occurrence of group calling (panhoots [ZPH], screams [ZSC], barks [ZBA], wa-barks [ZWA]) as a measure of high amount of chimpanzee activity around the baby and plotted it in Figure 16b. This measure was compared with the frequency of the vocali-

---

[1] Although on many occasions I felt that the neonates reacted not so much to another chimpanzee as such, but rather (see p. 49) to a black shape moving into the field of vision. To play it safe I omitted all contexts involving a chimpanzee from the group of "non-specific" stimulation.

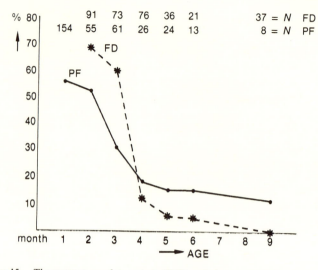

Figure 15.   The percentage of staccato's (STC) and uh-grunts (UHH) given as a reaction to "non-specific" stimulation for the two babies PF and FD.

zations staccato and uh-grunt per sample of 300 minutes over the age range of 4–12 months (Figure 16a). These two measures turn out to be highly correlated (Spearman Rank correlation coefficient, *r,* for FD = .86, *p* < .01; and for PF = .89, *p* < .01).

The conclusion that a shift occurred from non-specific to specific stimulation around the age of 3 months would be strengthened even more if it could be shown that during the first 3 months a correlation between the two measures in Figure 16 was missing or much weaker. Unfortunately, two (FD) or three (PF) measuring points are not sufficient for calculating a rank-order correlation coefficient. A possible solution would be to calculate a correlation coefficient for all months together. If the result would be a lack of correlation, then one may safely conclude that this lack of correlation stems from the first 3 months. Such calculations were made. The coefficient, *r,* for FD decreased enormously (*r* = .31, *p* > .05). Thus, the correlation disappeared. The coefficient for PF decreased a little (*r* = .86, *p* < .01), but not enough to make the significant correlation disappear. The latter is understandable if one realizes that the effect of non-specific stimulation on the correlation was lessened because PF was much more surrounded by chimpanzee activity during the first 3 months than FD.

DEVELOPMENT OF BITING (BIT), PLAYFACE (PFH), AND LAUGHING (LAC)

It struck me that, at least with good observation, during the neonatal period the mother paid little visual attention to her baby. Shortly after birth, she

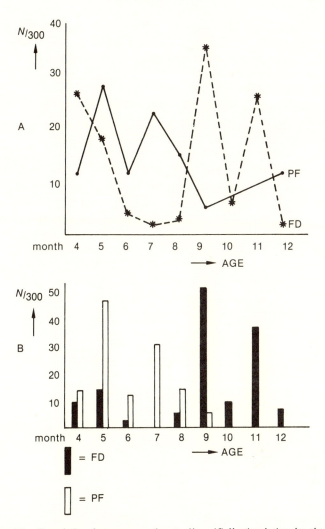

Figure 16. Correlation between reaction to "specific" stimulation by the baby and chimpanzee activity around the baby.
A) Number of staccato's (STC) and uh-grunts (UHH) per 300 minutes of good observation from the ages of 4–12 months for the two babies PF and FD.
B) Number of times group calling around the babies.

cleaned the baby. She also licked and gnawed the umbilical cord (Plooij, 1974). Later, she regularly groomed (GRO) the baby. While doing so, she only watched what she was doing, just as a human mother would do while administering body care. At other times, when she was doing other things not concerning the baby, she would glance down at her baby only briefly just after it vocalized. However, this was about all the visual attention she accorded him.

This lack of visual attention changed when the baby was 6-weeks-old. Then the three male babies observed started to bite on or at everything that touched their face or came in front of it. The development of this early biting, how it triggered the onset of mother-infant play, and how the mother responded to it and, in so doing, might influence further development has already been described (Plooij, 1979). Here I will consider some other aspects which were given little if any attention in the forementioned publication.

Peri-oral stimulation predominated as the mechansim releasing biting in the baby of 6 weeks (Plooij, 1979). It also played a major role in rooting before that age. For human babies, Prechtl (1958) has described in great detail how, when the peri-oral skin was tickled or touched, the head turned towards the stimulated side and simultaneously the mouth opened. With stimulation of the upper-lip there was retroflexion of the head. Following stimulation of the lower lip, the jaw dropped. The appearance of biting in chimpanzee babies at the age of 6 weeks fits well with the discontinuation of blind rooting. Slightly earlier, at the age of 4 weeks, the babies "changed nipple" during sucking for the first time. By the age of 6 weeks the "blind" rooting followed by sucking had disappeared and the baby went "straight on the nipple", as indicated also by the marked decline of whimpering in this context during the second month (Table 4 and pp. 60–63). Again, the same was reported for human babies by Prechtl (1958): the side-to-side head movement disappeared over development and was followed by the direct head turning response. He calls it the transition of a "stereotyped" motor pattern into a non-stereotyped motor pattern of environmentally controlled form. The biting of the chimpanzee babies at the age of 6 weeks was made possible by the direct head turning response elicited by peri-oral stimulation.

The orientation of the biting was very poor at first. Sometimes the baby bit its own limbs when they happened to be in front of its face at a time when something else (e.g., a branch) touched it. Such inappropriate orientation lasted for only 2 weeks.

The frequency with which "things" were present near the face of the baby was a major determinant of how often these "things" were bitten. I managed to observe and analyze the targets of one baby's (PF's) bites ($N = 50$) during the weeks 6–12. It bit its own limbs (hands and feet) 26 times. Moreover, 16 bites were directed at body-components of the mother, 6 at objects, and 2 at the sibling PM. In the 6 cases that an object was bitten the object did touch the baby's face. The 2 times that PF's sibling was involved, PM actually stroked its face one time and the other time put her finger into its mouth (FIM). All this implies that the baby did not make any discrimination between the "things" bitten, not even between physical and "social objects".

A facial expression called "playface" emerged at the same time as biting. In Appendix A both "playface-half" (PFH) and "playface-full" (PFF) are defined. In the early months I never observed playface-full; therefore, the following descriptions merely concern playface-half. It is my opinion that this facial expression resulted from and developed out of the peri-oral stimulation mechanism, namely when stimulation of the lower lip was involved. It was then that not only the mouth opened but also the jaw dropped. The following arguments led to this idea.

At the age of 6–12 weeks, only 17 of the forementioned 50 bites (34%) of baby PF were preceded by playface. This statistic is not in accordance with the idea that both biting and playface were predominantly released by peri-oral stimulation (Plooij, 1979). In order to understand this, the following explanation is pertinent. The lips of chimpanzee infants are incredibly flexible. Hayes (1951) described how she moved her finger along the lips of Viki and how a wave movement resulted in the lips going all around following the finger. If peri-oral stimulation occurred in chimpanzee babies of 6 weeks and older, not only did the mouth open and the head turn (or the jaw drop), but also the lips were retracted on the side where the stimulus was coming from. Furthermore, if the upper lip or the mouth corners together with the adjacent peri-oral regions were stimulated this did not result in a facial expression which one could call "playface". On the other hand, if the lower lip or adjacent region was stimulated it did. And finally, if the peri-oral region below the mouth corners was stimulated, a facial expression resulted which resembled playface in that the jaw dropped, but which was different from playface because the lower lip was drawn down asymmetrically towards the side of stimulation. During the pilot study I gave this facial expression a different name (playface-quart: Figure 17). Later I decided to combine it with playface-half (PFH). Thus, to conclude this section, if one assumes that the peri-oral stimulation is equally distributed around the mouth and if one divides the peri-oral region in the three sectors as illustrated in Figure 18, then one only would expect one-third of the bites to be preceded by a playface. However, one exception should be mentioned. From the very start (6 weeks), the playface was sometimes observed without any observable prior stimulus and without being followed by biting.

Other observations indicate that the mechanism eliciting playface extended the stimulus area caudally. Whereas, in the early mother-baby play (6–12 weeks), the mother merely caressed the peri-oral region of her baby's face or put her finger against or in its mouth (FIM; see Plooij, 1979), all three mothers started touching (TOU) and tickling (TIC) body parts of the baby other than the peri-oral region, around the age of 3 months (the neck-pocket, the belly, and the groin-pocket). This elicited playface as well. When the baby was tickled in the belly or the groin-pocket, the mouth was opened and the jaw was lowered. When he was tickled in the neck-pocket

Figure 17.   Playface-quart.

the head turned in that direction, the mouth opened, the jaw lowered, and the lower lip was retracted asymmetrically towards the side of the tickling (playface-quart: Plates XII and XIII in van Lawick-Goodall, 1967b).

Roughly at the same age (12 weeks), the release of playface and biting stopped having an "automatic" character. Initially (6 weeks) the baby bit on everything that touched or came in front of its face. By 12 weeks this had disappeared. Now the baby even started showing playface followed, for instance, by biting the hand of its mother, without being stimulated periorally or in any of the more caudal body parts. At a later age (pp. 70–74) it even showed playface when it saw a familiar individual approaching in the distance, with whom it had played before, e.g., the sibling.

A little earlier, beginning with the age of 2 months, the baby had already ceased showing playface towards physical objects before biting them (Table 5). Whereas 2 out of 6 objects (33%, which is the maximum incidence of playface preceding biting) were bitten with a playface over the age period of 6–8 weeks, over the age period of 3–6 months this was done in only 2 out of 49 times (4%). The opposite was true for body-components of the mother: the number of bites accompanied by playface increased from 7

Figure 18.   Peri-oral region divided in three parts. Only stimulation of part III causes playface-half (PFH). Stimulation of the right and the left extreme of part III causes playface-quart.

TABLE 5
Frequency With Which Different Targets are Bitten With or Without Playface (PFH) for Two Different Age Periods of the Baby PF

	Ages 6–12 Weeks		Ages 3–6 Months	
		PFH +		PFH +
Target	Bites	Bites	Bites	Bites
Self	26	6	6	4
Mother (PS)	16	7	115	91
Objects	6	2	49	2
Sibling (PM)	2	1	17	15
Total	50	17	187	112

out of 16 (44% over the age period of 6–12 weeks) to 91 out of 115 (70% over the age period of 3–6 months). The number of bites towards the baby's own body decreased to nearly zero. The baby behaved towards the sibling in the same way as it did towards its mother, as long as the sibling was within arm's reach. These data will be further discussed in later sections (p. 70 and 89–90).

Although the targets of biting preceded by playface narrowed down towards the body of the mother, I could not avoid the impression that the mother was not yet seen by the baby as a whole, as a "person", but merely as a collection of very interesting "social objects" (hands, mouth). However, the sudden extra attention to the face of the mother around the age of 3 months (Plooij, 1979) may have marked the beginning of the ability to react to mother as an individual. This brings us to the next section.

EARLY ESCAPE AND "FEAR OF STRANGERS"

Until the age of 4 months babies did not react to other individuals with any kind of escape behavior. Other individuals could approach, put their face close to the baby's face and even touch and pull the baby (though this was rarely allowed by the mother). As long as this did not result in any of the discrepancies that were mentioned in the beginning of this chapter (Table 4) the baby just looked back at that individual (LAT) or showed no reaction and continued to look around (LAR).

During the fifth month the babies even started to approach (APP) other individuals, grasp them (TAK) and smell at them (RUI). At the same time mother started to allow other individuals to interact more extensively with her baby. Consequently, the baby started to bite other individuals.

However, this is not to say that the baby did not differentiate between other individuals. It directed its behaviors selectively to different individuals. It vocalized (STC) towards adults (males and females) that came within arm's reach and looked at them (LAT). Then, after a while, it could go as far as to grasp (TAK) and smell (RUI) them. On the other hand, when a sibling came within arm's reach, the baby hardly vocalized (STC) and looked at her, but awaited her with half-playface (PFH) and was very likely to bite her (BIT) or to lead her hand towards its body (HAL). This is very much in line with the way the baby treated its mother: it never emitted a staccato (STC) to her and only looked at her face around the age of 3 months. Thereafter, it no longer looked at her face anymore when she was within arm's reach or closer. Infants other than a sibling were treated in a somewhat intermediate way; the baby did give a staccato and looked at them when they came within arm's reach. In that sense it treated them in the same way as it would treat adults. On the other hand, it began to bite these other infants after a while just as it bit its sibling or its mother (see Figure 19 a, b, c, and d).

This selectivity to different groups of other individuals (sibling, infants, adults) could, of course, be ascribed to these different groups being

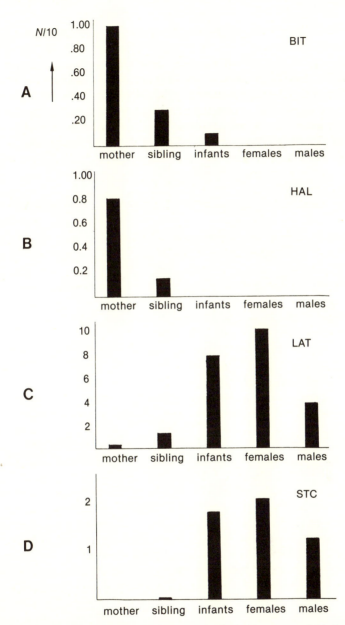

Figure 19. Selective behavior to different individuals. Frequency of 4 behavior-units per 10 minutes of good observation performed by the baby towards different individuals or groups of individuals. Data are pooled from months 3–7. Notice that the behavior-units biting (BIT) and handleading (HAL), which result in close bodily contact, are not performed towards adult males and females.

around the baby for different amounts of time. I checked this assumption and scan-sampled (Simpson & Simpson, 1977) data on the group-structure of the chimpanzees around the baby every minute. van de Rijt-Plooij (1982) compared scan-sampling every 5 minutes with scan-sampling using smaller intervals and found that 5 minute intervals produced the same end-result as intervals of 15 seconds. Table 6 gives the proportion of the time that each other individual was around the baby as well as the proportion of time each individual was within arm's reach of the baby. These figures are the means over four months (3–6).

TABLE 6
Proportion of Time That Other Individuals
Are Around Baby PF During Months 3–6.

	% of Time			% of Time			% of Time	
Adult Males	Around	Within Arm's Reach	Adult Females	Around	Within Arm's Reach	Infants	Around	Within Arm's Reach
SH	1.5	0	GK	3.6	0.1			
JJ	5.2	0	SW	9.1	0.1			
ST	7.5	1.7	GG	0	0			
FG	3.7	1.2	WK	9.0	0			
EV	5.2	2.9	FF	4.7	0.9	FD	4.7	0.5
HM	0.5	0	PL	7.6	0.1	PT	7.8	0.3
MK	2.9	0.4	NV	3.0	0	SS	3.0	0.2
HG	5.1	2.2	MF	0.8	0.1	MZ	0.8	0.1
CH	5.0	0	AT	0	0	AL	0	0
DE	2.8	0.1	NP	3.3	0.6	MU	3.7	0.5
GI	4.2	0	ML	16.4	1.0	GM	16.4	0.5
WW	5.4	0.1				GB	16.0	1.0
SF	5.1	0	FLO	11.3	1.1	FT	9.0	1.1
Total		8.6	Total		4.0	Total		3.7
			Mother (PS)	100.0	99.9	Sibling (PM)	91.3	26.1

The sibling stands out, indeed, as being around the baby for over 90% of the time. Furthermore, it is striking that the other individuals were around the baby for only a small fraction of the time. The Melissa family (ML, GM, GB) met the Passion family most frequently (16.4%). The FLO family (FLO + FT) ranked second, shortly followed by two young females without offspring (WK and SW). Of all the other individuals about half were around the baby for approximately 5% of the time whereas the other half were hardly ever seen.

Even when other individuals were around they still may have been "not there" from the point of view of the baby, because often they were at a distance of more than 15 meters. One could only be sure that babies really had "met" another individual if that individual had been within arm's reach.

If one took only the percentage of time that other individuals were within arm's reach of the baby, a different picture arose. Again the sibling scored highest although the percentage was surprisingly low (26%) and, again, there was the striking difference between the sibling and other individuals. Any one of them was within arm's reach of the baby for only 3% of the time at the most. The majority of the individuals fell below 1%. The most important difference was that four adult males (ST, FG, EV, HG) were most frequently within arm's reach of the baby (1-3%), as opposed to the former picture in which two families were most frequently seen around it. Added up, adult males were within arm's reach of the baby more than twice as much as either adult females or infants (8.6; 4.0; 3.7%; respectively). Nevertheless, the baby played (BIT) with other infants and not with adult males or females. Therefore, the possibility that the selectivity of the baby to different groups of other individuals could be ascribed to the "availability" of these other individuals can be ruled out.

Escape behavior was observed for the first time during the fifth month, in the context of the baby biting another infant (notably the sibling). As long as the other individual did nothing and simply allowed the baby to bite him or her, nothing happened. But as soon as the other only gently took hold of (TAK) the baby the latter resisted (VER) and immediately left (LVE) for its mother. Anything the other individual did was already too much to bear. The best strategy for another infant was to lie down and let the baby walk over him or her.

Leaving (LVE) was not the only escape behavior. In addition some more subtle behavior-units occurred. When the baby was already close to its mother and another individual grasped (TAK) or pulled (PUL) it the baby simply clung to its mother (CLM) or grasped her with one hand (TAM). If the other individual insisted and kept pulling or looking (LAT), the baby looked away from (LAT) the other individual.

In the sixth month escape behavior (CLM) could be elicited by the mere approach of another individual, whereas before that age the baby would have given a staccato and looked (age of 3-5 months).

Finally, during the seventh month, another individual merely looking at the baby (which had just grown into an infant now) elicited escape as well. Furthermore, for the first time the infant was observed to scream and avoid other individuals that merely approached it within arm's reach. In one example, the infant was in ventro-ventral contact (1) with its mother and avoided the other individual by going off the mother (3) and sitting behind her back while holding her (TAK)! This development towards more intensive escape-behavior-units was accompanied by an increase in frequency (Figure

20). It seems that by the age of 6 months the so-called "fear of strangers" had been developed. More about this will be said in the discussion.

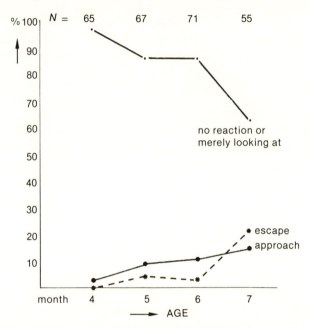

Figure 20.   Increase in early escape. Percentage of times that the baby performed one of three behaviors as a reaction to another individual approaching (APP) within arm's reach, looking at the baby (LAT), or touching (TOU), smelling (RUI), licking (LIK), and pulling (PUL) the baby.

MISCELLANEOUS

Finally, a number of developmental observations remain which seem incoherent at first sight. Nevertheless, I will present them in a simple, chronological order. In the discussion I will show that all these loose ends are very coherent when seen in the light of the model of early behavior development which I shall expand below.

At 2 weeks the baby PF was seen for the first time to be able to hold its head upright, although still very wobbly. Also, it no longer stared all the time: sometimes it looked around (LAR) or looked at (LAT). Thus, it controlled head and eye position fairly well.

At 3½ weeks pulling up (PUP) and thumb sucking (CHE) were observed for the first time. During travel the baby was now looking forward.

At 4 weeks changing nipple was observed for the first time.

At 5 weeks baby PF moved over the body of its mother. The impression was that it "wanted" to do a lot but was not able to achieve it. This resulted in much whimpering (ZWH).

At 5½ weeks PF was observed to look towards a sound for the first time. Reaching for (REF) was also observed for the first time. PF was not really looking around and did not stare any more. As the baby FD was born before I arrived in the Gombe National Park, there do not exist many detailed observations of it during the first month. However, already at the age of 5½ weeks it had been observed to hold its head upright, to look around (LAR), to look at (LAT), to pull itself up (PUP), and to reach for (REF) something (without touching it).

At 6 weeks directed head turning and biting occurred in PF. Blind rooting was not seen any more.

At 7 weeks baby PF was observed for the first time to scratch itself, albeit in a very wooden way: the whole hand was alternately flexed and stretched.

At 7½ weeks baby FD was observed to suck its thumb (CHE) frequently. In reaching for things it sometimes managed to get some leaves between its fingers. It was observed to make faces and push itself off (POF) the mother for the first time. The latter was done as follows. While lying in the prone position on the mother's chest (the mother resting in supine position) the baby tried to raise itself on all fours. In doing so it only reached a position in which it was leaning on the lower arms and in which the knees were still bent.

At 8 weeks PF frequently made faces. This started at 6 weeks, became very frequent at 8 weeks, and slowly disappeared thereafter. The hand could be brought to the face. "Reaching for" (REF) was sometimes followed by a touch (TOU) and the first clumsy grasp (TAK) was observed. The latter was done with an enormous overshoot. The baby sat (SIT), stood bipedally (STB) while holding its mother, pushed itself off (POF) the body of its mother, and was very well able to keep its head upright.

At 8½ weeks baby PF was struggling over (STR) frequently. It moved its hands in front of its face and with the eyes followed (FWE) an insect that flew through its field of vision as well as a termite (worker) walking on the ground at a distance of approximately 50 cm. For the first time it mouthed (SAB) something.

At 9 weeks baby PF moved its mouth parts (lips, tongue, jaws) in a wide variety of ways (i.e., smacking, moving its mouth as if it was chewing on something, etc.). For the first time it was observed to attend to the mother's face and was very clearly and frequently looking at sounds now. Rooting occurred less frequently. When in a large group, the baby spent much time looking at the different individuals, one after the other. It took great interest in the penis of a male who happened to be within arm's reach.

At 10 weeks baby FD moved all the time over its mother's body.

At 11½ weeks baby FD was frequently observed to stand bipedally (STB) and quadrupedally (STQ). It pulled itself up (PUP), holding the hair on its mother's belly, and stood bipedally for a few moments. Then either it fell back on its hindquarters or it went into a quadrupedal standing position. This was frequently followed by rolling over (ROO). Whether standing quadrupedally or lying on its back, the baby pulled itself up and the whole sequence was repeated many times. Baby FD was also observed to sit frequently. Its back was still very much bent, however, and it was sitting on the lower part of its back rather than on its buttocks. Finally, at this age, baby FD was observed to grasp a twig, watch it, drop it, and grasp it again (with a power grip). FD was also observed to look towards a sound.

At 12 weeks rooting had nearly disappeared. Baby FD was observed to make its first bipedal steps while holding its mother.

At 13 weeks baby PF made its first bipedal steps (WAB) while holding its mother, starting from a bipedal standing position (STB). It grasped objects smoothly and one could now speak for the first time of manipulating (MAN). Baby FD still showed jerky movements while grasping a grass-stem.

At 14 weeks baby FD was observed to make a few quadrupedal steps on the ground in between the legs of its mother. Furthermore, the behavior categories PUL, SLA, RUI, and DEF were observed for the first time.

At 15 weeks baby PF was making its first quadrupedal step (WAQ) in contact with the mother and it was observed for the first time to chew on something and swallow it (FED).

At 16 weeks the behavior categories PUL, SLA, RUI, and DEF were observed for the first time in baby PF. Baby FD was observed to make chewing movements. It was impossible to see whether it swallowed anything.

At 18 weeks baby PF was observed climbing (CLI) from the ventro-ventral to the ventro-dorsal position on the body of its mother for the first time. Now the baby manipulated (MAN) objects as much as it contacted them with its mouth (BIT, FED, SAB). For the first time baby FD was observed to move its hand through the hairs on the back of another individual. This could be the very beginning of the more complex grooming which developed at a later age. It was observed to swallow something it had been chewing. For the first time it was observed to walk quadrupedally alone and to climb (CLI) from its mother onto the branch of a very small, young tree.

At 19 weeks baby PF was walking quadrupedally (WAQ) alone. Furthermore, it was seen to move its hand through the hair of several individuals. Baby FD was observed to rise with a sudden movement on all fours, stand for a while and fall back on its buttocks. This was repeated several times.

At 21 weeks the following new behavior categories were observed: PEU, SHA, INS, LIK, HAL, TRA, and STE.

At 24 weeks two new categories were recorded: PLU and BEN. Baby FD was seen to run quadrupedally. It fell twice.

At 25 weeks GRO and TIL were observed for the first time.

DISCUSSION

The Main Sequence of Developmental Phenomena

The left column of the following list summarizes the main sequence of developmental phenomena which were presented in this chapter. In the right column a sequence of developmental phenomena as reported for human babies is presented because of the striking resemblance with the chimpanzean sequence, both in kind and timing. However, for the sake of argument, the reader is assumed to ignore this right column at the moment. We shall return to it later.

CHIMPANZEES

1. Blind rooting disappeared from the age of 6 weeks onwards and was replaced by "going straight on the nipple". This fits well with the appearance of biting at the age of 6 weeks. By the age of 12 weeks rooting had completely disappeared and biting stopped having the "automatic" character.

2. Making faces, including "playface-half" (PFH), and moving mouth parts emerged from the age of 6 weeks onwards, became very frequent around the age of 8 weeks, and slowly disappeared thereafter.

3. Various forms of body-position came under control from the age of 8 weeks onwards; the babies were observed to push themselves off

HUMANS

1. Prechtl (1958) reported the side-to-side head movement to disappear around the age of 6 weeks. This head movement was followed in the course of development by the directed head turning response. The rooting response can no longer be obtained after the age of 3–4 months (Paine, 1960).

2. The more complex social smiles in human babies begin to appear in the second month of life (Oster, 1978; Oster & Ekman, 1978). These involve a wide range of facial actions such as mouth opening, protrusion of the tongue, nose wrinkling, and lip actions such as tightening, pursing, protrusion or drawing down of the upper lip.

3. Human babies are not reported to sit free for some seconds and get into a standing position while supporting themselves during standing be-

CHIMPANZEES

(POF), sit (SIT), and stand bipedally while holding themselves (STB).

4. The first clumsy grasp (with an enormous overshoot) was observed at the age of 8 weeks.

5. A sudden and short-lasting increase in the interest in the face of the mother was observed around the age of 3 months. Attention to the mother's face was for the very first time observed at 9 weeks. In general, from the age of 8½ weeks the baby PF was observed to show interest for visual configurations such as the different individuals in the group, the penis of an adult male (pink against a black background), a termite walking on the ground, etc.

6. The vocalizations staccato (STC) and uh-grunt (UHH) were given in neonatal contexts of a kind which suggest that the production of these vocalizations is simply related to a sudden change in any of a very wide range of stimuli in several sense modalities: acoustic stimulation, change in illumination, a moving object, or unexpectedly being moved or touched. Furthermore, the data suggest that it is not a change in stimulus quality but merely a change in stimulus intensity which is influencing the behavior of the baby. Finally, the data strongly suggest that around the age of 2–3 months a shift takes place from reactions to an intensity change of ''non-specific'' stimulation to a selective responsiveness to ''specific'' stimulation (pp. 63–64).

7. The babies whimpered for qualitatively different reasons following separation from the mother at different ages. In the neonate, discrepancy from ventro-ventral and

HUMANS

fore the ages of 5 and 7 months, respectively (Touwen, 1976).

4. The palmar grasp was not observed before the age of 2 months (Touwen, 1976).

5. Kagan (1967) and Lewis (1969) reported the formation of a schema of the mother's face at the age of 3 months. The mother of one baby which participated in my study project on human babies (Plooij, 1978b) reported a sudden increase in interest for visual configurations, such as the shelved tins in a supermarket, after the age of 8 weeks. Beyond 1 to 2 months the baby is capable of focusing on qualitatively distinct features, figures, or patterns (Salapatek, 1975, p. 194).

6. McGuire and Turkewitz (1978) showed that babies of 10–15 weeks of age were responsive (in their finger movements) to the quantitative rather than the qualitative aspects of visual stimulation. This relationship between stimulus intensity and response direction disappeared somewhere between the age of 15–20 weeks.

7. Kagan (1972) reported that crying following separation from the parent may be mediated at different ages by qualitatively different sources of discrepancy.

CHIMPANZEES

nipple-contact caused whimpering. The 3–6 month-old baby whimpered when it was out of contact with the mother while the mother was out of sight. From 7 months onwards, the infant whimpered when the mother was out of arm's reach.

8. A selectivity in behavior towards individuals other than the mother was observed between the ages of 4 and 7 months (p. 70).

9. A preference for other infants over adults (p. 70) was observed at the same age.

10. The "out of sight out of mind" manner of behaving towards the mother as observed in babies of 3–6 months old (p. 62).

11. In between the ages of 3 and 4 months the babies were observed to make their first step while supported.

12. Around the age of 4½ months both babies started to walk quadrupedally and to climb. At the age of 5 months, a number of discrete motor-patterns were observed for the first time.

13. The first clearcut aversive reactions to strangers was observed at the age of 6 months.

14. Infants from the age of 8 months onwards were observed to follow other individuals (who interacted frequently with the infant, such as a sibling, an uncle or a grandmother) while whimpering.

HUMANS

8. Schaffer (1966), Bronson (1969, 1978), Campos et al. (1975), and Waters et al. (1975) reported differential behavior towards unfamiliar people up through the middle of the first year.

9. Lewis and Brooks (1974) reported positive reactions to strange children (e.g., smiling, trying to approach and cling) as opposed to negative reactions to adult strangers (e.g., frown, withdrawal, reaching for mother; almost no vocalizing, fretting or crying was observed in contrast with point 13).

10. Schaffer (1971) reported a "stimulus bound" fashion of behaving of infants of 6 months old.

12. Creeping on all fours was not reported before the age of 7 months (Touwen, 1976)

13. The "fear of strangers" phenomenon develops between the ages of 6–8 months.

14. Schaffer and Emerson (1964) reported multiple attachment in children.

Having depicted the changes in behavior during the first half year, I return now to the question posed in Chapter 1; whether it is possible to find evidence for the ontogenetic development of an increasingly complex, hierarchical organization of control systems underlying overt behavior.

I shall attempt to answer this question by searching in my data for different classes of consummatory stimuli with the help of the information about types of perceptual transformation (orders of control) as derived from Powers' (1973) hypothetical construct and using the three procedures as outlined in the introduction.

The Orders of Control in the Neonate

The data on the chimpanzee neonates support the notion that differentiation development is still predominating. On the one hand, the neonatal perception is still close to a total unity, which is indicated by the fact that a very wide range of stimuli in several sense modalities can elicit the production of the vocalizations staccato and uh-grunt. On the other hand, it was very difficult to observe discrete motor-patterns in chimpanzee newborns, notwithstanding the efforts to do so. As was shown in Chapter 3, the behavior repertoire of the chimpanzee newborn is very limited.

Sensations in the sense of Powers' model control the behavior of the neonate. One example is thermoregulation. In the chimpanzee neonate mountaineering and whimpering ("comfort-contact-search") start as soon as there is a discrepancy from ventro-ventral contact. No doubt this discrepancy causes a lowering of the temperature as measured at the skin of the ventral body surface of the baby[2]. This effect is enhanced by the hairlessness of that part of the neonate's body. Furthermore, mountaineering and whimpering persist as long as this discrepancy is present. The behavioral instruments which the chimpanzee neonate has at its disposal are very limited. If the baby, for some reason, slides out of the ventro-ventral position in such a way that mountaineering is of no help to get back into that position, there is no alternative available to the neonate but the help of its mother (whose attention is drawn by the whimpering). Without that help, the neonate would endlessly whimper and move with arms and legs in the air. These data can be interpreted as follows: The neonate is trying to keep a condition in the physical world constant, namely the temperature as measured at the skin of the ventro-ventral body surface. Thus, the set-value (consummatory stimulus) is the constant body temperature of the mother.

Another example is smell. Human neonates have been demonstrated to be able to recognize their mother by smell alone (McFarlane, 1975).

Sensations were defined in Chapter 1 as second-order perceptions controlled by second-order control systems (Figure 2).

---

[2] Undoubtedly, changes in tactual perception are also induced by this discrepancy. For the sake of argument, this aspect is omitted from the discussion.

Higher orders than second-order control of sensations are not functional in the neonate. This can be concluded from all three procedures through which one decides whether a particular type of perception is controlled or not. I shall discuss them successively.

Rigidity in the so-called "comfort-contact-search" in the chimpanzee neonate provides the first indication that no more than two orders of control are functional. The neonate continues behaving (mountaineering and whimpering) incessantly as long as a discrepancy exists from ventro-ventral contact. As soon as this contact is restored, this behavior stops. Thus one condition in the physical world (an optimal temperature) is kept constant. Variation from this single condition (fixed set-value) is counteracted. As shall be discussed further in the next section, this rigidity disappears around the age of 2 months, which indicates that a higher-order control system becomes operational and starts adjusting (varying) the reference signal for the second-order control system. This implies that before the age of 2 months the second-order control system was the highest system.

The speed with which the neonate's head oscillates from one side to the other during rooting provides the second indication that no more than two orders of control are functional. This occurs with a frequency of 2–3 Hz (Prechtl, 1958). If this figure is compared with the examples given in Chapter 1 (clonus = 10Hz; tremor = 3 Hz and overcorrection), the best fit for rooting would be to consider it as a result from an unstable second-order control system.

Further, the finding that the production of the vocalizations staccato and uh-grunt in the neonate is simply related to a disturbance, a sudden intensity change in any one of a very wide range of stimuli in several modalities, indicates that no more than two orders of control are functional. These disturbances cannot be counteracted by the neonate, partly because they are beyond its control (e.g., thunder, quickly moving shadow) or because their onset is very sudden. Therefore these stimuli result in an uncontrolled component of the first-order perceptual space (the latter is the whole collection of first-order perceptual signals and is illustrated in Figure 3; the uncontrolled component consists of the first-order perceptual signals marked "3"). Such uncontrolled components, in turn, may act as disturbances of second-order control systems. The resulting action of one or more second-order control systems can have disturbing effects on other second-order control systems and strong interactions among systems can make stabilizing of the whole array of second-order systems difficult (Powers, 1973, p. 112). I like to think of the staccato as the result of a destabilized array of second-order control systems. This idea is supported by the observation that as soon as a staccato was given, much less intensive stimulation was needed to produce a second staccato, and a third, etc. (pp. 49–50). The fact that the staccato is determined by intensity, regardless of the quality of the stimulation, is another indication that higher than second-order control systems are not yet active. The perceptual signals which feed into higher than second-order input function encode more than intensity only.

The Orders of Control After the Neonatal Period

Chimpanzee babies of 2 months and older showed overt behavior which cannot be directed at obtaining such simple consummatory stimuli as discussed in the foregoing section. For instance, to return to the example of thermoregulation, a discrepancy from ventro-ventral contact no longer elicited whimpering. Furthermore, finding a nipple through rooting and possibly via a temperature gradient disappeared. From this age onwards, the babies went straight on the nipple.

I am of the opinion that higher-order control systems start to rule the behavior of chimpanzee babies from the age of 2 months onwards. This can be concluded from the change of the speed with which the head oscillates during rooting and the change from rigidity to variability in the control of ventro-ventral contact (pp. 80–81).

Rooting was replaced by the direct head turning response combined with biting. Directed head turning clearly shows a lower frequency of oscillation; at this age a turn from one side to the other lasts about 2 seconds (in human babies; see Prechtl, 1958) whereas the same turn is performed 2–3 times per second during rooting. The fact that the chimpanzee baby of 2 months and older does not whimper anymore when ventro-ventral contact is broken implies that conditions in the physical world (e.g., temperature) are no longer kept rigidly constant but are allowed to vary.

These higher-order control systems must be third-order control systems. At the age of 8 weeks, the baby was observed to grasp (TAK) something for the first time. This occurred with an enormous overshoot, also called "purpose-tremor". Such an overcorrection is typical for an unstable third-order control system (Powers, 1973, p. 116), as was discussed before.

The remainder of overt behavior which emerged around the age of 2 months in chimpanzee babies can also be interpreted in terms of an organism with three orders of control. Making faces, moving mouth parts, the control of various body positions, and moving the hands to and from in front of the eyes may all be considered examples of the control of "bodily configurations" (proprioception; see Powers, 1973, pp. 121–123), and thus of third-order control. The interest in the face of the mother and in visual patterns in general indicates the ability to perceive visual configurations.[3]

---

[3] The reader may have noticed that the discussion jumped from body-control to perception. This may be a good point to remind one of the essential features of Powers' (1973) model which was mentioned earlier: each control organization controls its own perceptions. To control is to sense: in order to be able to control the bodily-configurations, these same configurations (coming from proprioception) must be perceived. There is no essential difference between the control of body-positions and the control of visual configurations. A similar notion was already expressed by Baerends (1956, p. 27). The main difference is that the body-positions are directly, and the visual configurations indirectly, controlled.

Finally, the shift from reactions to an intensity change of "non-specific" stimulation to a selective responsiveness to "specific" stimulation in the causation of the vocalizations staccato and uh-grunts suggests the ability to perceive acoustic as well as visual configurations.

The chimpanzee baby of approximately 2 months must be an organism with no more than three orders of control. The fact that fourth- and fifth-order of control (transition and sequence; see Figure 2) are not functional, yet, is indicated by the following observations. At the age of 7 weeks the baby PF was observed to scratch itself (SCS), but in a very wooden way: The whole hand was alternately flexing and stretching. This was only done at a body spot where the hand happened to be. The baby was not yet able to bring its hand to a certain spot on its body. This example shows how the baby at this age fails to make smooth transitions between one-arm hand configuration and the other. The occurrence of the above mentioned "purpose-tremor" is another example. Thus, fourth-order control is still absent. At the same age, the babies PF and FD were observed to "struggle over" the body of their mothers a lot. This indicates that they were not yet able to locomote in any sense and, therefore, fifth-order control systems also cannot be active at this stage.

Controlled Movement and Behavior-repertoire

I am of the opinion that fourth-order control of transitions (as defined in Chapter 1 and illustrated in Figure 2) emerges between the ages of 3–4 months. This is based on the following observations. The "purpose-tremor" and other jerky movements during grasping were not observed anymore after the age of 3 months in both babies PF and FD. From this age onwards, they could be said to manipulate (grasp smoothly). Furthermore, for the first time a number of controlled movements were seen which are smooth transitions between one body configuration and the other. Both babies PF and FD were, between the ages of 3–4 months, observed to make their first steps bipedally (WAB) while holding their mother, to make their first quadrupedal steps, and for the first time to slap (SLA) and pul (PUL).

The emergence of walking, climbing, and the other discrete motor-patterns towards the age of 5 months can be interpreted as resulting from yet another order of control being superimposed onto the already existing four orders of control. Fifth-order reference signals control sequences (Chapter 1 and Figure 2) in which lower-order perceptions occur. As for proprioceptions, sequences of transitions in posture are subject to fifth-order control. A short and familiar sequence of such transitions in posture is walking, according to Powers (1973, p. 139).

In order to select when or in what combination to produce certain controlled movements, fifth-order control is necessary, which can adjust fourth-order reference signals. Interestingly, selectivity in behavior towards individuals other than the mother was observed to arise from the age of 4 months onwards, followed by clearcut aversive reactions to strangers at the age of 6 months. I shall return to this later in this discussion as well as in Chapter 5.

In order to understand how walking or the other discrete motor-patterns may result from a fifth-order of control, the following is pertinent. Powers (1973, pp. 138–140) considers a sequence as a string of distinct elements. This string may vary in complexity. On the one hand, it may consist of simple repetitive movements involving just a finger or an arm. This would fit in nicely with the finding that pottering (PEU) or shaking (SHA) were observed for the first time in chimpanzee babies of 5 months. On the other hand, such a string may involve two or more limbs and a number of different movements which occur in such an order that they compose a complex pattern in time (in the same way as a sequence of pitches forms a melody). An example of such a sequence is walking (WAQ). Another example is picking a fruit off a tree (PLU).

Another characteristic of fifth-order control of sequences is that changes in the order in which the different movements occur result in an entirely different behavior category. There is clearly something more involved than just movement. Powers (1973, p. 138) gives the example of rotating a piece of newspaper held in the hands by inching the fingers around the edge of it. This inching of the fingers requires opening and closing the fingers, moving the hands towards and away from each other alternately, and the fingers of one hand releasing the paper, moving over and grasping it again while the fingers of the other hand are closed. A different order of the same movements could result in tearing the paper instead of rotating it. In a similar vein, one can imagine that a different order of the movements of walking results in jumping.

A third characteristic of fifth-order sequences, according to Powers, is that they are unitary. Or, in other words, they are short and stereotyped. This seems in contrast with common experience, because walking, for instance, may continue for minutes on end. However, when walking begins, an observer immediately, or shortly thereafter, gets an impression of "walking in progress," and this impression remains throughout. This implies that one walking sequence has been finished shortly after the beginning of walking (upon which an observer recognizes it) and is simply repeated many times thereafter as long as walking continues to happen. It may be this unitary aspect which makes us speak of *discrete* motor-patterns emerging around the age of 5 months in chimpanzee babies.

As an ethologist, I was trained to observe the stream of behavior as broken up in terms of discrete "behavior-elements", or "events", which are given separate names. Notwithstanding my efforts to do so, this was difficult to apply to neonates and slightly older babies, as was discussed before. It was relatively easy, though, to do this from the age of 5 months onwards. Thus, some change in the order with which the movements and postures (composing the behavior-elements) occurred must have caused this change in ease with which such behavior-elements could be recognized, and not some change in the observer. It is tempting to think that the ease with which behavior-elements could be observed in the stream of behavior of chimpanzee babies older than 5 months was due to these babies' new capacity to control fifth-order sequences from that age onwards.

Higher than fifth-order control systems were not yet present at the age of 5 months. This may be concluded from one of the three procedures presented in Chapter 1 for finding out what order of control is involved, namely the rigidity versus variability argument: as soon as higher (than fifth)-order control systems become operative, the reference signal for a fifth-order (sequence) control system starts being adjusted and variability in behavior is observed. Thus, one would have to observe a variety of different "short, familiar sequences" (or events, or behavior-elements). I did not observe this at the age of 5 months, but I did later at the age of 9–12 months. At the age of 5 months, 57 different behavior categories were observed (not only sequences, but mainly movements and postures). At 6 months, this number was the same. At 9 months, this number had rise to 68, and at 12 months it was 82–87 (two different individuals). Over the second year it only increased slightly (88–91). The sum of the frequencies with which the different categories occurred increased as well: per single "follow" (300 minutes of "good observation") this sum rose from approximately 1600 at 6 months, to 2400 at 9 months. Thereafter, it remained more or less constant. From these observations one would expect higher (than fifth)-order control systems to emerge between the age of 6–9 months. In Chapter 5, I will argue that sixth-order control systems may emerge between 7–9 months.

Differentiation Together with Ascending Development

The data support the notion that between the ages of 2 and 5 months ascending development takes place. One higher-order system after the other is superimposed over the two orders of control system which already exists at birth. Thus, an ascending integration into a hierarchy has definitely started at the age of 2 months.

Actually, ascending integration is likely to start even earlier. Although before the age of 2 months differentiation predominates, the second-order control system is present at birth and, thus, the ascending integration into a hierarchy must have started prenatally.

On a par with ascending development being present while differentiation predominates before the age of 2 months, differentiation may continue to exist while ascending development predominates after the age of 5 months. Even in (human) adults the perfectly integrated unity which is characteristic for neonates can still be observed (Condon, 1979), albeit less easily.

Neither differentiation nor ascending development is clearly present at first sight in the age period of 2–5 months, making this period some kind of "no-man's-land".

Thus, both types of development may be complementary aspects of one and the same developmental process, with each type being most "eye-catching" during a different age-range. The same opinion is also present in the writings of H. Werner (1959, pp. 32–33): an increasing differentiation together with a hierarchical integration ("zunehmender Differenzierung und hierarchischer Zentralisierung").

Yet, Kortlandt (1955) argued in his extensive review of the literature on differentiation versus ascending development that the latter is the rule and the former the exception. I cannot agree with this statement, for the following reasons.

Chimpanzee- (and other ape-) development is extremely retarded, as was discussed in Chapter 3. Consequently, the point in development at which isolated units of behavior such as walking have developed and at which the ensuing ascending development becomes most "eye-catching" lies much earlier in non-ape mammals and in birds. In fact, this point usually lies shortly after birth or hatching. Thus, studies of non-ape mammals and birds could not come up with anything else but ascending development, since they were all conducted after birth or hatching.

The following examples should support this argument. In most mammals this point in development lies a number of hours or days postpartum. For instance, Eibl Eibesfeldt (1950, 1951b) describes how several species of mice start to walk (with their belly off the ground) between 10 to 15 days of age. Oakley and Plotkin (1975) give roughly the same picture for the rabbit, the rat, and the guinea pig. In the squirrel (Eibl Eibersfeldt, 1951a) this point in development lies somewhat later (25–36 days). In contrast, the dromedary walks some 100–150 minutes after birth (Gauthier-Pilters, 1959). Baboons (Papio anubis) were observed to walk for the very first time at day 8 (van de Rijt-Plooij, personal communication). Rhesus monkeys were observed to walk from the thirteenth day onwards (Schneider, 1950, p. 541).

Developmental acceleration can also be used as an argument to show why differentiation development was usually reported to predominate in pre- and early postnatal studies. In non-ape species, development is so compressed and proceeds so fast before the point at which discrete motor-patterns such as walking develop that it must have been very hard to detect the different classes of consummatory stimuli (orders of control). Most species start walking at approximately 15 days (or earlier). If this figure is compared with the age at which chimpanzees start to walk (approximately 150 days), it appears that chimpanzee development is retarded by at least a factor of 10. The retarded and slowly proceeding development in chimpanzee

babies made it much more easy to detect the different classes of consummatory stimuli (orders of control).

Nevertheless, some studies of non-ape mammals came to my attention
which also support the existence of classes of consummatory stimuli controlling the behavior at different hierarchical levels. Cools and van den Bercken
(1977, pp. 129 ff.) report a morphine-induced, behavioral syndrome in cats.
The syndrome consists of a large number of successively appearing behavioral effects. Greatly simplified, this sequence is as follows. Within zero to
three minutes after the morphine injection irregular contractions in various
muscle groups (ears, tongue, neck, toes, limbs, etc.) appear. After 2–5
minutes, the cats make continuous attempts to sniff and lick. Continuous
changes in bodily position appear after 15–25 minutes. Next, the execution
of uncontrolled movements (head, body, limbs) occurs 15–30 minutes after
the injection. Thereafter (25–30 minutes), continuous attempts are made to
walk, climb, and groom. Finally (28–30 minutes), a chaotic sequence of attempts to sniff, lick, groom, walk, etc. occurs. The authors interpret these
findings "as the consequences of an intervention with organization marked
by the presence of hierarchically ordered comparators". They consider the
successively appearing phases as "a pathological, slow-motion picture of
what is normally going on;" the first phase (irregular contractions in
various muscle groups) reflecting reorganization at first-order control and
the last phase (chaotic sequence of attempts to walk, groom, etc.) reflecting
reorganization at sixth-order control. On a par with the opinion that this
syndrome is a slow motion picture of what is going on in real time, it may
also be looked upon as a speeded-up movie of what occurs in early development. Further work by Cools and van den Bercken (summarized in Cools,
1981a, b) on rats and socially living Java monkeys also supports the value of
Powers' concept of hierarchically distinct levels of cerebrally organized behavior. Interestingly, Golani et al. (1979) made similar suggestions based on
their study of recovery from akinesia in rats who were subjected to bilateral
electrolytic, hypothalamic lesions. After such lesions had been applied to
this part of the brain, the behavior controlled by it broke down. During
recovery, the behavior gradually re-integrated itself, revealing the levels of
organization involved. Fentress' (1980, 1983) detailed analysis of the very
early development of grooming behavior in mice are in line with the idea of
a developing hierarchical structure underlying the patterning of behavior.
Recent evidence from experiments on arm movements in (adult) rhesus
monkeys supports the hypothesis of a separate, fourth-order system controlling transitions in posture (Polit & Bizzi, 1979, pp. 192–193).

Reinterpretation of Some Literature

In the beginning of this discussion (pp. 77–79) a list of 2 columns was presented. The left-hand column gave the sequence of developmental phe-

nomena as reported in this publication. Let us return now to the right-hand column which gives a sequence of developmental phenomena as reported for human babies. This sequence shows a striking resemblance with the chimpanzean sequence in the left-hand column. Therefore, I am going to verify whether the sequence of human babies also fits the model of development presented above.

First, observations were found in the literature which, when reinterpreted, also support the notion that in the human neonate two-order control systems are functioning. For instance, Piaget and Inhelder (1969) advance the view that newborn babies do not yet differentiate between self and outside world. This view is in line with the notion that all first-order stimuli are perceived alike and that first-order perceptual signals from many different sources (exteroceptive as well as proprioceptive) contribute to a sensation. This is in accordance with Bower's (1974) notion that a nearly complete, intermodal unity exists in human newborns. Schneirla (1965) reviewed many studies on vertebrate behavior in neonatal stages (including humans) which indicate an appreciable degree of equivalence among sensory modalities. Lewkowicz and Turkewitz (1981) reviewed a considerable body of evidence indicating that newborn babies attend to the quantitative rather than the qualitative attributes of stimulation both within and across modalities, and they concluded that their sensory/perceptual world is rather primitive. Furthermore, they investigated intersensory interaction between auditory and visual stimulation in newborn infants and showed that visual preferences can be modified by immediately preceding exposure to sound. Prechtl (1958), in his early work on the head-turning response and allied movements in the human baby, reports that when, "after the development of adaptation (to tactual stimulation of a mouth corner), the arm on the stimulated side is lifted, a short series of responses will result, followed by renewed irresponsiveness" (p. 230). This may be reinterpreted if one realizes that "the effort intensity signals (first-order, kinesthetically perceived signals) are an integral part of controlled sensations" (Powers, 1973, p. 111). The experiment is inexplicable if one thinks of tactual input being processed in total isolation from the input from the other modalities. Only if one accepts that input from many different modalities may contribute to one, single sensation, is it possible to make sense of Prechtl's data: the same tactual stimulus combined with the lifted arm (all other parameters kept constant) is a new sensation for the baby, resulting in de-adaptation.

Further, the literature on human babies supports the notion that around the age of 2 months a three-order control system becomes functional. Salapatek (1975, p. 194) concludes that beyond 1–2 months the human baby is capable of visual pattern perception and of storing visual material. Visual patterns are considered to be "configurations", as was discussed above. Koopmans-van Beinum and van der Stelt (1979) studied the vocal behavior of human babies during the first year of life and presented an overview of the development both in phonation patterns and articulatory traits. They observed the first landmark of speech development between the ages of 6–9 weeks. It concerns the production of glottal stops in one expiration. These glottal stops result from keeping the muscles which close the larynx in a constant, contracted position. One may consider this to be the consequence of the ability to perceive and control third-order, proprioceptive configurations. In my study of the development of preverbal communication in human babies (Plooij, 1978b) a change was found in the arm-hand movements around the age of 9 weeks (Plooij, in preparation): from that age onwards one of the arms, in an obvious attempt to grasp something, could be observed from time to time to shoot into a particular position and stay, "locked" as it were, in that position for a short while before it started moving again. This particular position may result from a set-value for a proprioceptive "configuration".

The developmental phenomena during the first half year leading up to "fear of strangers" are strikingly similar in both chimpanzee and man. In an attempt to explain these phenomena the "discrepancy hypothesis" was used (Berlyne, 1960; Hebb, 1955; Kagan, 1970; most contributions in Lewis and Rosenblum, 1974). Simply stated, the hypothesis postulates that the ability to differentiate familiar from unfamiliar is sufficient to explain the phenomena. The baby is supposed to have built a "neuronal model", after repeated stimulation by the familiar (Schaffer, 1973), and to match any set of stimuli presented by an unfamiliar person or object with this model. The amount of discrepancy determines the reaction and takes on an inverted U-function: a certain amount of discrepancy is needed to arouse optimum attention but too much discrepancy induces fear-reactions and withdrawal. However, the theory does not explain how the baby develops this "neuronal model" and what subfeatures are important in this model of the familiar. A growing list of objections has been raised to this hypothesis (Bronson, 1978; Rheingold, 1974; Schaffer, 1971; Zegans & Zegans, 1972). The two main points of objection are the lack of a definition of discrepancy and the danger of circular reasoning as the amounts of discrepancy are postulated on the nature of the child's responses. As Kagan (1972, p. 74) himself points out, "the perspective of the viewer determines the definition of discrepancy". The perspective of the baby may change over development and with it the definition of discrepancy. Schaffer (1971) concluded that at least two processes have to be hypothesized, the onset of which appear in sequential order: (a) a perceptual learning mechanism, and (b) a response selection mechanism. In terms of the model presented here this perceptual learning mechanism involves a three-order control system. The baby starts to treat its mother as one entity after the age of 2 months, since only then has the perception and control of configurations developed. The interest in the chimpanzee mother's face as well as the formation of a schema of the human mother's face (Kagan, 1967; Lewis, 1969) may be thought of as resulting from the ability to perceive and control (visual) configurations. The response selection mechanism may be thought of in terms of the model presented here as the five orders of control system which appears later. This enables the baby to select what behavior to direct at the other individuals (as was discussed earlier). Bronson (1978) opposed a "learning" interpretation to the traditional "cognitive" explanations. He argued that learned aversions which have their roots in prior disturbing experiences may become an additional determinant in the phenomenon of "fear of strangers". Both explanations are incorporated in the model presented here. A separate level of memory is associated with each level of control (Powers, 1973, p. 208). This enables the baby not only to select its response to another individual but also to remember how that other individual behaved towards the baby.

In contrast with all the similarities, one difference between the chimpanzee and human sequence of developmental phenomena seems outstanding. Human babies in the western world are reported to sit, stand bipedally while holding themselves, and creep on all fours much later than free-living chimpanzee babies (Touwen, 1976). I am going to argue, however, that the earliest possible ages of onset in human babies may not differ from the ages reported here.

The ages of onset for sitting, standing bipedally while holding, and walking quadrupedally as reported here for free-living chimpanzees are confirmed by the literature both on other free-living (van Lawick-Goodall, 1968) as well as captive chimpanzee babies (Riesen & Kinder, 1952; Schneider, 1950; Steinbacher, 1941; Yerkes & Tomilin, 1935). Interestingly, however, Yerkes and Tomilin (1935) report that although the usual age of onset for quadrupedal walking in captive chimpanzee babies lies during the fifth month, a spread of 4–12 months occurs. In other words, the age of onset can be delayed considerably and well beyond the usual age of onset of most western human babies (Touwen, 1976, p. 48, Figure 15). Riesen and Kinder (1952) confirm this and they present data which show that the motor development of chimpanzee babies which are separated from their mother and raised in a nursery environment is retarded (see p. 171). Thus, the question arises whether the ages of onset in human babies could be earlier.

According to Geber (1958), the answer is affirmative. She examined 300 Ugandan babies with the Gesell tests for intelligence and found that at the age of 6–7 weeks all these babies could crawl and sit. Walking bipedally was reported to start between 6–7 months! This finding is partly confirmed by a study of 15 Nigerian babies (Whiten, Whiten, & Ibeh, 1980) who are reported to have brief periods of sitting on the ground (out of contact with mother) at the age of 3 months. All this is much closer to the findings on the free-living chimpanzees and in sharp contrast with the findings by Touwen

(1976) who reports the very first sitting with straight back not before the age of 6 months and walking bipedally not before the age of 10 months. Nevertheless, the ages of onset in western, human babies can be much earlier as well. In my study of the development of preverbal communication in western, human babies, one mother reported her baby to push himself off (POF) at the age of 9 weeks and to sit and stand bipedally while holding himself at the age of 11 weeks. At the age of 3 months that baby was already able to sit with a straight back. Furthermore, I once observed a baby walking bipedally at the age of 8 months. Zelazo, Zelazo, and Kolb (1972) report an earlier onset of walking bipedally alone depending on childrearing practices.

Thus, the developmental sequence of motor phenomena in human babies of our western world does not necessarily contradict the model as developed above. The earlier ages which are reported for different childrearing practices come very close to the ages of onset for the other milestones.

In one human baby I obtained observational evidence (Plooij, in preparation) that it could perceive and understand spoken words from the age of 5 months onwards. This observation was confirmed independently by van der Stelt (personal communication) for another baby from the age of 6 months onwards. This early age is not surprising in view of the finding that word comprehension precedes word production in the early lexical development of young children (Benedict, 1979). This author reports one baby (Graig) which already comprehended 10 words before the start of the study at the age of 9 months. According to Powers (1973) perception of words may be considered to result from fifth-order control.

"Babbling" emerges in human babies of approximately 6 months of age. Koopmans-van Beinum and van der Stelt (1979) redefine babbling as "production of chains of repetitive articulatory movements during continued or interrupted phonation in one breath unit". These authors reject other definitions of babbling on the grounds that the descriptive tools in most investigations proved to be too limited to describe the whole range of infant utterances, because their method is derived too directly from the adult linguistic system. Redefined in such a way, babbling consists of short sequences of transitions between vocal tract figurations and, consequently, may be considered to result from fifth-order control as well.

Earlier Concepts of Levels of Integration

The concept of hierarchy of levels of organization (orders of control) is already old (Kortlandt, 1955; Schneirla, 1949, 1953). In fact the concept is based on biologically sound and evolutionary solid principles (Tavolga, 1974). One may find elaborations of this concept in, for instance, the writings of Kortlandt (1940 a, b, 1955), Baerends (1941), Tinbergen (1942, 1950), Hinde (1953), Dawkins (1976), and Fentress (1976 a, b, 1980, 1983).

The idea that this hierarchy consists of negative feedback control organizations is not new either. Kortlandt (1955, pp. 171–172) speaks of hierarchically organized "appetites", where an appetitie is defined as "the performance of a specific activity (consummatory act) or the presence of a specific external object or situation (consummatory stimulus) which causes the ending of a variable sequence or series of activities (instrumental acts or appetitive behavior) leading to this particular activity or simulus". Dawkins (1976) translates "hierarchical organized appetites" into "hierarchically nested stopping-rule programs". Miller et al.'s (1960) and Pribram's (1976) TOTE sequence is in full accordance with the idea of negative feedback control organizations.

The more general formulation by von Holst and Mittelstaedt (1950) of their "reafference principle" shows great resemblance with the model presented here. Their center Z1 is similar to my first-order control system and the centers which are superior to center Z1 can stand for second- and higher-order control systems. Their efferent series of impulses are similar to my first-order output signals and the reafference stand for my first-order perceptual signals. The fact that their efference-copy and the reafference cancel one another out in Z1 is similar to my first-order perceptual signal and reference signal being compared in the first-order comparator function. One minor point of difference here is that my first-order output signal results from comparison between reference signal and perceptual signal, whereas the efferent stream (E) and the efference-copy (EC) of von Holst and Mittelstaedt (1950) split before this comparison takes place.

Evidence that one order of control after the other is superimposed, during development, onto an already existing hierarchy can also be found in the literature (Kortlandt, 1955). Although this study only presents evidence for the existence of hierarchical levels from the fifth-order control of behavior patterns onwards, Kortlandt (1955, p. 234) discussed the possibility of a further hierarchical ramification below this level of control. Dawkins (1976, p. 18) developed a similar argument for sensory systems in which "pattern recognizing units share subcomponents which recognize subfeatures which their key-stimuli have in common."

The model of early development as presented here does not conform with the model of early sensorimotor development which is usually ascribed to Piaget (1952, 1954). In the latter model, a set of hereditary structures (such as the eye but also reflexes such as the sucking reflex) are postulated which are defined as isolated assemblages. They are uncoordinated. Only during stage 2 (1–4 months) does coordination take place. For instance, the sucking reflex is modified to become part of a primary circular reaction (thumb-sucking). Furthermore, the hand-eye coordination takes place (Piaget, 1952, pp. 25–53).

Mounoud (1976) reports, however, that another point of view is also ascribed to Piaget. According to this point of view, the set of hereditary structures form an undividable whole: a first level of whole organization or coordination. Mounoud (1976) elaborates this point of view and describes a postnatal process in which a dissociation of the initially coordinated whole into substructures takes place, followed by recoordination. He manages to reinterpret the original observations of Piaget on sucking, hand-eye coordination, and thumb-sucking in terms of this process. The point of view is very much in line with the idea that the differentiative type of development submerges into an ascending type of development between the ages of 2–5 months, as was argued earlier in this discussion. Mounoud's (1976) notion that the dissociated substructures recoordinate in a new level clearly indicates this and reminds one strongly of Kortlandt's (1955, pp. 240–241) concept of reprogression. Furthermore, Mounoud's (1976) definitions of "system of treatment" and "system of representation" are strikingly similar with the definitions of output function and input function, respectively. He mentions the relationship between developmental psychology and neurophysiology as one of the origins of his theoretical modification and clearly states that development at the sensorimotor level is made possible by the appearance of new "instruments" resulting from maturation of certain nervous centers. Nevertheless, he does not specify his neurophysiological sources any further and does not make clear how one should envisage the new levels emerging after the age of 2 months.

Now that the model presented here has been shown to apply to man and chimpanzee, it is likely to apply to other, non-ape mammals as well. As was argued before, the development of the first five levels of control goes much faster in non-ape mammals and usually occurs pre- or peri-natally. This may be the reason why the developmental stages as described above have not been recognized in other mammals. The studies of early development of grooming in mice (Fentress, 1980, 1983) do not contradict this model so far. If such studies would finally support the model presented here, this would open new ways of testing it. As Goldman (1976) pointed out, behavioral analysis has been an important tool in the understanding of the development of various parts of the nervous system, since behavior is a definitive measure for differentiation of neural structure. Thus, an effort could be made to relate behavioral evidence for a newly emerging order of control with neuroanatomical data.

5

Early Infancy: 6–12 Months

The remainder of my observations provide evidence for the emergence of two other, higher orders of control (control of relationships and programs in Figure 2). These will be discussed in Chapters 5 and 6, respectively. The procedure, as followed in Chapter 4, shall be maintained. First the original observations will be presented. In the present chapter these will appear under the following headings:

1. Excursions.
2. Anomalous motor-patterns.
3. Object-play and social gestures.
4. Sociosexual Behavior.

This may seem a very heterogeneous collection of subjects. Yet, it will be shown that the wide variety of data presented under these four headings can be understood from the emergence of only one more higher-order-level of control and/or from a conflict between two incompatible control systems of that same level.

EXCURSIONS

Introduction

As was shown in Chapter 4 (Table 4), broken contact with the body of the mother no longer elicits whimpering (ZWH) at the age of 7 months. From that age onwards, only a discrepancy from "within arm's reach" (code 4, p. 24) of the mother causes whimpering. Consequently, on the one hand the infant starts going away from its mother (making "excursions"), whereas, on the other hand, it seems as if there lies an invisible, critical borderline (circle) around the mother which is not easily crossed.

van de Rijt-Plooij (1982) has shown that with increasing age the infant spends more and more time in the circle around the mother, until around the age of 18 months it spends the largest part of its time in it. Towards the end of the second year, the circle begins to expand and simultaneously a smaller, concentric circle around the mother appears which marks the inner borderline of a "ring" in which, from then on, the infant spends the largest proportion of its time. This shift reminds one of the progression of a wave on the water surface, concentrically away from a spot where a stone was thrown in (Figure 21). The diameter of this "ring" becomes larger over the years until the infant starts leaving its mother altogether between the ages of 7–10 years (Pusey, 1978, 1980).

This long-term development of the chimpanzee infant's independence serves as the background for the topic of my concern: what are the mechanisms responsible for the changes observed in the development of excursion-behavior? Simpson (1974) presented data on five free-living chimpanzee infants between 3 and 7 years old, indicating that the probability that an infant who is apart from its mother will return to her side is not constant through the time the two spend apart. Similarly, he reported that the process generating a rhesus monkey infant's returns are not Markovian (Simpson & Simpson, 1977). On the other hand, Dienske and Metz (1977) did find that the termination rates of on-mother bouts as well as off-mother bouts ("excursions" in my terminology) were constant, suggesting the opposite. This is reason enough to examine the problem again.

Methods

Before presenting my data, a short digression is needed to explain the construction of the log survivor function which is used as a statistical tool in this section as well as in Chapter 6. Furthermore, the rationale for interpreting such functions is presented.

The question posed in this section (namely, what are the changes over early development in excursion behavior and where do these changes come from) has to do with changes in the processes generating an infant's return to mother after it left her. The only data available are descriptions of "off-mother" and "on-mother" sequences using a time scale with 15-second units. When the causal analysis of behavior cannot be made deterministic (by eliminating all obvious sources of environmental noise), recourse has to be taken to stochastic models.

A survey of some simple stochastic processes as models for behavior sequences is given by Metz (1974, 1977). In this survey the stochastic processes are ordered according to the assumptions made. At one extreme end, there are the assumptions that the behavior acts are point-events, that their occurrences are independent Poisson processes, and that the behavior acts are distributed in time completely randomly, because at each instant the orga-

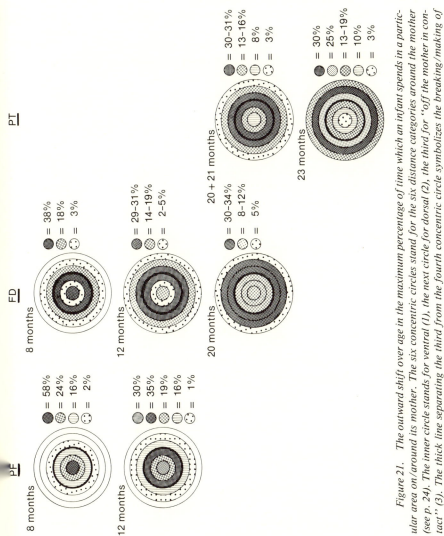

Figure 21. The outward shift over age in the maximum percentage of time which an infant spends in a particular area on/around its mother. The six concentric circles stand for the six distance categories around the mother (see p. 24). The inner circle stands for ventral (1), the next circle for dorsal (2), the third for "off the mother in contact" (3). The thick line separating the third from the fourth concentric circle symbolizes the breaking/making of contact. The fourth, fifth and sixth circles stand for distance categories 4, 5 and 6.

nism decides randomly, with constant probabilities, which act it will perform. Towards the other end, the assumptions move step by step away from complete randomness. The assumption nearest to complete randomness is that the behavior acts cannot be considered point-events, but that all behavior changes occur randomly, i.e., the starts of the different acts follow independent Poisson processes. A second step away from complete randomness is the assumption that the transitions between acts are random except for a dependence on the current act: the organism knows what it is doing now, but nothing more. In terms of probability theory this is a Markov chain, the acts being its states. Although the survey continues towards stochastic processes that are increasingly removed from complete randomness, I stop here, because Markov chains are the subject of dispute between Simpson and Simpson (1977), and Dienske and Metz (1977).

For continuous time Markov chains it can be shown that the durations of the states are independently exponentially distributed (Metz, 1977). Thus, the semi-logarithmic plotting of the survivor function of the durations of one state produces a straight line (Metz, 1974, pp. 16–17).

Turning this argument around, one could say that, if the log survivor function of the duration of an observed behavior forms a straight line, these durations are distributed exponentially and the termination rate of these durations (the probability that a duration that already has lasted t seconds terminates between t and t + dt) is constant. Or, in other words, duration termination is random. A concave (convex) log survivor function indicates a decreasing (increasing) termination rate.

Thus, plotting the log survivor function provides a simple graphical means for judging whether the original frequency distribution of durations of a behavior is exponential and, thus, the termination rate is constant. If not, it provides information in what direction (increasing or decreasing) the termination rate diverts from being constant. Various statistical means to test whether a log survivor function differs significantly from a straight line are given by Dienske and Metz (1977, p. 32, Appendix). I used the statistic K. The use of the statistic L was not considered in view of the fact that this test is very sensitive to recording errors in the duration of bouts: The time base underlying my data is too rough (Metz, personal communication).

In my study, the log survivor functions were constructed in the following manner. All durations of the excursions of an infant at a particular age were measured in terms of the number of 15-second time markers passed. This resulted in a frequency distribution with the following classes: 0, 1, 2, ... n time markers passed. Then, this frequency distribution was transformed into a survivor function by estimating, for every time class t, the probability that a duration lasted longer than that time class (by dividing the number of durations that laster longer than t by the total number of durations of the distribution). Finally, this survivor function was plotted semilogarithmically after calculating the logarithms of these probabilities.

Data

Both Simpson and Simpson (1977, p. 730) and Dienske and Metz (1977, pp. 12–13) report nonhomogeneity of the data over one day: There are times when there are runs of relatively long visits to the mother ("rest" periods) and other times when short visits are bunched together, which means that visits to the mother and excursions quickly alternate. The latter periods are called active periods or active states. In these periods Simpson (1979) found a homogeneous distribution of visits in rhesus infants of 6- and 16-weeks-old.

Inspection of my own data revealed a third group as well: periods were present in which there were runs of relatively long excursions. These periods seem to be age dependent: at the age of 8 months, when the infants begin to go on excursions reasonably frequently, these periods are absent, but towards the second half of the second year they are invariably present. Thus, it seems that the active states are split over age into two periods: one in which visits to the mother and excursions alternate quickly and another in which there are runs of comparatively long excursions (Figure 22).

In order to check whether this impression was correct, the data were further analysed in the following way. Through scan-sampling (method of sampling in which an observer keeps, so to speak, his or her eyes closed for a fixed interval only to open them briefly to observe, after which the eyes are closed again; Simpson & Simpson, 1977) with an interval of 5 minutes it was scored whether the infant was "on excursion" (= out of contact with the mother, indicated by +) or not (indicated by −). For every single "follow" (for definition see pp. 25–27) this results in a sequence of plus and minus signs. A sequence of two or more identical signs is called a run.

The choice of this 5-minute interval is crucial. It is long as compared with the mean duration of the excursions or the visits to the mother (see Table 10). This prevents too many runs of plus or minus signs as a result of one single excursion or one visit. Thus, if runs of plus and minus signs are actually found, this has to be the result of periods in which relatively long excursions or visits to the mother are clustered.

To test whether statistically significant runs occurred in the sequence of plus and minus signs the one-sample-runs-test (Siegel, 1956, pp. 52–58) was used. The null hypothesis is that the order of the plus and minus signs is random.

Tables 7, 8, and 9 give the result for the three infants PF, FD, and PT respectively, covering the age span of 8–23 months. The higher the numerical value of a negative z, the stronger is the indication that bunching occurs. In more then ⅔ of the samples the null hypothesis could be rejected in favor of the conclusion that some bunching due to lack of independence occurs. The samples in which no significant bunching occurs are found only before the age of 16 months. To begin with, no significant bunching is found before

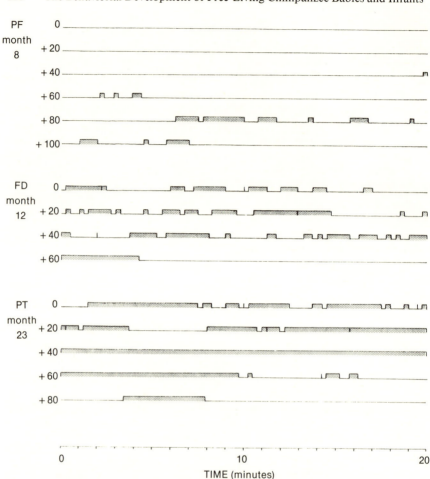

Figure 22.   Change over age of the temporal distribution of excursions.

month 9 (in PF, Table 7) or 10 (FD, Table 8). Between month 10 and month 16, the significant bunching disappears again in all three individuals at least once. Thereafter, significant bunching is found without exception. Thus, the assumption seems warranted that the active states show over the age span of 8–16 months a change from periods in which visits to the mother and excursions alternate quickly, into periods in which comparatively long excursions predominate.

From this finding that the active periods contain increasingly more long excursions it follows that the termination rate of excursions must be expected to show a developmental trend as well: during the active periods at an early age (in which visits to the mother and excursions alternated quickly) the termination rate of the excursions should be constant, whereas during the active periods at an older age (in which comparatively long excursions predominate) the termination rate of the excursions should not be constant anymore.

In order to check whether the termination rate of excursions follows this developmental trend the log survivor functions of the durations of the excursions were plotted for a series of ages. The analysis was restricted to those months which in the one-sample-runs-test (see Table 7, PF, months 8,

TABLE 7

One-sample-runs-tests on scan-sampled (interval of 5 minutes)
excursions of the infant PF at different ages.

AGE month	r	n1(−)	n2(+)	z	p
8	8	80	2	8.28	
9	21	82	16	− 2.54	.0055
10	11	86	4	3.12	
11	12	81	6	− 0.15	.4404
12	18	59	11	− 0.71	.2389
13	29	76	24	− 2.35	.0094
14	17	60	18	− 3.77	.00011
15	28	84	25	− 3.15	.0008

+ = excursion
− = no excursion
r = number of runs
n1 = number of scan-samples that infant was not on excursion
n2 = number of scan-samples that infant was on excursion
z = see formula (4.7) in Siegel (1956, p. 57)
p = probability that the null hypothesis is correct

TABLE 8

One-sample-runs-tests on scan-sampled (interval of 5 minutes) excursions
of the infant FD at different ages. For legend see Table 7.

AGE month	r	n1(−)	n2(+)	z	p
8	24	62	16	− 0.86	.1949
9	28	42	22	− 0.52	.3015
10	18	53	31	− 5.22	< .00003
11	12	48	11	− 3.02	.0013
12	34	47	40	− 2.22	.0132
13	37	39	48	− 1.53	.0630
14	35	39	40	− 1.24	.1075
15	36	45	56	− 3.02	.0013
16	36	30	39	0.27	.3936
17	32	53	40	− 3.10	.0010
18	29	56	61	− 5.65	< .00003
19	29	42	104	− 6.46	< .00003
20 +	71	62	136	− 2.51	.0060

TABLE 9

One-sample-runs-tests on scan-sampled (interval of 5 minutes) excursions of the infant PT at different ages. For legend see Table 7.

AGE month	r	n1(−)	n2(+)	z	p
12	27	60	27	− 2.84	.0023
13	32	27	21	− 2.19	.0143
14	43	56	51	− 2.22	.0132
15	14	20	15		n.s.
16	14	19	25	− 2.67	.0038
17	19	31	35	− 3.71	< .00011
18	27	30	56	− 3.12	.0009
19	28	56	45	− 4.64	< .00003
20 + 21	46	63	58	− 2.82	.0024
22	35	32	76	− 2.56	.0052
23	36	33	68	− 2.15	.0158

9, 12. 13; Table 8, FD, months 9, 10, 12, 13) surrounded a rise in the p-value above 0.05, and to those months just before and after the development of the "ring" in Figure 21 (FD, month 20; PP, months 20 + 21, 22, 23).

The results are shown in Figure 23. At a very young age the log-survivor, function is a straight line (PF, month 8) or a nearly straight line (FD, month 9: the chance that the null hypothesis of a straight line is correct is 700 times larger than in most other samples). Thereafter, the log-survivor functions of both PF (months 9 and 12) and FD (months 10 and 12) differ very significantly from straight lines and become concave (decreasing termination rate). At month 13 they become once more nearly straight (PF, month 13) or straight (FD, month 13), but thereafter they return to the concave shape (FD, month 20; PT, months 20 + 21, 22, and 23). Thus, these data confirm the suggestion made on the basis of the one-sample-runs-test: the termination rate of the excursions follows a developmental trend from being constant to not being constant any more.

Embedded in this developmental trend is an additional phenomenon. The first part of all the concave functions up to the age of 21 months is straight. This part forms ⅔ or more of the entire distribution[4]. At the ages of 22 and 23 months the straight part has disappeared. It is safe to conclude from this straight first part that the distribution is a mixture of at least two separate populations of data. According to Metz (1974) such data suggest that there are two different time-periods involved in the excursions of the infants, indicating the existence of two different internal states or phases.

1. The infant returns soon but the probability of return is constant over these short excursions. In other words, termination of these

---

[4] Unfortunately, it is not proper to cut off the tail of the distribution and test the first part for linearity (Metz, personal communication). Visual inspection is so convincing here, however, that any statistic, if it existed, would only reveal the obvious.

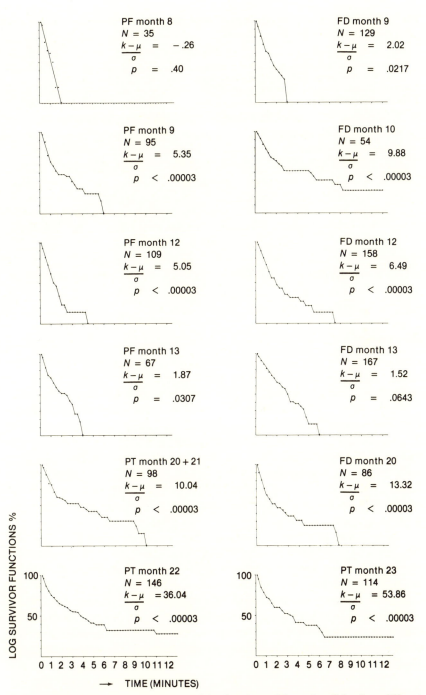

Figure 23. Log survivor functions of the durations of "excursions" for three different infants over age. Excursions are periods which start when the infant breaks contact with its mother and finish when the infant makes contact again. Each point in a graph gives the logarithm of the number of excursions (as percentage of the logarithm of the total number of excursions) which last the time indicated on the abscissa, or longer.

short excursions is random. These periods must be the same as the periods found after visual inspection of the raw data in which the infant quickly alternates between excursions and visits to the mother.
2. The infant goes on excursion and stays away a long time. The probability of return is unlikely to be constant. Visual inspection of the log-survivor functions reveals two possibilities: either the tail is wobbling, or, in one case (PF, 13 months), in which most long excursions were rather equal in duration, a sharp increase in termination rate occurred between 3-4 minutes.

The existence of two phases is further supported by data (Table 10) which show that, with respect to the mother, the infant comes frequently and relatively briefly in distance categories 3 and 4 and, on the other hand, infrequently and for relatively long periods in distance category 6. Thus, the infant is either close to its mother and may break and take up contact frequently but unpredictably, or the infant goes further away from its mother and stays away for a long time.

Discussion

Concluding, one may say that a very young infant can be in two different states concerning the control of the distance to its mother: it is either mainly on its mother for long periods of time or it shuttles backwards and forwards between "in contact" (category 3) and "within arm's reach" (category 4), making and breaking contact frequently and in an unpredictable way. Then, after some ups and downs, a third state can be observed as well, from the age of 15-16 months on: the infant is mainly far away (category 5 and 6) from its mother and its behavior is predictable in the sense that the probability it will return soon after it left its mother is low. Finally, towards the end of the second year (22, 23 months) the state in which the infant frequently shuttles between distance categories 3 and 4 disappears, making its behavior far more predictable: either it is on mother for some time or it is on excursion for a long period.

The contrast between the findings of Simpson and Simpson (1977) on the one hand (showing that the termination rate of the excursions is not constant) and Dienske and Metz (1977) on the other hand (termination rate of excursions is constant) appears to be resolved by the present findings. The occurrence of time periods in which the infant drifts randomly around its mother, making and breaking contact all the time, is age dependent and finally disappears. And, indeed, Dienske and Metz (1977, p. 5) have studied only very young macaques (± 1-3 months) whereas Simpson and Simpson (1977, p. 726) studied their monkeys over a wider age range (0-6 months). Interestingly, Figure 5 from Simpson and Simpson (1977, p. 730) is marked by a developmental trend in their data similar to the one I find in mine;

TABLE 10

Frequency of entrance into and mean duration of stay in the six distance categories between mother and infant. The extreme categories (1 and 6) are entered relatively infrequently and the infant stays relatively long in them. The middle categories (3 and 4) are entered frequently and the infant remains relatively shortly in either one of them.

Distance Category	Mean Duration (sec)			Frequency		
	FD (12 months)	PF (15 months)	PT (20 months)	FD (12 months)	PF (15 months)	PT (20 months)
1	131	177	69	38	21	19
2	27	116	53	37	77	66
3	47	32	36	135	67	142
4	47	42	30	182	118	202
5	57	39	27	48	39	76
6	215	86	210	2	3	5

moreover, the lower scores observed hardly differ from the calculated scores, suggesting that the processes generating these scores may have been Markovian. In view of my data, it is attractive to postulate that the lower scores are due to behavior displayed by very young infants.

What biological sense can be made of the fact that the periods of drifting around the mother (producing straight lines in the log-survivor functions) are randomly distributed during a limited number of months (8–21 in chimpanzees)? I do not believe in "random generators" inside the organism as an explanation of these data. Take, for instance, the example of an untrained bowman aiming for a target. He hits everything around it except the target itself. The result of his shooting is statistically random. Still, nobody would say that this end-result was generated randomly. Another, and even better, example is a kitten playing with wool and producing an enormous mess. The end-result may be chaotic, but it is by no means generated randomly. In order to get out of this dilemma it is necessary to make a distinction between statistical non-randomness and order (Bohm, 1969). However, it may be clear that the chaotic end-result cannot help in any way to formulate what kind of order is present. Consequently, the straight lines in themselves (of the log-survivor functions) cannot help in any way to make sense of the data.

The value of plotting the data in this way is that it uncovers changes with age: the transition from a straight line to a concave curve with a straight beginning around the age of 9 months, and the transition from the latter to a completely concave curve after the age of 21 months. However, the causation of these changes remains unknown.

In order to learn more about this causation it is necessary to know what the infant is controlling. The model presented in the foregoing chapter to find the consummatory stimuli may be of help here too. In the general discussion an effort will be made to place the data of this section in a wider, biologically meaningful framework. But first the description of the behavioral development in early infancy shall be continued, because of the mutual relations concerned.

ANOMALOUS MOTOR-PATTERNS

Introduction

Three of the motor-patterns which developed around the age of 5 months may be called anomalous: rearing (STE), tilting (TIL), and trampling (TRA). They are remarkable because of their form: two tendencies seem to be simultaneously present in all three of them. First of all, a tendency to approach and, secondly, a tendency to withdraw. In rearing, the infant's torso goes up instead of forward while the bent elbows and wrists indicate withdrawal. With tilting, withdrawal is apparent because the infant moves its hand more upwards than it pulls the hand towards itself. Finally, trampling is a kind of locomotion on the spot.

In between the seventh and ninth month, six more motor-patterns were observed for the first time which were anomalous as well: branchswaying (BRS), gymnastics (GYM), pirouetting (PIR), slapstamping (SLS), stamping (STA), and somersaulting (SUM). These patterns occur to the observer as peculiar because they are not straightforwardly functional in one sense.

Similar motor-patterns in adult individuals are gathered under the name "charging display" (CHD). Some of the patterns are exactly the same in adults as they are in infants, such as branchswaying (BRS), slapstamping (SLS), and stamping (STA). One pattern (GYM) shows a striking resemblance with the adult pattern "tree-leaping" (TRL) and I think it reasonable to suppose that the one (GYM) is a forerunner of the other (TRL).

Bygott (1974, 1979) gives a description of all the adult male forms of displays. In his description it becomes clear that the most prolonged and intensive, non-vocal displays are given when an individual is likely to attack another individual but is simultaneously afraid to do so (see 1974, Chapter 4.6 and Appendix C, 3).

Following a common trend in ethology, one would say that these displays result from a conflict between the tendencies to attack and to escape. However, attack has not been observed yet in infants of this age. Therefore, a more parsimonious hypothesis is that the eight anomalous motor-patterns result from a conflict between the tendencies to approach and withdraw. Hinde (1974) lists the following types of evidence on which particular tendencies are usually postulated:

1. The situation.
2. The behavior which accompanies the motor-pattern.
3. Sequential and temporal correlations.
4. The nature of the motor-pattern itself.
5. Independent manipulation of the separate factors controlling the motor-patterns.

So far, I used only type 4 in considering the form of the motor-patterns rearing (STE), tilting (TIL), and trampling (TRA). The same type of evidence can be used for the motor-pattern somersaulting (SUM). However, the form of the other four patterns (BRS, GYM, SLS, STA) is not so very suggestive. Therefore, I turned to the other types of evidence to find out whether my working hypothesis could be verified or not.

The Situation

When a chimpanzee infant is on excursion it is very likely to perform eight of the aforementioned nine anomalous motor-patterns (tilting is excluded here, of course) when it comes close to the "borderline" of its range around the mother. This may occur when the infant is exploring the environment and has left its mother without an overt, previous interaction with her. When there has been an interaction such as biting and tickling, the infant may run away from its mother, perform one of the eight motor-patterns out of her arm's reach, and then return to her to resume the interaction. It is not always the infant that goes away from the mother: the mother also may increase the distance by a few meters, for instance in the process of collecting food while the infant is manipulating an object. Then the infant may be observed to perform one of the eight motor-patterns before or while reducing the distance. Apparently, in this example, the infant experiences a conflict between, on the one hand, staying on the spot and continuing what it was doing and, on the other hand, following the mother.

Other individuals can be involved as well. A typical situation which may be observed is the appearance and subsequent approach of another individual. Then, if the infant is off the mother, it may perform one of the eight anomalous motor-patterns; gymnastics especially is observed frequently in this situation. If the approaching individual comes very close, the infant will return to the mother. If, on the other hand, that individual settles somewhat further away, the infant is likely to approach a little, perform one of the motor-patterns (usually stamping or slapstamping) and return again.

While manipulating objects, the infant may perform these motor-patterns as well, not only tilting, which was discussed earlier, but also one of the other patterns. If one knows that biting insects, to name one thing, could be under every stone it becomes understandable why an infant would be afraid of manipulating stones. And, as I discussed in Chapter 4, the infants are able to remember painful events from the age of 5 months onwards.

Independent Manipulation of the Separate Factors Controlling the Motor-patterns

This type of evidence stems from a study which was carried out before I even thought of going to Africa. During 1969 I conducted a study on the formation of "number-concept" in a 4–5-year-old captive, male chimpanzee named Koos (Plooij, 1970). At that time I did not know that the Hayeses had done a similar study on their female chimpanzee Vicki, because that part of their work was only published in 1971 (Hayes & Nissen). Some aspects of the design of their experiments and results are surprisingly similar.

I do not need to go into a detailed description of the set-up of the study in order to make my point here. It should suffice to say that the design was a visual multiple-choice apparatus, which contained a row of 10 boxes. On top of each box-lid there could be placed a white stimulus-field with a number of black dots in it. The number of dots varied from 1–10, the dots themselves varied in size, and the pattern of dots varied. The appropriate response for Koos was to open the lid of the box with five dots on top of it and the reward was a piece of fruit inside that box.

I trained Koos such that he behaved in the following way: he came and sat in front of the apparatus after which the stimuli appeared (see Kelleher, 1958). Then he walked along all the boxes one or more times looking at the stimulus fields on top of them. Thereafter, he made his choice and raised one of the lids. If his choice was correct he got his reward by taking the fruit out of the box and left the apparatus in order to eat it. Thereafter, he usually manipulated the toys that were in the room with him. Sooner or later he returned to the apparatus in order to produce another set of stimuli and the same procedure started all over again. If, however, his choice was incorrect, he was not allowed to make a second choice (the incorrect boxes were locked) and the stimuli disappeared. In that case, Koos had been trained to leave the apparatus without a reward. He could come back any time thereafter in order to produce a new set of stimuli and have another trial.

A negative trial was very distressing for Koos and he sometimes had a temper-tantrum (TEM) after having made a mistake. Normally, after he had mastered the particular problem he was being trained on, he "worked" fast. He would come back to the apparatus immediately after he had eaten his fruit, parade only once along the set of stimulus fields, and make his choice without any delay. On the other hand, he "worked" slowly when he was not able to master a particular problem and continued to make mistakes: he would parade a few times instead of one time, then he would alternately touch the lids of the boxes with, for instance, five or six dots on top of them without raising them. Thereafter he would show a preference for one of the two boxes and he would continue touching that lid repeatedly without raising it. In between two touches he would pirouet on the spot. One time he did this 53 times before lifting the lid (correct in that case). This touching and pirouetting was broken by periods during which he scratched himself (SCS) all the time. Occasionally, he groomed (GRS) himself frantically for a few seconds.

The relevant part of all this for my working hypothesis is that Koos showed one of the anomalous motor-patterns, namely pirouetting, in an experimentally induced conflict situation. It is clear that Koos must have experienced a conflict between opening and not opening that particular box, between wanting that piece of fruit and being afraid to fail.

If, somehow, one could reduce one of the two supposed tendencies experimentally, one would expect the anomalous motor-patterns to disappear. Therefore, I did the following. Whereas Koos during the first phase of the study had not been allowed to make a second choice, I now switched to a corrective method in which the boxes were not locked any more and Koos was allowed to make a second choice. In that way he always got his reward. Immediately, the frequency of pirouetting decreased enormously together with the latency-time (the time needed to make a decision) which is plotted in Figure 24. After 15 series of 25 trials the pirouetting had completely disappeared.

Later, for some other reason, I started to use the non-corrective method again and immediately the pirouetting reappeared while simultaneously the latency-time increased (see arrows in Figure 24). As soon as the corrective method was used again the pirouetting disappeared and the latency-time decreased. This was repeated twice and every time I obtained the same results. It is my opinion that by taking away the factor causing the tendency to leave, the conflict was resolved.

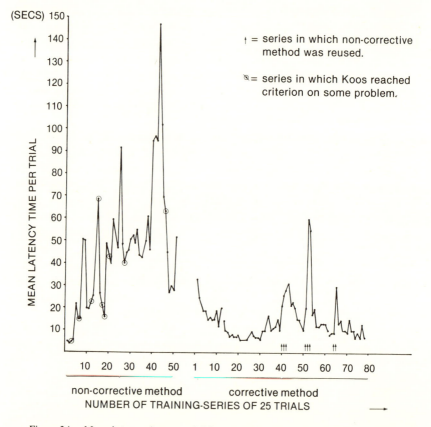

Figure 24.   Mean latency-time per trial for a number of consecutive training-series with the chimpanzee juvenile Koos. The first 51 series, during which the non-corrective method was used, consist of a number of problems of increasing difficulty. Whenever Koos reached criterion on one of these problems the latency-time decreased only to rise even higher with the next problem. A long latency-time was due to the excessive performance of anomalous motor-patterns. When the corrective method was started the latency-time decreased. Whenever the non-corrective method was re-used (see arrows), the latency-time increased promptly.

Taking away the factor causing the tendency to approach also resolved the conflict: if the non-corrective method was continued when a problem was offered which Koos could not solve, Koos would finally flee from the testing apparatus, not to come back any more. Then the pirouetting stopped as well.

Thus, the working-hypothesis that the anomalous motor-patterns result from a conflict between the tendencies to approach and withdraw appears to be supported by these data on experimentally induced pirouetting.

Temporal Correlation with Approach and Withdrawal

Another type of evidence on which particular tendencies are usually postulated is obtained from a temporal correlation between the anomalous motor-patterns and behaviors which clearly result from the tendencies involved. For example, the experimentally induced pirouetting correlated temporally both with approach and withdrawal to an equal amount. It was preceded by withdrawal and followed by approach many times in succession. One would expect the other anomalous motor-patterns also to correlate temporally with approach and withdrawal. Therefore, I analyzed this correlation for two different, anomalous motor-patterns from my field notes.

In this analysis, first of all the target towards which the anomalous motor-patterns were directed had to be found. I could usually decide from the infant's looking behavior whether it was directing its attention to a particular target. Either the infant was watching this target for a long period of time (LAT), or it directed regularly recurring glimpses (GLI) towards it. The target could be, for instance, the mother, (an)other chimpanzee(s), baboons, insects such as termites, or an object. It was not always possible to pinpoint a target. This is not to say that there was no target. It may simply have remained hidden from the observer. Such cases resulted in a remainder group which was scored as "no target was observed" (see Table 11 and Table 12).

If the target was observed, the temporal correlation between an anomalous motor-pattern and approach towards or withdrawal from the target was measured in the following way. Approaches or withdrawals were defined to be temporally correlated with an anomalous motor-pattern if they occurred during the performance of that motor-pattern (for instance, approaching while stamping) or immediately before or after that performance (for instance, approaching, stamping, withdrawal).

Four combinations of approach and withdrawal were observed to occur in temporal relation to an anomalous motor-pattern. These combinations were:

1. neither approach nor withdrawal (= "on the spot")
2. approach only

TABLE 11

Frequencies with which the anomalous motor-patterns stamping (STA) and slapstamping (SLS) associate temporally with approach and/or withdrawal. For further explanation see text. The columns with a plus sign are double samples. The sample of PF at the age of 7 months was analyzed but not included in the table, because PF did not yet perform these anomalous motor-patterns.

STAMPING or SLAPSTAMPING

Individual	FD	FD	PF	FD	PF	FD	FD	FD 12+	PF 12+	FD 20+	PT	TOTAL
Month	7	8	8	9	9	10	11	13	13	20+	20	
No target observed		1	1			3	1	3	2	12	5	28
'on the spot'				2	1		1	8	2	35	8	57
approach		2	1	1			1	3	9	25	10	52
withdrawal						1	1	1	1	18	5	27
approach + withdrawal	1	1					1	4	5	43	27	82
TOTAL	1	4	2	3	1	4	5	19	19	133	55	246

TABLE 12

Frequencies with which the anomalous motor-pattern gymnastics (GYM) associates temporally with approach and/or withdrawal. For further explanation see text. The columns with a plus sign are double samples. The sample of PF at the age of 7 months was analyzed but not included in the table, because PF did not yet perform this anomalous motor-pattern.

GYMNASTICS

Individual	FD	FD	PF	FD	PF	FD	FD	FD 12+	PF 12+	FD 20+	PT	TOTAL
Month	7	8	8	9	9	10	11	13	13	20+	20	
No target observed	1	1	1			10	3	8	3	32	19	78
'on the spot'					2	2		13	3	22	13	55
approach	1	3				3	3	15	2	31	12	70
withdrawal		1			3	3	1	14		28	16	66
approach + withdrawal		11			3	6	2	30	3	37	27	119
TOTAL	2	16	1	0	8	24	9	80	11	150	87	388

3. withdrawal only
4. approach plus withdrawal

Locomotion towards or away from the target was used to define whether approach or withdrawal had occurred. However, cases also occurred in which a target was within immediate reach of the infant (inanimate objects such as small stones; small animals such as ants and termites). Then no locomotion was involved, but only a directed movement of some body part. Usually the infant would touch (TOU), smell (RUI), and manipulate (MAN) the object or small animal before and after the anomalous motor-pattern. Thus, both approach and withdrawal occur in temporal relation to anomalous motor-patterns directed at such targets in the same way as approach and withdrawal accompanied the experimentally induced pirouetting discussed in the foregoing section. Therefore, when one of the anomalous motor-patterns was aimed at an inanimate object or small animal, it was counted as temporally related to both approach and withdrawal.

The two anomalous motor-patterns for which this analysis was executed were slapstamping (SLS) or stamping (STA), and gymnastics (GYM). Table 11 and Table 12 show the frequencies with which, respectively, these anomalous motor-patterns occur in temporal relation to the four possible combinations of approach and withdrawal, if a target was observed. The analysis was done from month 7 (the age at which the anomalous motor-patterns were observed for the first time) to month 12 + 13, as well as for one older age (month 20). For every age, the records of two different individuals were taken. Months 12 and 13 were taken together in order to obtain larger samples. For the same reason month 20 of FD is a double-sample.

The column totals show that these motor-patterns only rarely occur during the second half of the first year. By the time the infants are 1 year old, however, they perform them quite frequently. The frequency increases further over the second year. Therefore, only the frequencies of months 12 + 13, and 20 and the total column are discussed further.

In the total column of Table 11 and Table 12 one can see that both stamping or slapstamping as well as gymnastics are frequently temporally related to approach plus withdrawal. This is in accordance with the working hypothesis that the anomalous motor-patterns result from a conflict between the tendencies to approach and withdraw. However, the frequencies with which the other four combinations mentioned in the tables go together with the anomalous motor-patterns are not very low. The fact that "approach only" and "withdrawal only" also occur in temporal association with the anomalous motor-patterns deserves some special attention. It is possible to understand that these temporal associations occur if one realizes that not only the tendencies to approach or withdraw influence the behavior of the infant, but also the situation surrounding it. For instance, the target is not always immobile and may move away from or towards the infant resulting in "approach only" or "withdrawal only", respectively. Accepting the argument that the situation surrounding the infant variably influences its behavior, one would expect the number of times that "approach only" relates temporally to an anomalous motor-pattern not to differ too much from the number of times that "withdrawal only" is associated with that motor-pattern. This is true for gymnastics (see Table 12) but not for stamping or slapstamping (Table 11). The latter motor-pattern relates temporally more with approach than with withdrawal. This fact indicates that the balance between the tendencies to approach and withdraw varies and is different for the two motor-patterns. Conversely, this would imply that depending on the value of this balance between approach and withdrawal, one or the other anomalous motor-pattern should be performed.

Discussion

The data appear to support the working hypothesis that the anomalous motor-patterns result from a conflict between the tendencies to approach and withdraw. I have already remarked that a common trend in ethology would be to explain the occurrence of such apparently "irrelevant" motor-patterns as a result of interaction of more complicated behavioral systems, such as those for attack and for escape, in accordance with the so-called "conflict hypothesis" postulated by Tinbergen and some of his co-workers. Baerends (1975) has evaluated this conflict hypothesis as an explanatory principle for the form of displays. Although he tends to adhere to the idea that the conflict usually takes place at relatively high levels (he is exclusively referring to display behavior in adults) he realizes that "the hypothesis leaves open the possibility of considering conflicts between very restricted systems...as origins for signal behavior..." (p. 193), and further states: "The simplest possibility of a conflict is probably one between two opposite orientation components during locomotion" (p. 193). I like to entertain the idea that in chimpanzee infants a conflict between opposite orientation components is the first type of conflict to develop and the only one existing at least up to the age of 12 months. Higher order systems which are usually postulated as causal mechanisms underlying the functional grouping of behavior elements (see Baerends, 1976) only develop after the age of approximately 1 year. By the age of 7 months the chimpanzee infant cannot yet be said to be "eating" (see Chapter 6). Functional groups of behavior such as aggressive behavior, sexual behavior or nest-building (NES) are still absent.

Since the tendencies to attack and to escape cannot be involved in the causation of the anomalous motor-patterns performed by the very young infants and in view of the fact that the adult "charging display" (CHD) patterns are identical with these motor-patterns, it is not parsimonious to assume that the tendencies to attack and escape must play a role in the causation of the adult "charging displays". If attack and escape would play a role, their effect may be thought to be ultimately restricted to inducing a conflict between two opposite orientation components. The advantage of this point of view is obvious: many situations in which "irrelevant" behavior occurs (not only in young but also in adult individuals) can be observed where overt approach and avoidance behavior is present but overt attack and escape behavior is not. The most important argument against this point of view, as presented by Baerends (1975, pp. 194 ff.), is that elements other than just orientation components are often found to be involved in displays which do not occur in simple exploratory behavior and thus suggest an interaction of higher-order systems. To evaluate this argument, a better specification of the kind of accompanying elements than hiterto given is needed. Among them are autonomic responses. One such autonomic response in chimpanzees is "hair on end" (HAI). It accompanied the anomalous motor-patterns in the young infants as well as the charging displays in adults. However, Baerends (1975) mentioned not only autonomic responses. More detailed attention to these other responses as well as the autonomic responses is needed in order to settle this issue for chimpanzees.

OBJECT-PLAY AND SOCIAL GESTURES

Object Against Body

From the age of approximately 9 months on, a group of behavior-categories was observed for the first time which is best characterized by the name "object against body". This group is split into different categories according to the body-spot against which the object is placed (see Appendix A: OIN, ONP, OOH, OTB, OTP).

Later in life, this "object-against-body" behavior can still be observed, though not as frequently as during the first 2 years. It is especially seen when an individual is confronted with a new object. In the Gombe the chimpanzees were sometimes introduced to new objects (which they would never find in the natural environment) through the presence of human observers living there: a piece of plastic, an empty vegetable tin, etc. At such an occasion a typical sequence could be observed. Initially the chimpanzee would stay away from it and only watch. Soon he or she would carefully approach, and walk around it. This would be followed by prodding, poking, and pushing; jumping back once in a while. Thereafter "sniffs finger" (SFI), smelling (RUI), and licking (LIK) could be observed, followed by manipulating (MAN). Then the individual would do the "object-against-body" behaviors, after which the object was abandoned. All this lasts approximately 15–20 minutes. It is as if the developmental sequence which lasted months is repeated here in a matter of minutes. Similar exploratory sequences have been described for captive chimpanzees by Menzel (1964).

One aspect of this whole phenomenon (both the slow, developmental sequence and the fast, exploratory sequence) fascinates me: apparently, an object is fully "known" only after all possible information about that object is processed through all possible perceptual nerve-ending-surfaces. Not only the eyes, the ears, or the nose contain important receptor-surfaces, but also the skin of the entire body.

As far as I know, these "object-against-body" behaviors have not been reported in the human literature. However, I found out that human children also start to perform these around the age of 9 months. I observed my own daughter performing object in neck (OIN) and object against clitoris (OTP) when she was not yet 9-months-old. A second baby (a boy), which I observed weekly (see Plooij, 1978b), performed object in neck (OIN) for the first time at the age of 11 months with various objects. The mother of this baby reported him to perform object against penis (OTP) for the first time when he was just over 9-months-old. These observations were confirmed by my colleague J. van Orshoven (personal communication) from observations on his own children. It is clear that tactile perception takes an important place in the child's perception of its world. Therefore, it is surprising to find that it has been little studied (see Bullowa, 1979, pp. 39–41) and more research of this modality is badly needed.

More knowledge about tactile perception is also important because the tactile sense not only plays a role in the exploration of the inanimate world, but in interactions with other individuals. The same body-spots which are involved in the "object-against-body" behaviors (the back of the neck, the neck-pocket, the belly, and the groin-pocket) also play an important role in the chimpanzee mother-baby play (see pp. 64–70) and later in playwrestling (PWR) with mother and with other individuals. Furthermore, these body-spots play a role in some of the social gestures which appear for the first time around the age of 9 months and which shall be discussed in the next section.

Social Gestures

Together with the emergence of behavior-categories directed at objects, the chimpanzee infants started to use a number of gestures which were directed at other individuals.

"Begging" (BWM, BWH) was observed for the first time at the age of 9 months. If a baby wanted the mother's food, it simply grasped it. To begin with the mother allowed this. Soon, however, she passively prevented the baby from taking the food by not letting go of it, or by withdrawing her hand from its advances. In such cases the baby (or young infant) kept trying to obtain the food directly, without ever looking up into the mother's face. This changed with the onset of begging: the infant touched the mother's hand or mouth and looked intermittently at her face (eyes) and hand (or mouth). Thus, the infant no longer attempted to attain its goal directly, but used its behavior communicatively and indirectly for that purpose.

The initiation of play-tickling sessions with the mother by using gestures whose values had been established in earlier sessions was observed from the age of 11 months on. This ability had developed as follows. When the mother tickled her baby, it defended (DEF) itself: if the mother tickled the belly, for instance, the baby arched its back and pulled up its legs so as to repel the stimulation with hands and feet. If she tickled the baby's neck-pocket, it bent away while bringing its hands backwards over its shoulders towards her hands or head, trying to push them away. This resulted in a characteristic posture. Around the age of 11 months, chimpanzee infants started to initiate play sessions by directing this posture ("hands around head" = HOH) towards their mother or other individuals.

A comparable developmental sequence was observed in the context of grooming. When grooming her baby, a chimpanzee mother frequently put it in a characteristic posture as described in Appendix A under "puts arm high" (DAO). In order to groom its sides and armpits, she took its arm and pulled it upwards. By the age of 6½ months an infant was observed to adopt this posture unaided while its mother groomed it. At the age of 11 months an infant was observed who came up to its mother, sat down in front of her and adopted this posture ("arm high" = AOH). Almost predictably, its mother started grooming.

Yet another gestural example may be described literally as "lies down on back" (GOR): an individual lies down on its back while keeping its head lifted and extending its hand and arm towards another individual whom it is also looking at. The meaning of these gestures becomes clear if one knows how very young infants interact with older infants. In the first half year of life chimpanzee babies hardly interact with anyone but their mother. When they finally start making excursions away from their mother and towards other individuals, interactions can only be sustained if the other adopts a very passive role: as soon as a "stranger" takes hold of the infant's arm (in order to pull it close and cuddle it, for instance), the infant withholds and retreats. Apparently, it does not like to be restrained in these situations. The only thing the older individual can do to maintain the interaction is to lean backward and allow the infant to walk over him and lie on top of him. It is in this context that the older individual leans backwards and extends his arm. This gesture, "lies down on back", is usually given at a distance of a few meters—the reason for this probably being that the younger infant would retreat towards its mother if the older individual were to approach it. This gesture was observed in chimpanzees as young as 12½ months towards younger infants.

With the onset of begging between the ages of 9 and 12½ months, followed by the use of the other gestures initiating tickling (HOH), grooming (AOH), and approach (GOR), it may be assumed that the chimpanzee infant understands the role of its mother (and others) as an agent and that it possesses a true communicative ability, as was argued earlier (Plooij, 1978a).

SOCIOSEXUAL BEHAVIORS

In all primates there exists a significant overlap between behavior elements or patterns which are usually present in the hetersexual copulatory context and which appear in other social situations as well. Such behavior elements are called sociosexual (Hanby, 1976). The only elements I will describe here are presenting (PRE), mounting (MOU), and thrusting (THU). "Presenting and mounting, though obviously related in context, appear to have different developmental sequences" (Hanby, 1976, p. 16). Therefore, I will describe one after the other.

Presenting

> Presenting is seen in more social situations and has even more postural variations than mounting. Possibly due to the variety of postures and situations for presenting, there has been great difficulty in interpreting this social signal and describing its development (Hanby, 1976, p. 19).

According to Hanby, a distinction must be made between holding still with rump oriented to the other (or the more distinctive approach with rump or genital area "presented" to the other) on the one hand, and crouching when approached on the other hand. The latter category (CRO) has more to do with holding still and avoiding interactions altogether and is observed frequently in confined conditions only. The first two modifications concern the proper presenting pattern (PRE) which is discussed here.

The frequency with which presenting was observed per sample is very low. There were even a fairly large number of samples in which presenting was not observed at all.

Presenting was first observed at the age of 10 months in infant FD. Clumsiness, malorientation, and bad timing are striking aspects[5]; soon these disappear. Thus, experience is needed in order to present properly.

Presenting functions more in a social than in a sexual context. Often it is a social gesture. I conclude this from the fact that female infants present to other females as well as males and from the fact that, if presenting has no

---

[5] These aspects express themselves in, for instance, not turning fully around after having approached another individual, as a consequence of which the infant is presenting "sideways". Or, in another example, turning around too far away from the presentee, as a consequence of which the infant has to approach further while walking backwards, upon which he falls on his hindquarters.

effect in eliciting a reaction from the partner, one of the other gestures which emerge from the age of 9 months on are tried as an alternative, such as hands around head (HOH; pp. 116–118). The more social nature of presenting may also be clear from the reactions of the presentees: in nearly half the observations ($N = 39$) the presenting infant is not even touched, the presentee simply looking at the infant or not reacting at all. Once a presentee was observed to lower its face towards the infant. In roughly one quarter of the observations the presentee groomed, embraced, or played with the infant. Only in the remaining quarter was the presenting infant mounted or inspected, sometimes in addition to one or more of the other reactions.

Mounting and Thrusting

Penile erections in male babies were observed from the age of 1 month on. Thrusting was observed for the first time at the age of 13 months, when PF thrusted on the back of his mother.

Mounting together with thrusting was seen from the age of, respectively, 17, 18, and 20 months on in the infants PT, FD, and GM. Some general conclusions are:

1. Female infants mount. However, male infants mount much more frequently. Male infants were never mounted.
2. From the earliest appearance mounting may also occur in non-copulatory contexts.

The youngest age at which mounting was seen by different authors varies considerably, from 9 months (van Lawick-Goodall, 1968) through 15, 17, and 18 to 20 months (my own observations above, and Tutin, 1975). Hanby (1976, p. 11) suggests that the differences in the earliest appearance of mounting depend on the ongoing group setting. Van Lawick-Goodall's observations were done on chimpanzee infants under high density. My data stem from observations under much more dispersed conditions.

I was left wondering what the crucial differences were between these two conditions. Could it be that experience with adult females in oestrus played a crucial role? In order to answer this question, data was needed on the frequency and duration of associations between the infants and adult females in oestrus.

For this purpose I used the so-called "travel-and-group-charts" of my "follows". These charts recorded where the target-chimpanzee traveled in the park and what other individuals were associated with him/her. These records were collected during the whole day and were not restricted to the periods of time I had "good observation". Consequently, these samples were larger than 300 minutes and varied from 500 to 1400 minutes. Table 13 shows the results.

TABLE 13

Total time (minutes) per sample that the infants were in the company of adult females with a swelling (SWE) who were associated with one or more adult males. The numbers between brackets are the number of minutes the particular infant was observed to be in the company of a tumescent female while I was following another infant.

AGE month	TIME (mins) in company of adult females with swelling who are associated by adult males				
	PF	FD	GM	PT	SS
1	95	0			
2	120	0			
3	195	0			
4	40(+15)	210(+15)			
5	45(+5)	60(+10)			
6	45	0(+60)			
7	60	0			
8	30	60			
9	0	35(+15)			
10	0	75	0(+210)		
11	0	0	30(+60)		
12	0	0	330		
13	0	0	0	10(+45)	
14	0	0(+10)	0	5(+60)	
15	0	0	45	0	
16		0(+75)	5	0	
17		45	135	0	
18		0(+480)x	5(+45)	0(+45)	60(+45)
19		95	0	30(+75)	60(+10)
20		0	0(+30)	0(+25)	0
21			0	75	0
22			70(+150)	55	0
23			0	0	0(+5)
24			480	0(+30)	0
25					5xx
26					0
27					0
28					0(+10)
29					90
30					150(+5)

x nearly all males and 5 females with swelling

xx NV cycles again

The samples in which the mothers did not associate with "sexual groups" form the majority. Sexual groups consist of sexually receptive females surrounded by males. Furthermore, if the mothers joined such groups, they usually did so for short periods. Nevertheless, from 9 months on (the age at which mounting was observed for the first time by van Lawick-

Goodall, 1968), two of the three male infants were seen in the vicinity of sexually receptive females. And yet, mounting was not observed until several months later.

Why did the two infants not mount when they were 9 months old? Could it be that the infant has to observe copulating conspecifics before it is able to perform mounting itself? It was striking that FD was seen to mount for the first time after he had been in a large sexual group (five sexually receptive females and all adult males) for 8 hours. Furthermore, FD mounted frequently when playing with objects after he was seen in this large sexual group whereas he put "objects against penis" (OTP) long before. The other infant, PT, was observed to mount objects only after he was observed to mount females. The importance of the social example for the onset of mounting is discussed in the next section.

Discussion

Presenting (PRE) does not exclusively subserve the sexual function. It functions very much as a more general social communicational signal in the same way as the gestures initiating tickling, grooming, approach, and the gift of food are social (pp. 116–118). This corresponds with the fact that presenting is first observed at the same age as all these other gestures (10–11 months for presenting and 9–12.5 months for the other gestures). Just as the other gestures such as "putting arm high" (DAO) and "arm high" (AOH) (pp. 116–118) are interlaced with and derive their meaning from interactions during early development, so is presenting interlaced with being restrained, having the hips held, and the genitals and the perineal area inspected (Hanby, 1976). It cannot be denied that presenting may initiate mounting or inspecting, but it initiates other interactions much more frequently. Presenting as a way of asking to be mounted is just one of several meanings which presenting can have, depending on the context.

Tutin and McGinnis (1979) report that "female juveniles were seen to present, both to peers during play, and to adult males during greeting, from the age of 4 years on, but this behavior was "uncommon". My data contradict this statement because female infants from the age of 14 months on were observed to present to all age/sex classes from babies to adults.

Chimpanzee male infants are capable of mounting when 9-months-old (van Lawick-Goodall, 1968). In my opinion it is no coincidence that this age of 9 months is the earliest ever reported. It goes together with the appearance of the various forms of "object against body", the use of social gestures, and presenting. It is tempting to think of mounting as just another way of relating things and individuals alike to an important body part, in the same way as the various forms of "object against body" and categories such as handleading (HAL) and "hands around head" (HOH) do to two other important body spots (the neck and the belly). Related ideas are expressed by Golani (1976, p. 112) in relation to sequences of mammalian courtship, agonistic, and play behavior. His concept of kinetic field and ideas of biological relativistic space (p. 113) may be very helpful in the study of the development of social and sexual behavior. I propose to forget about the the adultomorphic idea of "sexually motivated behavior", and suggest stressing the fact that infants relate to the physical and social world with their whole body in general and with certain body spots in particular. The infant seems not so much focused on copulation with intromission, but more on bringing inanimate and animate objects in contact with a particularly sensitive body spot. Mounting is only one of various ways to do so. Quotes from Bruner's (1974) article on the nature and uses of immaturity are pertinent here. He stresses the chimpanzee's lack of "interest in the goal of the act being performed and by its preoccupation with means" (p. 25). . . . and further states, "The acts themselves have a self-rewarding character. They are varied systematically, almost as if in play to test the limits of a new skill" (p. 27). This has been commonplace to ethologists for a long time (Kortlandt, 1955). The observation that various forms of "object against body" (pp. 115–116) and mounting of objects are frequently performed in early infancy and then disappear (see also Tutin, 1975, p. 124) supports this idea.

The variation in age of onset of mounting needs explanation. Contrasted with the early age of onset reported by van Lawick-Goodall (1968: 9 months) for infants living under high density, I observed a late onset of mounting for infants living in more dispersed conditions (17, 18, and 20 months). This late onset of mounting was confirmed by Tutin (1975: 15, 17, and 20 months) who observed in Gombe under the same, dispersed conditions. A late onset of mounting cannot be ascribed to lack of opportunity. Two of the three male infants I observed had opportunities to mount sexually receptive females from 9 months on. However, they were not seen to use these opportunities. In contrast, after mounting was observed for the first time, it "was repeated at almost every opportunity the infant had to interact with a receptive female" (Tutin, 1975, p. 125), although the opportunities were equally scarce as before the onset.

I suggest that the lack of social example could be a sensible explanation. My data are suggestive in this direction if one realizes that, although the infants were in the company of tumescent (SWE) females, this did not last long enough for them to witness adult males and females copulating. This notion is supported by the independent data of Caroline Tutin (1975). She followed maximally tumescent females and found that mothers with infants were infrequently seen to associate with receptive females (Tutin, 1975, Table 5.5). It could be possible that mothers with small infants tend to avoid sexual groups.

The point of view that lack of social example can explain the late onset of mounting is indirectly supported by the data on mounting objects.

Whereas objects were put against the penis or clitoris (OTP) from 9 months on, they were only mounted after "mounting females" had started. I suggest that, before the onset of mounting, the infants simply did not know that relating things and swellings to their penis or clitoris could be done in the adult way as well.

A further argument in favor of the opinion that social example is crucial consists of the recent findings (Goy, 1964; Goy & Goldfoot, 1973; Hanby, 1976; Wallen et al., 1977) that sexual hormones do not seem to be necessary for the expression of sociosexual patterns in infancy. Social experience seems to be the determining factor since castrates who had the greater social experience mounted and thrusted much more frequently than intact males with less social experience.

The findings of Phoenix (1978) support the findings of Goy and Goldfoot and show that early experience may have long-lasting effects. He demonstrated that the mean "sexual performance" level of laboratory-reared (adult) rhesus males is significantly below that of males born in the wild whereas testosterone levels in the two groups do not differ significantly.

However, differences in the frequencies with which various sociosexual patterns are performed by infants of the different sexes are clearly present. This is understandable from recent research on fetal steroids and brain development in rhesus monkeys by Resko (1973, 1974). It seems that testosterone either per se or as a prohormone regulates sexual differentiation of the brain prenatally.

The role of social example and social experience in early infancy appears to be very important for the development of non-distorted sexual behavior, not only for chimpanzees (Davenport, 1979; Plooij, 1979) but for many primate species (Hanby, 1976). All too often there is a delayed and distorted development of social patterns in humans, at least in our western society, producing all sorts of unwanted side-effects such as disrupted individual relationships as a "mild" example and rape as one of the more severe examples. I cannot help but wonder at this point what effect various upbringing strategies in our western culture, such as the closed bedroom door and the prevention or forbidding of any expression of sociosexual patterns in early infancy, may have on later development. Not all cultures restrict sociosexual behaviors as our culture does and more comparative research between human cultures is badly needed.

GENERAL DISCUSSION

The Main Sequence of Developmental Phenomena

The left column of the following list summarizes the main sequence of developmental phenomena which were presented in this chapter. In the right column a sequence of developmental phenomena as reported for human babies is presented and, again, the resemblance is striking.

CHIMPANZEES

1. From the seventh month on, no behavior was observed in the infant which showed that out of sight was out of mind (see pp. 60–62). From then on the infant was able to go *away from* its mother and go *back to* her and it apparently knew that the mother was *behind* it. The various behavior categories grouped under the label "object against body" appear towards the age of 9 months. All these categories imply the control of a relationship between an object and a certain body spot: object *on top of* head (OOH), object *in* neck (OIN), object *into* neck-pocket (ONP), object *against* belly (OTB), etc.

2. From the age of 7 months, a discrepancy from "within arm's reach" (= 4) causes whimpering. Until the age of 9-10 months the young infant stays close to its mother, making and breaking contact frequently and in an unpredictable way. When the infant grows older, it makes progressively larger and longer excursions away from its mother at the expense of the short and unpredictable ones. Towards the end of the second year, the infant's excursions are far more predictable: either it is on its mother or it is on excursion for some time.

HUMANS

1. From Piaget (1952) we know that human infants are occupied in the control of relationship from the middle of the third sensory-motor stage (thus approximately 7 months) on: hitting two objects *against* each other and memory of position, for instance. By the age of 9–10 months (stage 4) the human infant is able to put a cover *over* an object, a ball *into* a container, and searches for a hidden object *under* a cloth or *behind* a screen. Although the achievement of most of these abilities of the infant are usually placed in stage 4 (9–11 months), their very first appearance (in which I am interested now) is earlier. This was reported by Piaget himself according to Ingram (1978, p. 264): "It is perfectly normal that these first behavior patterns of the fourth stage are constituted sporadically from the middle of the third state", thus approximately 7 months.

2. After the age of 8 months, children are concerned with the distance to their mother (Bronson, 1972; Morgan & Ricciuti, 1969). Nine-month-olds possess the cognitive ability to perceive distance arrangements (Lempers, Flavell, & Flavell, 1977). Kagan (1974, p. 241) reports that crying and sustained inhibition of play to maternal separation, which only appear after 8 months, increase in frequency and duration through 2 to 2.5 years of age, *after which they decline* (emphasis is mine). "This age function has the same form in middle-class Cambridge children, infants from an institution in Athens, and poor ladino infants from Antigua, Guatemala".

CHIMPANZEES

3. In between the seventh and the ninth month, six anomalous motor-patterns were observed for the first time (BRS, GYM, PIR, SLS, STA, and SUM). These patterns may be considered to result from a conflict between two opposite orientation components.

4. From the age of 9 months on, social gestures such as "begging" (BWH, BWM), "hands around head" (HOH), "arms high" (AOH), and "lies down on back" (GOR) are used. The infants may be assumed to possess a true communicative ability (Plooij, 1978a).

5. Sociosexual behaviors such as "presenting" (PRE) "mounting" (MOU), and "thrusting" (THU) emerge around the age of 9 months (at the earliest).

HUMANS

3. To my knowledge such anomalous motor-patterns have not been reported in the human literature for babies of this age. At a later age comparable patterns can be observed (personal observation).

4. Trevarthen and Hubley (1978) review the considerable evidence concerning the growth of a fundamental mechanism of infant personality and person-perception by infants around the age of 9 months. "There is a seemingly endless list of new achievements at this age, all of which require the baby to identify with and reciprocate attentions of others" (p. 221). For instance, they cite Melanie Klein to be the first to postulate infantile neuroses: "She observed that after 9 months the baby was capable of remorse for causing pain to a loved one (depressive position) (p. 223). This requires that the infant develops a concept of relationship between a distinct self and another (object relation). Interestingly, this is the age at which an infant first shows self-consciousness in a mirror" (Amsterdam, 1972).

5. Lewis (1965) reports the age of 8–10 months for the onset of pelvic thrusts in human infants directed towards the mother's body.

The resemblance in the sequences of developmental phenomena of both chimpanzee and human infants is supported by the literature on captive apes. Wood et al. (1980) and Redshaw (1978) compared cognitive development during the sensory-motor period in human infants with the cognitive development in chimpanzee and gorilla infants, respectively. Both found that, during the first year of life, the similarities were pronounced and that all three species follow much the same course of development—passing through the same stages in similar order without a systematic difference in the rate of development. Chevalier-Skolnikoff (1977) comes to the same conclusion after her application of a Piagetian model for describing and comparing socialization in monkey, ape, and human infants.

Control of Relationships

There is a consensus in the human literature that somewhere between 7 and 9 months of age a special cognitive competence emerges among western infants, which underlies a seemingly endless list of new achievements. Kagan (1974) considers it as an activation of hypothesis and the ability to "think" (Kagan, 1972). Schaffer (1974) looks upon it as the ability to *relate* different stimuli to one another (emphasis is mine). Trevarthen and Hubley (1978) speak of a fundamental mechanism of infant personality and person perception and "change in structures of intelligence at a deeper level".

It is tempting to think that the wide variety of developmental phenomena which was discussed in the foregoing section result from this cognitive competence. But then all these phenomena should at least have one thing in common. The common denominator may be that all these phenomena have something to do with the control of "relationships": the relationships which the infants are occupied in during the third and fourth (Piagetian) stages, the distance-relationship between the infant and its mother, and the relationship between a distinct self and another individual ("object relationship").

The developmental phenomena of the chimpanzee infants may also have the control of such relationships in common. The "object against body" behavior categories could not have been performed without the perception and control of a relationship between an object and a certain body spot. The way in which the infants go on excursion and whimper when a discrepancy from "within arm's reach" arises indicates the permanent control of the distance relationship between mother and infant. The performance of the social gestures and the sociosexual behaviors demands the ability to relate certain body parts to the other individual or certain body parts of that individual.

The sixth-order control system in Powers' (1973) model perceives and controls relationships (see Figure 2, Chapter 1). Relationships are defined as those invariants that appear in collections of independent events (short, familiar sequences = fifth-order perceptions) and lower-order perceptions. Examples given by Powers (1973, pp. 155–159) are space-time relationships, cause-effect relationships, but also the logical concept "and" as a relationship, to name a few.

Therefore, I suggest that the special cognitive competence which emerges between 7 and 9 months is this sixth-order system becoming functional for the first time. The previous chapter discussed how towards the end of the first half year the organization underlying the baby's perception and behavior could be thought of as a hierarchy of five orders of control. Apparently, between 7–9 months yet another sixth-order control system is superimposed onto this hierarchy.

Finally, I would like to point out that the developmental phenomena described range from relationships in the physical world as described by Piaget and others to phenomena in the social realm. Looft and Svoboda (1975, p. 59) point out that "Freud's orientation was almost exclusively 'child-society', while Piaget's orientation has been 'child-object'. Consequently, a dualism has evolved." It may be worthwhile to try and abandon this dualism from our models and theories on early development. In the hierarchy of negative feedback control systems which, it is suggested here, underlie overt behavior during early development, the various orders of control are not limited to any functional domain which human observers have ever selected for classification.

The Anomalous Motor-patterns

When in the foregoing section the control of relationships was discussed the anomalous motor-patterns were not mentioned. Yet, these patterns develop approximately at the same age as the other developmental phenomena for which the control of relationships was proposed. Thus the question arises whether these motor-patterns might have anything to do with the control of relationships.

The performance of the anomalous motor-patterns was discussed earlier (pp. 114–115) in relation to the ethological conflict hypothesis. The opinion was expressed that the occurrence of these motor-patterns could more parsimoniously be explained in terms of a conflict between a tendency to approach and a tendency to withdraw. This is in fact synonymous with a conflict between two incompatible distance relationships. Phrasing it in the latter way has the advantage that the emergence of the anomalous motor-patterns after the age of 7 months can also be interpreted in terms of sixth-order control of relationships, just as the list of all the other new achievements which emerge after that age. Therefore, this explanation is explored a little further.

First it should be pointed out that the definition of conflict as given by Powers (1973) shows great resemblance with the ideas about conflict found in the ethological literature (Baerends, 1975, 1976). These resemblances are:

1. A hierarchy of negative feedback control systems is involved.
2. Conflict is defined as a competitive encounter between two control systems.
3. This conflict between control systems is not limited to any level of integration.

In order to understand the performance of the anomalous motor-patterns in terms of a conflict between "two incompatible distance relationships'', Powers' (1973) ideas about conflict must be elaborated a little further. Conflict can occur only when two control systems control the same kinds of variables, so closely related that they are essentially one variable. In effect, the two control systems attempt to control the same quantity, but with respect to two different set-values. For one system to correct its error the other system must experience error. There is no way for both systems to experience zero error at the same time. Therefore the output of the systems must act on the shared controlled quantity in opposite directions. If both systems are reasonably sensitive to error, and the two set-values are far apart, there will be a range of values of the controlled quantity (between the set-values) throughout which each system will contain an error signal so large that the output of each system will be solidly at its maximum. Over this range of values the controlled quantity cannot be protected against disturbance anymore.

The basic mechanism behind conflict is response to disturbance. Any moderate disturbance will change the controlled quantity, and this will change the perceptual signals in the two control systems. As long as neither set-value is closely approached, there will be no reaction to these changes on the part of the systems in conflict. When a disturbance forces the controlled quantity close enough to either set-value, however, there *will* be a reaction. The control system experiencing lessened error will relax, unbalancing the net output in the direction of the other set-values. As a result, the systems in conflict will act like a single reference system having a ''virtual set-value'', between the two actual ones. A large dead zone will exist around the virtual set-value, within which there is little or no control. If nothing disturbs the controlled quantity of a conflicted pair, an equilibrium point will be reached somewhere between the set-values. A lower-order system responds as if to a single set-value that is the average or vector-sum of the conflicting ones; that is what creates the virtual appearance of a virtual set-value. If the disturbance is nothing more than a result of one's ongoing behavior, that behavior will be disrupted by what Powers (1973) calls an ''automatic resistance'', an inhibition to at least some aspect of it. In humans, this resistance is felt as a reluctance to carry out the behavior leading to some goal.

The kind of behavior ensuing from this interaction is of the type which in the ethological literature is classified as ambivalent behavior, i.e., as a combination of—or a compromise between—intention movements of functionally opposed behavior patterns. The ethological literature is full of examples of such behavior. Powers' (1973) ideas about conflict are thus compatible with this ethological concept.

Arguments have been given that in chimpanzee infants the anomalous motor-patterns can be considered as ambivalent behavior. Let us take the examples of somersaulting (SUM) and pirouetting (PIR). It has already been stated that the form can be explained as a conflict between opposed orientation components. A similar causation can be argued with respect to the situation in which the patterns occur. For instance, an infant may make a somersault (SUM) when, while traveling with its mother, it gets ahead of her. Afterwards, it sits down and waits. If we assume that the distance between the mother and the infant is the quantity which is controlled by two conflicting sixth-order control systems, the set-value of one of these systems could be "ahead of mother" and the other "staying with mother" (distance = 0). Then, according to the model given above, a virtual set-value will result in between these two set-values with a dead-zone around it (Figure 25). As long as the infant remains inside this dead-zone, no change will be induced, since little or no control exists within this dead-zone. Thus, the infant keeps running ahead of mother. However, as soon as the infant crosses the boundary of the dead-zone, control is exerted again (automatic resistance). Then, as was explained above, a lower-order system (such as a fifth-order system controlling a short sequence such as walking) responds to a virtual set-value which is the average of the conflicting ones. From the resulting disruption of coordination the anomalous motor-patterns result.

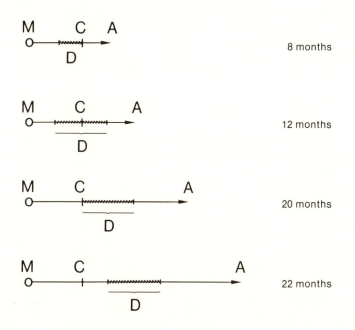

Figure 25. Outward shift of the dead-zone (D) in the control of the distance between mother and infant over the age range of 8–22 months.
M = set-value "ventral on mother".
A = set-value "away from mother".
C = dividing line between "in contact" and "out of contact".

A nice aspect of this way of explaining the anomalous motor-patterns is that it is done in terms of systems controlling the external input, which is relatively easily measurable. The position of the mother (one of the set-values: distance = 0) and of the infant can be registered continuously, thus also the distance between them. The other set-value ("ahead of mother") can be estimated from the data collected on the average distance at which infants distance themselves from their mothers at each particular age. In this study distances could not be measured continuously, but had to be scored in rather gross, digital categories. Therefore, this is research which must be done in the future.

So far I do not quite understand why at any particular moment one or the other anomalous motor-pattern should be performed. It was argued earlier that this may depend on the value of the balance between approach and withdrawal. In terms of the model of conflict between two incompatible distance relationships this may depend on which boundary of the dead-zone is crossed. However, in order to answer this question adequately, much more research is needed in which the distances are measured continuously, as was argued above.

Termination Rates of Excursions

The developmental changes in the termination rates of the chimpanzee infant's excursions (pp. 95–106) can also be interpreted in terms of the conflict between two incompatible distance relationships. I assume, again, that the distance between the mother and the infant is the quantity which is controlled.

The first distance relationship is proximity to mother. The infant never allows the distance to its mother to increase beyond its control. I assume that there exists a set-value "being ventral on the mother" which is controlled by a sixth-order system. And yet, the infant is not ventral to the mother all day. Besides rest periods, during which the infant is ventral, there are active periods during which the infant leaves the mother. This is not to say that the just-mentioned set-value ceases to exist. Instead, I assume that other systems become active resulting in what is usually called "exploring the environment" (social or physical) and resulting in another distance relationship to mother which is in conflict with the first-mentioned distance relationship (being ventral to mother). One could say that these systems becoming active have their own set-value as far as the distance to mother is concerned.

If nothing disturbs the controlled quantity, an equilibrium point will be reached somewhere between the set-values. As the infant becomes capable of going farther and farther away from its mother without meeting unsolvable problems on its return, this equilibrium point will come to lie farther and farther away as well. Around this equilibrium point there is, still according to the model, a large dead zone or a range of values over which there is little or no control. Here the controlled quantity cannot be protected anymore against disturbance.

Now, in my opinion, this "dead zone" overlaps the dividing line between "in contact", and "out of contact" from the age of 8–21 months. This can be concluded from Figure 21 where it is shown that the infants spend the largest proportion of their time in one or both of the distance categories surrounding this dividing line. Consequently, it is not surprising that the crossing of this dividing line (being the start or the finish of an excursion) occurs unpredictably (see Figure 23). Finally, as soon as this dead zone shifts so far away from the mother over the course of development that it no longer overlaps this dividing line, no constant termination rate of excursions should be observed and the infant should spend the largest proportion of its time farther away from the mother. This, again, is fully supported by the findings: Figure 21 shows the development of the first "ring" between the age of 20 and 23 months and the constant termination rate of excursions disappears completely and rather abruptly from the age of 22 months on. Figure 25 visualizes the whole process.

Stranger Anxiety Versus Fear of Strangers

According to Escalona (1968, p. 10), there exists confusion in the human literature about these two phenomena: "With a few notable exceptions, communication between psychoanalysts and other behavioral scientists has been unsatisfactory. This is even true of the definition of the phenomena under discussion. For instance, the notion of 'stranger anxiety', as used by psychoanalysts is frequently equated with 'fear of strangers' by psychologists; most of the academic work on the topic fails to recognize that what is postulated by psychoanalysts is a fear of losing the mother which manifests itself in the response to strangers under certain—and only certain—conditions." In the light of this it is interesting to note that, according to the model developed in this book, these two phenomena are mediated by two quite different processes. The "fear of strangers" phenomenon was suggested to result from the emergence of a fifth-order control system (pp. 89–90), whereas the phenomenon of "stranger anxiety" may be interpreted to result from the sixth-order control of the distance relationship with the mother.

6

Beyond One Year

INTRODUCTION

The repertoire of discrete movement patterns develops from the age of 5 months on, as was discussed in Chapter 4. Yet, until the age of 9 months, all of the behavior categories either involve the control of events (short, familiar sequences: e.g., TAK or WAQ) or relationships (e.g., OIN). None of the categories represent functional sequences of behavior in which discrete types of behavior have been integrated. It was not yet possible to say: "the infant is eating now", or "the infant is nestbuilding".

In the field I had the impression that the behavior of infants of 20-months-old was far more "predictable" than the behavior of very young infants. What changes in the behavior of the infants lead to this impression? Why is it that one is able to say that an infant of 20-months-old is "nestbuilding" (NES), "fishing" (VIS), or eating, whereas this is totally impossible for infants of 9 months? After all, nestbuilding and fishing are still incomplete if compared with the way adults build nests and fish for termites; the infants have another few years to go before their skills come anywhere near those of the adults. Is my adult way of observing fooling me or has there been a real change in the behavior of the infants? The differentiation of begging and feeding has been already accounted for and is completely present from the age of 9 months on. Thus, that cannot explain the afore-mentioned field impression that the infant's behavior is more predictable at a later age. There should be more to it.

Thinking about it, I was struck by the fact that termite fishing, nest-building, and eating can be described by programs in the same sense as "eating porridge with a spoon" is defined to be a program (see Powers, 1973, pp. 160–168). It involves a definite list of relationships brought about one after the other: first put spoon *into* the porridge, shovel some porridge *onto* the spoon, put the spoon *into* your mouth (and not *against* your eye), etc. A program is represented by a seventh-order perceptual signal (see Figure 2 in Chapter 1).

The program is not a list. It is a *structure* and at the nodes of this structure are tests or decision points (if-statements): a point where the list of operations being carried out is interrupted and some state of affairs is perceived and compared to a reference state of affairs. Sometimes such choice points may form a "tree". In this tree the *network,* not the particular path followed, is the organization in question.

Programs can be organized to obey any imaginable rules: not only deduction, but superstition, grammatical rules, expectations about the consequences of behavior in the physical world (models), experimental procedures, mathematical algorithms, recipes for cooking and chemistry, and the strategies of business, games, conversation, and love-making. "Plans and the structure of behavior", by Miller et al. (1960) is a good textbook of seventh-order behavior. (See Powers, 1973, pp. 160–168).

In chimpanzees, eating, for instance, may involve locomotion *towards* a fruit, picking (PLU) or bit-pulling (BIP) it *off* the branch, biting (BIT) a piece *off* the fruit and chewing and swallowing (FED) it, et.

Could it be that yet another reorganization takes place somewhere between the ages of 9 and 20 months, combined with another class of invariance? Or, to be more specific, that seventh-order of control (programs) emerges (see Figure 2, Chapter 1)?

If this were to be the case one would expect the behavior categories, which are needed to bring about the aforementioned relationships, to cluster in time as soon as reorganization had taken place, whereas they should not do so before. This is something that can be analyzed from my notes.

METHODS

First of all, the behavior categories which may be needed to bring about the list of relationships of the program eating have to be chosen. For this purpose my knowledge of eating as it is performed by adult chimpanzees was used. The following categories were chosen: biting at (BAT), bit-pulling (BIP), biting (BIT), chewing and swallowing (FED), looking at (LAT), pottering (PEU), picking (PLU), reaching for (REF), and mouthing (SAB).

In the search for "eating-bouts" the following procedure was used. In the transcriptions of my running commentary, first chewing and swallowing (FED) was located. From that point a search was started, forwards in time. As soon as a behavior category was found which was not mentioned in the list above, the eating-bout was defined to be finished. In order to find the beginning of the eating-bout a second search was performed, backwards in time and in a similar way. As soon as another behavior category (as compared with the ones listed above) was found, the beginning of the eating-bout was located.

After having located all the eating-bouts in a sample, the duration of the bouts as well as the intervals between them were measured in terms of the number of 15-second time-markers crossed.

DATA

The duration of the eating-bouts does not change very much over development. The median is usually two (once three) time-markers ($=30\pm15$ seconds) and the mode one or two. The spread becomes slightly larger as development proceeds: Eating-bouts may last up to 13 time-markers ($=195$ seconds) at the age of 6 months and up to 24 time-markers ($=6$ minutes) at the age of 20 months.

The intervals between eating-bouts give a more interesting picture. In Figure 26 the log-survivor functions of these intervals are given for three different infants at the age of 6, 9, 12, and 20 months. The reasons for plotting the interval lengths as log-survivor functions are similar to the ones

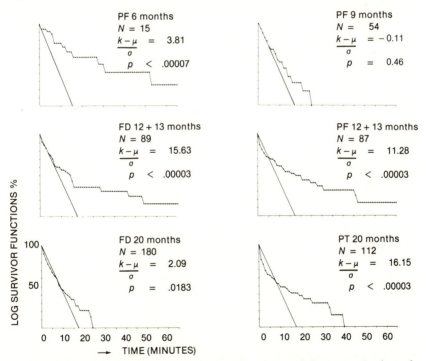

Figure 26. Log-survivor functions of the lengths of intervals between eating-bouts for three different infants at the ages of 6, 9, 12, and 20 months. Each point in a graph gives the logarithm of the number of intervals (as percentage of the logarithm of the total number of intervals) which last the time indicated on the abscissa or longer.

given in the beginning of Chapter 5, and the statistic K for testing linearity was used.

In the course of this series of graphs a change in form occurs around the ninth month. Only at this age does the graph not differ significantly from the straight line, meaning that the termination rate of the intervals between eating-bouts is constant. Both before as well as after this age all graphs do differ significantly from a straight line, albeit in a different way (the straight line belonging to the graph of PF at the age of 9 months is reproduced in all the other graphs as a visual aid). Before 9 months, the beginning of the log-survivor function is convex whereas the beginning of all the graphs after the age of 9 months are concave.

This means that at the age of 6 months the infant occasionally eats, but this eating is isolated in time. The intervals between the eating-bouts tend to be large. Once the infant has eaten, it is not likely to do so soon thereafter. At the age of 9 months the infant eats more frequently, but its eating behavior is not predictable. When it stops eating it may resume this activity soon thereafter, or not for a long time. At the age of 1 year and older, two groups of intervals between eating-bouts have differentiated: either the infant stops eating for not much more than 1 minute or it stops eating for a long time. The group of short intervals should result from periods in the sample during which eating-bouts are clustered together. The emerging of such periods must have contributed to my field impression that one could say: "the infant *is eating* now".

DISCUSSION

The only value of such data, as was stressed already in Chapter 5, is that some change has been shown to have occurred by the age of 12 months. The process underlying this change remains unknown. More research is needed to uncover it.

The emergence of seventh-order of control of programs is a serious candidate to serve as a guide for future research. It creates a link with the idea of a "syntax" of behavior (later also referred to under names such as plan, program, grammar) as suggested by Lashley (1951).

Not many human studies have been done on the ontogenetic development of "programs". The works of Bruner (1970), Connolly (1970, 1973), Elliott and Connolly (1974), and Greenfield (1978) are exceptions. Similar studies should be done on chimpanzees in the future. The observations as recorded in this study are not fine enough for such analyses.

I established that, for instance, nestbuilding (NES) was observed for the very first time at the age of 12 months in chimpanzee infants, the same age as the assumed emergence of seventh-order of control. In the study on human babies and infants which is still in progress, typical examples of "programs" as wide apart as "eating-porridge-with-a-spoon" to "vacuum-cleaning" were observed to emerge around the age of 12 months as well (Plooij, in preparation).

It may be a fruitful line of research to compare the early development of sentence grammar with the early development of "programs" in other functional domains in order to answer the question of how unique the language faculty really is. The emergence of complex motor "programs" such as eating-porridge-with-a-spoon or vacuum-cleaning in human babies of 12 months coincides with the first production of spoken words and the "language readiness". Sentences are considered by Powers (1973) to be strings of words (fifth-order perception) in relationship (sixth-order control). Thus, grammar is one example of seventh-order control. So are games, the recipes for cooking and chemistry, the strategies of conversation, etc. But these domains (with the possible exception of pattern recognition) have not been studied formally to the same degree as sentence-grammar (Marshall, Newcombe, et al., 1980).

In the discussion on the changeover between differentiation and ascending development (pp. 1–6) I have already touched on the possibility of a synthesis between the concept of system as used in the ethological literature (Baerends, 1956, 1976; Hinde, 1953; McFarland, 1971, pp. 205–206) and the concept of control systems as discussed in this publication. I like to entertain the idea that the ethological concept of system and the concept of seventh-order control system as discussed here have much in common. A similar idea was expressed by Tinbergen (1951, p. 121 ff.), who stated that ethologists have been considering higher levels of integration. If we again look at his attempt at a synthesis between Weiss' (1941) concept of nervous hierarchy and the ethological concept of the hierarchical structure of behavior (see Tinbergen, 1951, p. 125), it can be said that Tinbergen's second level (fighting, nesting, etc.) is similar to the seventh-order control of programs as discussed above. Continuing this comparison, Tinbergen's third level can be considered similar to the fifth-order control of short sequences as discussed in Chapter 4. In between Tinbergen's second and third level, I have proposed an additional, sixth-order of control. It is clear that this publication ends where a great deal of further research is needed. However, I hope to have shown that such an undertaking shall be worth its while for chimpanzees as well as man.

Summary

INTRODUCTION AND STUDY AIMS

This study aims to achieve an ontogenetically oriented understanding of behavioral phenomena during early development (first 2 years) of free-living chimpanzees. For this purpose, six chimpanzee babies and infants were observed in the Gombe National Park, Tanzania. Furthermore, comparisons are made between the results of this publication and the human literature with the intention to uncover aspects of human behavior which would remain unnoticed without such a comparison.

The main question which dominates this publication is whether it is possible to find out what type of organization is underlying the developing behavior. Two opposed lines of thought concerning development (differentiation versus ascending development) are considered. Neither type of development fits all facts. Rather, one type of development (ascending development) seems to replace the other (differentiation), which is not surprising if one considers that, after a number of parts have differentiated from the total unity, this unity would be lost if these parts were not integrated by a system which is hierarchically superior to these parts.

It is argued that around the age of 2 months the changeover takes place between differentiation and ascending development. This point of view raises the problem that it is difficult to specify the supposed system (integrating the differentiated parts), because discrete behavior patterns which are used in the search for the existence of systems in adult organisms do not yet exist in chimpanzees under 5-months-old.

Another way to find these systems is suggested, namely the search for consummatory stimuli, which stop all ongoing activity aimed at restoring set-values derived from these consummatory stimuli. In order to illustrate what is meant by "a search for consummatory stimuli", data and literature on thermoregulation in neonates are presented. However, the consummatory stimuli which rule the behavior of chimpanzee babies older than 2 months are less easy to find.

As a lead to finding these consummatory stimuli, Powers' (1973) hypothetical construct is presented. This construct is a functional block diagram of the organization of the human nervous system. It stands model for the way in which overt behavior is regulated. This regulation of overt behavior results from the control of perception, since the regulation is aimed incessantly at reaching or maintaining certain set-values in perception. Not all these set-values belong to the same level. They are hierarchically nested and higher-order set-values are able to adjust lower-order ones.

Additionally, three procedures aimed at finding the consummatory stimuli are discussed: the study of reactions to disturbances, the speed of control systems, and rigidity versus variability of behavior.

GENERAL METHODS

The study-area, the study-population, and the study-subjects are described. The observations under natural conditions were made in terms of a list of behavior categories and a list of environmental categories which exerted influence on the subjects. The way in which these lists were assembled and the criteria which were used to define the behavior categories are spelled out. These criteria change with age. Before the age of 5 months only a few motor-patterns could be defined. Most other categories concern the end-result of motor activity and not the motor activity itself. After the age of 5 months, an increasing number of motor-patterns could be distinguished. These were defined according to form. Only much later (at the age of 12 months) was it possible to define behavior categories according to function. Another factor which played a role in defining the behavior categories was the finding that it was impossible to describe the behavior of the whole organism in terms of mutually exclusive categories. Instead, categories concerning body parts were defined and the behavior of the whole organism was described in terms of a sequence of combinations of such categories. Data collection, sampling, and observer reliability are described.

PERINATAL PERIOD

During the prenatal period self-protective behavior by the mother was absent. Only during the last day before parturition the mother restricted her movements and avoided social activity. The construction of a "daynest" was found to be the best indicator of parturition being due.

Some anatomical aspects of the newborn baby such as hairlessness, skin-pigmentation, skin color, and tooth-eruption are dealt with. Furthermore, the limited behavior repertoire of the chimpanzee neonate is described. Extra attention is given to the waking recurrences, to the activities of sucking, clinging, mountaineering, and rooting and to the vocalizations effort-grunt, staccato, uh-grunt, whimper-ho, and whimpering.

The waking and sucking cycles of one chimpanzee baby are described and the difference between this baby and captive chimpanzees are compared with the differences between human babies of different caretaking environments.

During the daytime of the first week of life the free-living baby was fast asleep for at least 20 minutes every 3 hours. In between, the baby was frequently awake (more so during the morning than during the afternoon) and several sucking recurrences occurred. Whereas the captive chimpanzee babies slept almost all day, the free-living baby had it eyes open 30% of the time.

After the first week, the baby was awake twice as much and for much longer periods. This contrasts strongly with the captive babies who still slept during most of the day. Sucking had become more frequent and more irregular. Sucking-bouts emerged in those parts of the day during which the baby was fast asleep in the first week.

The differences between the free-living chimpanzee baby and the captive ones are similar to the differences between human babies of different caretaking environments. The caretaking environments are compared. The features which appear to cause the observed behavioral differences in the newborn babies are discussed. These are: body position (horizontal versus upright), caretaker (single versus multiple), and feeding (demand versus schedule).

The helplessness of the newborn chimpanzee baby was considerable. It was not able to cling properly and its life depended on the maternal support. Furthermore, its thermoregulation system was not yet able to prevent hypothermia. The helplessness of the chimpanzee newborns equals the helplessness of the human babies (and the other ape babies) much more strongly than the helplessness of monkey babies. This remarkable difference is related to developmental retardation. It is argued that human babies would not loose the "grasping reflex" soon after birth if only the baby caretaking routines would give it a chance.

Three vocalizations and the conditions which elicit them are described. Two of these vocalizations, the effort-grunt and the staccato, are very useful to measure the striking individual differences in activity/reactivity soon after birth.

EARLY LIFE: BABIES

A description of the overt behaviors which are typical for the age range of 2–6 months is given. The changes in behavior during this age span receive extra attention.

The conditions which elicited the vocalization "whimpering" (ZWH) changed qualitatively over age. The neonate whimpered when a discrepancy from ventro-ventral contact or nipple-in-mouth arose. By the age of 3 months this had changed to the mother being out of contact and out of sight and when the baby had become an infant (7 months) only the mother being out of arm's reach was still able to evoke whimpering.

A change in conditions evoking the vocalization "staccato" (STC) was observed as well: around the age of 3 months there is a shift from intensity determined stimuli to more complexly determined stimuli.

Biting and playface developed from the age of 6 weeks on. Laughing developed a few weeks later.

The early biting triggered the onset of mother-baby play: contingent upon when bitten, the mother started to tickle the baby and this biting-tickling grew into an alternating interaction, in which both mother and baby could take their turns many times in succession. The early biting at the age of 6 weeks was made possible by the directed-head-turning response and elicited by perioral stimulation. It only developed after the "shocky" rooting had disappeared and after the baby had started to go "straight on the nipple". The frequency with which "things" were present near the face of the baby was a major determinant of how often these "things" were bitten. The baby's own limbs were bitten most frequently. Body components of the mother came second, physical objects third, and a sibling fourth. This implies that the baby did not make any discrimination between the "things" bitten, not even between physical and "social objects". At the age of 2 months this changed. The range of targets narrowed down to body components of the mother. The impression could not be avoided, though, that the mother was not yet seen by the baby as a whole, but merely as a collection of very interesting "social objects". This impression was changed around the age of 3 months when the baby showed a sudden, intense interest for the mother's face.

The facial expression playface-half may be considered to develop out of the perioral stimulation mechanism around the age of 6 weeks, namely when stimulation of the lower lip is involved. Around the age of 3 months the release of playface and biting stopped having an "automatic" character and the mechanism releasing playface expanded the stimulus area caudally.

Escape behavior as a reaction to other individuals was not observed until the fifth month of age. From the fourth month on, however, the baby directed its behaviors selectively to different individuals. From this it is concluded that the baby differentiates between the mother and the sibling on the one hand and other adult individuals on the other hand. Other infants take an intermediate position. The possibility that this selectivity of the baby in its behavior to different groups of other individuals can be ascribed to the "availability" of these other individuals is ruled out.

During the fifth month escape behavior was elicited as soon as another took hold, even if only gently, of the baby. In the sixth month the mere approach of another individual was already enough. Finally, during the seventh month, another individual merely looking at the infant elicited escape as well. By the age of 6 months, the so-called "fear of strangers" seemed to have developed.

A number of miscellaneous developmental facts from the first half year of life are presented in chronological order.

DISCUSSION CHAPTER 4

First of all, the main sequence of developmental phenomena is summarized. Thereafter, the data are interpreted in terms of the hierarchically nested classes of consummatory stimuli with the help of the three procedures as outlined in Chapter 1. The data support the notion that between the ages of 2–5 months a hierarchy of negative feedback control organizations develops.

Notwithstanding this evidence in favor of ascending development, it is argued that both types of development are complementary aspects of one and the same developmental process, with each type being most "eye-catching" during a different age range. The reason why most studies conducted so far concluded in favor of only ascending development may be that these studies were all conducted postnatally or posthatching. Furthermore, it is pointed out that the changeover between the two types of development can be observed more easily in the apes because their whole development is so much retarded. Nevertheless, a few studies in non-ape mammals are discussed which support the ideas about development as discussed in this publication.

The sequence of developmental phenomena as reported in this publication is compared with a sequence of developmental phenomena as reported in the human literature. The resemblance is striking. The human sequence also appears to fit the model of development as presented here. Some additional human literature is reinterpreted in terms of this model.

In contrast with all the similarities, one difference between the chimpanzean and human sequence of developmental phenomena seems outstanding. Western, human babies are reported to sit, stand bipedally while holding themselves, and creep on all fours much later than free-living chimpanzee babies. It is argued, however, that the earliest possible ages of onset in human babies do not differ from the ages reported in this publication and that the delay in onset is related to Western childrearing practices.

Finally, earlier concepts of levels of integration are discussed. It is argued that the model presented here applies to the development of non-ape mammals as well and that an effort should be made to relate the behavioral evidence for newly emerging, hierarchical levels with neuroanatomical data.

EARLY INFANCY: 6–12 MONTHS

A wide variety of data presented under the four headings "excursions", "anomalous motor-patterns", "object-play and social gestures", and "sociosexual behavior" can be understood from the emergence of only one more level of negative feedback control systems being superimposed onto the already existing hierarchy between the ages of 7–9 months, or from a conflict between two incompatible control systems of that same level.

Excursions are those periods of time during which the infant is out of contact with its mother. The changes in excursion-behavior over development are described and statistically tested. From the age of 7 months on the infant went on excursion without whimpering (ZWH). The control of the distance to its mother was typical: It shuttled backwards and forwards between distance category 3 and 4, making and breaking contact frequently and in an unpredictable way. This random drifting around the mother was age dependent and disappeared after the age of 21 months. Another state in the control of the distance to the mother was observed from the age of 9–10 months on in which runs of relatively long excursions occurred. This state did not disappear after the age of 21 months.

Nine anomalous motor-patterns developed from the age of 5 months on, three patterns around that age, and another six between the ages of 7–9 months. These patterns are peculiar because they are not straightforwardly functional in one sense. With four different types of evidence it is shown that these motor-patterns result from two opposite orientation components. The model of conflict as presented here is compared with the "conflict hypothesis" as developed by Niko Tinbergen and associates.

"Object-play" stands for a group of behavior categories which was observed from the age of 9 months on. All these categories imply the control of a relationship between an object and a certain body spot. Although these behaviors are not reported in the human literature, they can be observed in human babies of the same age.

Together with the emergence of these behavior categories directed at objects, the chimpanzee infants started to use a number of gestures which were directed to other individuals. With the emergence of these gestures it may be assumed that the chimpanzee infant possesses a true communicative ability.

Sociosexual behaviors emerge around the age of 9 months as well. The development of presenting, mounting, and thrusting is described. The general social nature of these behaviors is stressed. The late age of onset of mounting (15–20 months) in infants living under dispersed conditions as opposed to early age of onset (9 months) in infants living under high density is discussed. The simple explanation that an earlier age of onset would have been observed if only more intensive observations would have been done was practically ruled out. The puzzling, late onsets may be explained if one stops thinking of mounting as sexually motivated behavior. This is in accordance with recent findings that sexual hormones are not necessary for the expression of sociosexual behavior in infancy. Contrastingly, social experience seems to be the determining factor. The alternative notion of mounting as just another way of relating things and individuals to a certain body spot is discussed. Nevertheless, male infants mount much more frequently than do female infants. This can be understood from recent research on fetal steroids which has shown that testosterone either per se or as a prohormone regulates sexual differentiation of the brain prenatally.

In the discussion these findings are compared with developmental phenomena as reported in the human literature for babies of the same age. Again, the resemblance is striking.

A special cognitive competence which is reported in the human literature to emerge between the ages of 7–9 months and to underly the seemingly endless list of new achievements at this age, is discussed. It is argued that this cognitive competence has to do with the control of "relationships". Furthermore, it is suggested that this new cognitive competence results from the emergence of one more level of negative feedback control systems being superimposed onto the already existing hierarchy.

A model of conflict in the control of two mutually exclusive relationships is presented in order to put the developmental changes in the infant's excursion-behavior around its mother in a wider, biologically meaningful framework. In the light of this model it is argued that the phenomenon "stranger anxiety" is quite different from the phenomenon "fear of strangers" and mediated by a control system of a different level of hierarchy. The same model of conflict helps to explain the performance of the anomalous motor-patterns.

BEYOND ONE YEAR

The behavior repertoire expands over the second half of the first year. Yet, until the age of 9 months, all the behavior categories involve the control of either motor-patterns or relationships. None of the categories represent functional sequences of behavior in which discrete types of behavior have integrated. From an analysis of time intervals between eating-bouts it is concluded that some change occurs towards the age of 12 months. Furthermore, sequences of nestbuilding behavior was first observed at the age of 12 months as well.

In the discussion, it is suggested that the emergence of one more level of negative feedback control systems which enables the control of programs (= a definite list of relationships brought about one after the other), may explain these observations. This concept of seventh-order of control is compared with the concept of system as used in the ethological literature and the similarities are discussed. Further lines of research are suggested.

Appendix A

List of Abbreviations, Names, and Definitions of Behavior Categories

AOH   arm high
> Raising one arm high in the air combined with scratching, with long strokes, from elbow to side across the armpit or vice versa. If the side is directed towards another individual, this usually elicits a grooming response (Figure 27 A).

APP   approaching
> Locomoting in the direction of.

ARA   arm raise
> Raising the arm, which initially hangs more or less down, forwards with usually a rather quick, jerky movement. The fingers are flexed slightly and the palm of the hand may be oriented towards the other individual and upwards (Figure 27 B) or away from the other individual and downwards (Figure 27 C). The arm stops rising at a more or less horizontal position. The hand may swing further upwards. The other individual is never seen to be struck.

ATH   aimed throwing
> Overarm throwing in a forward direction, while looking at the target.

AVO   avoiding
> Locomoting away from an individual that is approaching or following.

BAL   balancing
> Balancing an infant on the planar- and palmar surfaces of feet and hands respectively while lying on the back and constantly moving the vertically stretched arms and legs downwards and upwards a little. Additionally the infant may be moved sideways towards the ground, up again, and towards the ground on the other side in a semi-circle movement (Figure 27 D).

Figure 27.

A = AOH   C = ARA   E = BAR   G = BOB   I = BIS
B = ARA   D = BAL   F = BEC   H = BEN   J = BKI
              + PFF

BAN   banging
        Holding an object with a power-grip and slamming it on some sur-
        face.

BAR   bipedal armwaving and running
        Rising to a bipedal position, while facing another individual (often
        a baboon as well), and raising one or both arms rapidly into the air.
        This is followed by running bipedally towards the other individual,
        waving arms in the air (Figure 27 E).

BAT   biting at
        Opening the mouth by parting the jaws and moving the head to-
        wards another individual, lips may or may not be withdrawn. At
        the end of this forward movement the head may slightly drop and
        the jaws may partly close. In other words: to make an attempt to
        bite, to snap with the teeth at.

BCO   breaking contact
        Moving out of contact with another individual without locomo-
        tion. Usually a shift of weight of the torso is responsible for this.

BEC   beckoning
        Raising one or both arms forwards and upwards rather sweepingly
        and stiffly with the elbows more extended than in the "arm raise"
        (ARA). The hands are hanging down rather limp. This movement
        is held at the end of the upward swing while the individual stares
        fixedly at the other individual and may rock (Figure 27 F and also
        Figure 28 A).

BEN   bending away
        Flexing elbow and wrist and at the same time drawing both arms
        close to its body and leaning slightly away from the stimulus, usu-
        ally another chimpanzee (Figure 27 H).

BIP   bit-pulling
        Taking something in between the teeth and pulling it off the sub-
        strate with a jerk of the head.

BIS   bipedal swagger
        Adopting an upright- or semi-upright posture and shifting the body
        weight, often rhythmically, from one foot to the other. During this
        swaying movement the chimpanzee may or may not be locomoting
        and the feet may or may not be lifted from the ground. The bipedal
        swagger is often combined with hunched shoulders (see HHC) and
        the arms are held out from the body (Figure 27 I).

BIT   biting
        To cut into, pierce, or nip (anything) with the teeth (Oxford English
        Dictionary). In babies and young infants (up to the age of 15
        months), in contrast with older individuals, it was impossible to

observe the difference between gnawing (GNA) and biting (BIT). They did put their teeth onto another individual's body part and pressed with their jaws but a reaction of pain was never observed in the other individuals. This may have been because the babies and young infants were not strong enough to inflict pain. This opinion is strengthened by the impression that they apparently put all their force into the biting. Once I observed a painful reaction (withdrawing of the finger) in another individual who was herself a young infant (the biting baby was 5-months-old). Van Hooff (1971) used the aspect of "holding on for a while" to distinguish biting from gnawing. For all these reasons gnawing was never and biting was always scored until the age of 15 months (Figure 27 D).

BKI   bite-kissing
Holding an appendage of another individual in the open mouth (see Figure 27 J, also Figure 30 A). This appendage may have been put or may have been taken into the mouth.

BOB   bobbing
Standing briefly on the feet (bipedally) and raising the body slightly from the horizontal position whereafter, as a continuation of the movement, dropping back onto four limbs and flexing the elbows until the chest is nearly touching the ground. The chimpanzee then jerks itself back to the bipedal position prior to repeating the entire sequence several times. Usually these movements follow each other rapidly. This description is of bobbing in its most extreme form. Usually the elbows are flexed and straightened while the hands remain on the ground (Figure 27 G). Up to 10 bobs are normal. The bobbing individual may bob when another individual passes, or it may hurry towards the other individual to bob. Often the bobbing individual seems to actually get in the way of the other individual who is walking along, the bobber backing away and bobbing as he does so. Mostly seen in adolescents.

BOW   bowing
Approaching another individual and crouching (CRO) while facing the other. The elbows are markedly more flexed than the knees.

BRA   brachiating
Locomoting above the ground through vegetation: hanging from the hands and moving hand over hand. The body may be facing or sideways to the direction the chimpanzee is going (van Lawick-Goodall, 1968, p. 180, Fig. 5).

BRN   branching
Taking hold of a branch or young sapling and shaking it with rather jerky movements of the arm. The chimpanzee may be sit-

ting or standing and the movements may be slight or vigorous (Figure 28 A).

BRS   branch-swaying
Standing bipedally, holding a growing branch or a palm-frond with both hands and swaying forwards and backwards vigorously (Figure 28 B, and also Figure 28 E). When the same behavior occurs in a tree, the whole tree may sway as well.

BWH   begging with hand
Placing one or both hands around or under the lips, or chin and lips, of another individual that has food in his mouth (Figure 28 F, and also Figure 28 G). Or touching the hand of the other individual containing the food, or touching the food itself.

BWM   begging with mouth
Protruding the lower lip towards the lips of another individual from close distance when the other is chewing something (Figure 28 H). This behavior is often seen in infants when they are asking for their mother's food. The mother may pass food into the infant's mouth but she does so only after having chewed on it for some time herself and after the food has been transformed into a wadge (Figure 28 J).

CAL   camel-look
Sitting and looking up into the air, face slightly averted from another individual that is in sight. It is a way of ignoring the other individual. The camel-looking individual will wait until the other makes the first move or gesture. Then he will react to it.

CAR   carrying
Carrying an infant on the palmar surface of one hand, walking bipedally or tripedally. The infant does not cling itself (van Lawick-Goodall, 1968, p. 227, Fig. 19 C).

CHA   changing nipple
Ceasing to suck from one nipple and switching to the other side without being involved in another activity during this switching.

CHD   charging display
A category covering a wide variety of behavior units which are defined elsewhere in this list, such as: throwing (THO), dragging (DRA), branch-swaying (BRS), slapping (SLA), stamping (STA), flailing (FLL), drumming (DRU), raking (RAK), bipedal armwaving and running (BAR), and tree-leaping (TRL). The chimpanzee may walk or run bipedally, tripedally, or quadrupedally. A charging display is always accompanied by hair erection. When an infant and his mother were the target of my observations, it was impossible to always observe the behavior of other chimpanzees in great

Figure 28.

A = BRN   C = CLI   E = BRS   G = BWH   I = CLM

B = BRS   D = CLM   F = BWH   H = BWM   J = BWM

detail (Chapter 2). Therefore, if any of the above mentioned behavior units were used by other individuals, the category "charging display" was used for convenience.

CHE   chewing
Sucking on wrist, hand, thumb, fingers, feet, etc.

CLI   climbing
Locomoting above the ground through vegetation (Figure 28 C). This unit excludes walking bipedally (WAB) or quadrupedally (WAQ) on thick horizontal branches and brachiating (BRA).

CLM   clinging to mother
By grasping and holding onto her hair with the hands and sometimes the feet as well (Figure 28 D, and also Figure 28 I, and Figure 29 F).

CLN   clinging to an individual other than the mother.

COB   chin on chest
Sitting motionless, the chin lowered on the chest, while looking at something. Often seen in mothers looking down on their small infants toddling around. One could not help but have the impression that the mothers were feeling very affectionate towards their infant. This impression may have arisen because the mothers were likely at such a moment to start an interaction with their infant such as grooming or tickling. Sometimes this behavior unit was seen in chimpanzees looking "absent-mindedly" ahead in the distance.

COM   compressed lips
Pressing the lips tightly together so that the upper-lip is bunched up and protrudes beyond the point where the lips meet (Figure 29 A, and also Figure 27 F and I, and Figure 29 K, Figure 30 F, Figure 31 F, Figure 34 C, and Figure 35 J).

CON   covers nipple
Withholding an infant from access to a nipple by pressing a hand or an arm between the infant and the breast.

COP   copulating
Intromission of the penis into the vagina combined with thrusting (THU). May be accompanied by mounting (MOU). However, sometimes a male squats behind a female with both hands on the ground leaning back (Figure 29 B). Because it is very difficult indeed to observe intromission, often only mounting and thrusting were scored.

CRA   cradling
Bending the knees and pressing the feet or knees against/under the torso of the baby. Method of holding a baby securely, especially

Figure 29.

A = COM
B = COP + CRO
C = EHU
D = EHD
E = DAB
F = CRA
G = DRU
H = DEF + TIC
I = DAN
J = DAO
K = DRA

when a mother cannot use her hands and arms for support. In this way the baby rests in mother's groin-pocket (Figure 29 F, and also van Lawick-Goodall, 1968, p. 224, Figure 18). Babies are very poor at clinging during the first two months of life.

CRO   crouching
Lowering the body by flexing the arms and legs until the body is (in an extreme case) in a horizontal position touching the substrate (female in Figure 29 B, and also Figure 31 G, Figure 32 B, Figure 32 F, Figure 32 H).

CRU   crutching
A way of locomoting, usually used to go downslope: swinging legs and body through the arms while *leaning* with the hands on the ground (van Lawick-Goodall, 1968, p. 178, Figure 2c and d; also, the adult male in Figure 29 E).

CRY   crying
Varying sequence of high and low pitched pure screams. Usually giving by infants and juveniles.

CTA   contacting
Moving into contact with another individual and without locomotion. Usually a shift of weight of the torso is responsible for this.

CUP   cupping
A mother puts her hand near her nipple, sometimes four fingers under and the thumb above the nipple, while the infant is sucking. Usually this is followed by gently pushing her infant off the nipple.

DAB   dabbing
Touching the face of an approaching individual with the back of the flexed fingers whereafter the touching hand is withdrawn immediately. This sequence is repeated a number of times in quick succession (Figure 29 E). Dabbing usually occurs together with bobbing (BOB).

DAN   dangling
Hanging under and holding a substrate (e.g., a branch) with one or two hands. Body may swing (Figure 29 I, and also Figure 29 F).

DAO   putting arm high
After having lain down her infant in a horizontal position in her lap, a mother takes hold of an arm of the infant and stretches it beyond the tip of its head. This enables her to groom the infant's side, armpit or inner-arm (Figure 29 J).

DEF   defending
Bringing hands and, if possible, feet towards the body-part which is being stimulated by tickling or gnawing in order to repel tactile

stimulation. The most favorite body-parts are: the belly, the neck-pocket, and the groin-pocket (Figure 29 H). The infant may also arch its back while its belly or groin-pocket are being stimulated. When its neck-pocket is tickled the infant may round its back and neck away from the source of stimulation.

DRA   dragging

Walking or running while holding an object or an individual with one hand in such a way that it drags along the ground (Figure 29 K).

DRU   drumming

Making one or several rapid backward and upward kicks with each foot alternately on an object (buttressed tree; barrel outside one of the buildings; metal, resonating wall of a house; other trees). The hindquarters are normally higher than the shoulders during drumming. The object may also be hit with the hands or the chimp may leap up the object (buttress, barrel), grab it with the hands, and kick forward with the feet (Figure 29 G).

DSC   dreamscream

Faint, high-pitched sound during sleep. The eyes are closed, moving or not. Only observed in babies.

DTG   pushing against ground

An infant of 20 months and older taking thin, long objects such as a grassstem or a twig between thumb and indexfinger and pushing it against the ground. An imitation of adult "termite-fishing".

EFF   effort-face

Forehead showing horizontal wrinkles, eyes wide-open, lower-lip retracted downwards (sometimes asymmetrically). Mainly observed in chimpanzee babies (Figure 35 L).

EHD   extending hand, palm downwards

Holding a hand towards another individual by extending the arm, wrist, and hand in a more or less horizontal position, and stretching the fingers while the handpalm is directed *downwards*. The other individual is not being touched (Figure 29 D).

EHU   extending hand, palm upwards

The same as extending hand palm downwards (EHD) except that the palm of the hand is directed *upwards* (Figure 29 C).

EMF   embracing, full

Embracing another individual by holding both arms around him (Figure 30 A and B).

EMH   embracing, half

Embracing another individual by holding one arm around him (Figure 30 C).

Figure 30.

A = EMF	C = EMH	E = FLI	G = FLP	I = GFO
B = EMF	D = FIM	F = FLL	H = GFC	J = GLC

EYC   eyes closed
The eye lids are closed.

EYO   eyes open
The eye lids are open though there is no gross movement in the eyes and the head.

FED   feeding
Chewing *and* swallowing something.

FIM   finger in mouth
Putting a finger, often the indexfinger, into another individual's mouth (Figure 30 D).

FLI   lipflip
Folding the upperlip backwards over the nose. The pink inside of the upperlip is visible (Figure 30 E).

FLL   flailing
Holding a branch or handful of vegetation firmly in one hand and locomoting forward (usually tripedally running) while constantly raising the handful and slapping it on the ground (Figure 30 F).

FLP   flapping
Raising one arm and hand and making a downward slapping movement of the hand in the direction of another individual (Figure 30 G).

FOL   following
Locomoting towards an individual that is already locomoting away.

FRE   freezing
Stopping all movements suddenly while slightly crouching (CRO).

FSP   full-speed
The speed of any locomotion is scored on a three-point scale. Full-speed is topspeed.

FWE   following with eyes
Moving the eyes (often together with the head) in the same direction as some object or individual.

GAL   head between arm and body
An infant approaching its mother from either side and pushing its head between her arm and torso in order to pass through and gain ventro-verntral contact. This behavior unit is used only if the mother pushes her arm against her body and thus prevents the ventro-ventral contact.

GAM   gambolling
Galloping type of locomotion, seen especially in young infants: the infant suddenly moves forward, both hands off the ground. When its hands reach the ground both legs move forward simultaneously

while the hindquarters, as a consequence, may be moved up a little. The start and end of the movement are abrupt. There may be one or more of these "forward jumps" (van Lawick-Goodall, 1968, p. 181, Figure 7b).

GAT   gathering
Grasping an infant and placing it into ventro-ventral position.

GFC   grin-full-closed
Withdrawing the mouth-corners and, thereby, retracting the upper- and lower-lips horizontally (grin) in such a way that both upper- and lower-anterior teeth are revealed (full). Often the gums are revealed as well. The teeth (jaws) are not parted (closed) (Figure 30 H and also the individuals pictured on the left side in Figure 32 C, Figure 33 G, Figure 33 H).

GFO   grin-full-open
The same definition as for grin-full-closed (GFC) except for the teeth (jaws) which are parted (open) (Figure 30 I, and also Figure 30 G, Figure 34 J, and the individuals pictured on the right side in Figure 32 C, F, and Figure 33 G, H).

GLC   grin-low-closed
The same definition as for grin-full-closed (GFC) except for the anterior teeth of which only the lower ones are revealed (Figure 30 J). This is often the expression that follows whimpering (ZWH) and precedes crying (CRY). It has been referred to as "cry-face" by van Lawick-Goodall (1968).

GLI   glimpse
Looking at something (or some individual) for less than one second.

GNA   gnawing
Tickling with the mouth: inhibited form of biting. After opening the mouth and, usually, covering the teeth with the lips, touching the body of another individual with the mouth and making quick nibbling movements with the jaws (Figure 31 A). Under the age of 15 months this behavior unit was not used because it was very difficult to *observe* the difference between biting and gnawing in babies and young infants.

GOR   lies down on back
Lying down on the back while keeping the head lifted from the ground and extending the arm and hand towards another individual while looking at that individual (Figure 31 E).

GRL   grooming leaf
Picking off a leaf (seemingly at random and with a sudden impulse), holding it in one hand and making grooming movements with both thumbs while often pushing the lower lip to the leaf sur-

Figure 31.

A = GNA	C = GRL	E = GOR	G = HHC + ROL	I = HNH
B = GYM	D = HAH	F = HHC	H = HNM	J = HOH
				K = HPF

face as is done in grooming another individual or in self-grooming. Nothing was ever observed to be on the leaves groomed in this way (Figure 31 C).

GRN   groan
Long, drawn-out rough grunt.

GRO   grooming
Allo-grooming: picking through the fur of another individual. Usually, both hands and lips are used: one hand mainly pushes the hairs apart whereas particles may be picked up with the other hand or with the lips (the individual pictured on the left side in Figure 27 A and also the mother in Figure 29 J).

GRS   self-grooming
Picking through one's own fur.

GRU   infant-grunt
Low intensity tonal call of various kinds in the baby.

GYM   gymnastics
A variety of conspicuous and exaggerated motor-patterns which seemed unnecessary for locomotion. Nothwithstanding the explosion of movement and locomotion, the individual is staying more or less on the spot. Characteristic motor-patterns are: dangling from one hand and possibly one or two feet and swinging from the right to the left or forwards and backwards. In the process of doing so, the infant might change from dangling from the hands to dangling from the feet and during this change "making birds-nest" is often observed. Brachiating in a very exuberant way is also shown frequently (Figure 31 B). Although there is some overlap, "gymnastics" is not the same as the behavior element named as such by van Hooff (1971) or as the pattern "locomotor play" named by van Lawick-Goodall (1968): units such as somersaulting (SUM), pivoting, rolling over (ROO), and activities with objects are excluded by the above given definition.

HAH   hand holding/shaking
Grasping a hand which is extended towards the "handholder" by another individual, and holding it for a while or even shaking it (Figure 31 D).

HAI   hair on end
Hair erection or piloerection (Figure 27 F, I, Figure 29 K, G, Figure 30 F, Figure 31 F, Figure 34 C, G, J, K, Figure 35 E, J, K).

HAL   hand leading
Taking the hand of another individual and bringing it into contact with his own body.

HAP   hair pulling
       Holding the body, especially the skin or hair, of another individual
       and giving vehement tugs. In doing so the animal may occasionally
       pull out tufts of hair.

HAW   taking arm away
       A mother taking her arm or hand, which prevented access to the
       nipple, away.

HCA   hoo-call
       A vocalization very much like the hoo-whimper but higher pitched.
       Also, the pouting of the lips is far less obvious.

HEK   heel kicking
       Lying on the back while holding an infant in ventro-ventral embrace
       and kicking gently and repeatedly with the heels on the infant's tor-
       so. When the male does this he is usually pressing the infant against
       his erected penis.

HHC   hunching
       Rounding the back, pulling the shoulders up and forwards, draw-
       ing the head down, holding the upper arms slightly outwards and
       forwards and the forearms slightly upwards. The chimpanzee may
       sit, stand bipedally or quadrupedally (Figure 31 F and also Figure
       31 G, Figure 34 C).

HIN   hand in neck
       Placing the hand in the neck of another individual, often an infant,
       in a non-abrupt manner.

HNF   hand to face
       A baby or an infant looking up into the face of another individual
       and touching that face. Touching the mouth is excluded: see HNM.

HNH   hand to hand
       Bringing the hand to the hand of another individual. This is part of
       the mother-baby play: the mother tickles her baby (TIC), then
       retreats her hand (RHA). This evokes the baby to reach for that
       hand (HNH) and the mother then, suddenly and with a touch of
       unexpectedness, pokes (POK) or tickles (TIC) her baby again. This
       sequence may be repeated several times (Figure 31 I).

HNM   hand to mouth
       Chimpanzee baby or infant looking up into the face of another in-
       dividual and touching the other's mouth. This is part of the
       mother-baby play in the same way as HNH except for the fact that
       the mother tickles her baby with her mouth (GNA) instead of with
       her hands (TIC) (Figure 31 H).

HOH   hands around head
       Raising the arms and placing the hands around another individual's
       head while sitting with the back towards the other (Figure 31 J).

HPF   horizontal pout-face
       Pushing the lips forward into a pout while slightly retracting the
       lip-corners in such a way that the pout becomes lengthened hori-
       zontally. There is still some degree of funnelling in the front (Fig-
       ure 31 K). When the lip-corners become more retracted the face
       grades into the lower-closed-grin (GLC).

HPH   hup-hup
       A mother gently and rhythmically moving her forearm up and
       down while the infant is lying horizontally on top of that arm.

HSP   acceleration (half-speed)
       The speed of any locomotion is scored on a three point scale, accel-
       eration being the middle point. This means the individual is loco-
       moting faster than he normally does although he is not using the
       maximum of his abilities. Absolutely speaking, the speed belonging
       to any of the points on this scale varies with age/sex classes.

HWO   hitting with object
       Holding an object (e.g., a stick or a stone) in one hand, raising it
       into the air above the head and moving it down in the direction of
       another individual or object (van Lawick-Goodall, 1968, p. 204,
       Figure 16).

IBA   infant-bark
       Intense vocalization in younger infants and babies. Sounds like a
       bark.

INS   inspecting
       Sniffing, licking, or touching the genitals of a female or a male
       (Figure 32 A). After touching, the tip of the finger which was used
       is frequently sniffed (SFI; Figure 32 B).

ISC   infant-scream
       Scream by a baby or a very young infant. This scream is higher
       pitched than the adult screams.

ISQ   infant-squeak
       Short, high pitched, intense vocalization in a baby or a very young
       infant. The pitch does not rise or lower but stays level.

IWA   infant wa-bark
       Wa-bark vocalization by a baby or very young infant.

JUM   jumping
       Moving through the air from one substrate to the other: pushing off

Figure 32.

A = INS   C = MOU   E = LEG   G = OKO   I = OIN
B = INS + SFI   D = ONP   F = MOU   H = MOU +   J = OMK
                                                                                     COP +
                                                                                     HHC

from one substrate by flexing the legs and bending the torso forwards, rounding the back, the head held up looking in the direction of the jump and then, abruptly, stretching the legs and torso while moving the arms forward. The individual may catch hold of a substrate in the air (e.g., a branch) with one or two hands, or he may land on his feet and, thereafter, on his hands as well (van Lawick-Goodall, 1968, p. 179, Figure 3 and 6).

KOT   vomiting
The act of bringing up and ejecting the contents of the stomach by the mouth. Does occur in all age/sex classes, young babies not excluded.

LAC   laughing
Staccato-rhythmic breathing which easily develops into rhythmic, sometimes hoarse, grunting. The inhalation may be vocalized. The grunts may be given at a rather irregular rate. Within one burst of grunts the rate often suddenly accelerates and decelerates again.

LAF   looking away from
Avoiding eye-contact by turning away the head, thereby "cutting off" the sight of another individual. If the other individual repeatedly forces eye-contact on a baby or an infant, this baby (infant) ultimately may hide its face in its mother's hair.

LAR   looking around
Moving the eyes. The head may move as well. Small pauses in the eye/head movements of less than 1 second are ignored.

LAT   looking at
Fixing the eyes on some individual or something for more than 1 second, not moving the head.

LEG   leg bending
Mother chimpanzee standing quadrupedally with one lower leg slightly back, bent at the knee. The infant uses the calf as a "mounting block" to climb onto mother's back (Figure 32 E).

LFI   licking finger
Licking the tip of the finger with which something has just been touched.

LIE   lying
Being in a postrate or recumbent position: bodily posture (van Lawick-Goodall, 1968, p. 201, Figure 14 b, e, f).

LIF   lifting and slamming
Lifting another individual off the ground by grabbing a limb and/or body hair and slamming him down again. This may be repeated several times (van Lawick-Goodall, 1968, plate 8b).

LIK   licking
Touching something or some individual with the tongue. The tongue may be moved along the object or individual.

LIP   lipsmacking
Opening and closing the mouth rhythmically. As the mouth is opened there is a smacking sound as the tongue is withdrawn from the palate.

LIU   lying upon
Lying down into a ventro-ventral position upon another individual who is in a recumbent position, and staying here motionless for a while.

LOB   lowering back
A mother lowering her hindquarters in front of her infant in such a way that she is nearly sitting, leaning forward on her hands.

LUP   looking up
An infant or baby looking up into the face of its mother or into the face of another individual.

LVE   leaving
Locomoting away from an individual which itself is not locomoting.

MAN   manipulating
A variety of hand-activities which have the power-grip in common. Examples are: turning an object around, shoving an object along the ground, breaking an object, etc.

MHA   moving hand
Gently and variably moving the hand or foot in which an infant or baby is biting. An infant may even start playwrestling with the hand or foot. The individual who is "moving hand" may look elsewhere while doing this (Figure 29 H and Figure 31 I).

MON   mountaineering
Extending the arms and opening the hands combined with flexing the legs, alternating with flexing the arms and closing the hands combined with extending the legs. This may result in progression up the mother's body. This behavior unit was observed in chimpanzee babies only. Prechtl (1953) defined a similar behavior unit for human babies except for one difference: the legs of the human babies in supine position do not seem to participate in the mountaineering whereas the legs of a chimpanzee baby do. However, the legs of a human baby in the prone position in ventro-verntal contact with an adult caretaker *do* participate in the mountaineering in the same way as the legs of a chimpanzee baby (personal observation on my own daughter of 4 days and older). Casaer (1979, p.

21–22) describes motor-patterns in arms and legs of the awake human newborn in the prone position which resemble mountaineering strongly.

MOS mock-smile
Retracting the lip-corners while pressing the lips tightly together. The teeth are not visible.

MOU mounting
"Any position or posture which involves one individual climbing (wholly or partly) onto another (Figure 32 C and F). Mount postures are not necessarily equivalent to copulatory postures: the copulatory posture typically does not include the male resting his weight on the female." (Hanby, 1976, p. 4). For a comparison between mounting, copulating, and hunching over, see Figure 32 H.

MOV moving
Gross movements of arms and legs. No regularities observed. Probably equivalent to "mass-movement", as can be found in the human literature. Only observed in young babies.

MRP with back wrist
Rubbing or hitting objects with the back of a bended wrist.

NES nestbuilding
Bending branches towards and under oneself. After having bent them, a foot is placed on top of the branches in order to keep them in place (van Lawick-Goodall, 1968, p. 198, Figure 13b). The difference of nestbuilding of young infants and adults is the end product. Adults build a platform of bended and broken branches that can be used to lie down and sleep on (the "nest"; van Lawick-Goodall, 1968, plate 3a and b). The end product contains complexly interwoven branches and twigs (van Lawick-Goodall, 1968, p. 197, Figure 12). Young infants are unable to make such an end product. As soon as the infant moves its foot the branches unfold themselves.

NEU nose-gesture
Rubbing the nose or the eyebrows, moving the back of the hand once from one side to the other.

OIN object in neck
While sitting, bringing an object over and behind the head, grasping it with the other hand and holding it against the neck and the shoulders (Figure 32 I). Also: rolling with the back of the upper torso on top of an object bringing the hands behind the head. If an object is too large to move, an individual may lean against it with neck and shoulders, bringing his hands behind his head and holding the object.

OKO   standing on head
        Approaching another individual and somersaulting in front of him
        in such a way that he is standing on his head while he is leaning
        with the back of his torso against the other (Figure 32 G).

OMK   open mouth kiss
        Pressing the opened mouth against another individual's opened
        mouth (Figure 32 J).

ONP   object in neck-pocket
        Pressing an object against the side of the neck and between the
        lower-jaw and shoulder or chest (Figure 32 D).

OOH   object on head
        Placing an object with two hands on top of the head and holding it
        there for a while. Usually, the individual is sitting (Figure 33 A).

OTB   object against belly
        Pressing an object against the belly or chest (Figure 33 B).

OTP   object against penis
        Pressing an object against the (usually erected) penis or clitoris
        (Figure 33 D).

PAT   patting
        Rapidly repeatedly contacting another individual with the palmar
        surface of the hand.

PBB   pressing bottom in belly
        Pressing the bottom against the lower ventral surface of another in-
        dividual's torso. The other may be sitting or standing bipedally.

PEN   erection of the penis

PEU   pottering
        Scratching a substrate with the tip of the thumb, the index-finger,
        or the middle-finger.

PFC   putting face close
        Putting the face within a range of 20 cm's of the mouth or the
        hands of another individual while looking fixedly at that mouth or
        those hands (Figure 33 E).

PFF   playface full
        Keeping the mouth in a wide open position, slightly retracting the
        mouth corners, sliding back the lips, so that upper and lower teeth
        are bared. This facial expression easily grades into a full open grin
        (Figure 27 D and also Figure 31 A).

PFH   playface half
        Keeping the mouth in a moderate to wide open position slightly
        retracting the mouth corners, maintaining the lips in their normal,
        relaxed position so that the upper teeth remain wholly or partly

Figure 33.

A = OOH	C = PFH	E = PFC	G = PRE	I = PRE
B = OTB	D = OTP	F = PFH	H = PRE	J = PKI
				K = PKI

covered by the upper lip. Sometimes the upper lip is pulled down and inwards to cover the upper teeth completely. The lower teeth are bared (Figure 33 C and F).

PIN   pinching
Taking a bit of skin between the thumbnail and the side of the index-finger and twisting it.

PIR   pirouetting
Progressing in a series of tight circles. Most of the time the individual is quadrupedal or tripedal, sometimes bipedal (van Lawick-Goodall, 1968, p. 181, Figure 7f)

PKI   pout-kiss
Pouting the lips slightly and pressing them against or briefly laying them against the torso, the face or the limbs of another individual (Figure 33 J and K).

PLU   picking
Taking hold of some (plant) material and pulling it off the substrate.

PLW   play-walk
Walking quadrupedally with a rounded back, the head slightly bent down and pulled back between the shoulders, taking small, somewhat stilted steps. Often there is a side-to-side movement as the individual progresses.

POF   pushing off
A chimpanzee baby pushing itself up by stretching the arms. This happens when the mother is lying on her back and results in a gap between the belly of the baby and the belly of the mother.

POK   poking
Pushing one or more finger tips with a sudden movement onto the belly or into the neck-pocket of another individual. Same effects as with tickling (TIC).

PRE   presenting
Orienting actively or remaining oriented more or less passively with the hindquarters towards another individual. See Figure 33 G, H, I.

PTF   pout-face
Pushing lips and lip-corners forward in a pout. The lips are together except right at the front where they may funnel out a little (Figure 34 A and also Figure 29 C, D).

PUL   pulling
Taking hold (with hand or foot) of an object or any part of another individual's body and moving the hand (or foot) towards oneself without moving the trunk in the opposite direction.

Figure 34.

A = PTF	C = RAK	E = RFA	G = ROL	I = STA
B = PUN	D = RFA	F = SHA	H = SNE	J = ROL
				K = SLS

PUN   punching
Hitting an object or another individual with the back of the flexed
fingers (middle phalanx). See Figure 34 B.

PUP   pulling up
Extending the arms and opening the hands, followed by flexing the
arms while closing the hands. This is done while the mother's torso
is in a vertical position and this may result in progression up the
mother's body.

PUS   pushing
Contacting something or another individual with hand or foot followed by moving that hand or foot with accelerating speed away
from oneself.

PWR   playwrestling
Two (or more) individuals grabbing hold of each other and often
rolling over as they are biting (BIT), gnawing (GNA), tickling
(TIC), or defending (DEF), without losing contact. If there is quite
an age difference (infant-adult) between two partners the younger
one may play wrestle with the hand of the other who may be moving the hand only (see MHA).

RAK   raking
Sweeping movements with straight arms amongst ground vegetation. Usually prior to charging display (CHD). See Figure 34 C.

RAO   running away with object
Taking an object (objects of any size or kind are being taken) and
running away from another individual while looking back at that
other individual.

REF   reaching for
Holding the hand(s) or foot (feet) towards another individual. The
hands are in the normal semi-flexed position and the arm is in a
position somewhere in between pronation and suppination.

RFA   relaxed face
No clearly observable muscle contractions in the face. The lower
lip either touches the upper-lip or droops. If the face was relaxed
nothing was scored (Figures 34 D, E, and also the mother in Figure
28 D, 29 H, 31 I, 32 E, G).

RHA   retreating hand
Retreating the hand which is being held or bitten by another individual. This is part of the mother-baby play: the mother tickles her
baby, then retreats her hand. This causes the baby to reach for that
hand and the mother then, suddenly and with a touch of unexpect-
edness, pokes or tickles her baby again. This sequence may be repeated several times.

ROC   rocking
Moving the torso from the left to the right or forwards and backwards repeatedly. Rocking normally starts with almost impercep-
tible movements of the head while the chimpanzee is sitting. See
Figure 27 F.

ROL   rolling
"Rolling-over" another individual or an object by leaning over the
other in a bipedal position, grasping him with both hands, and
pulling him towards oneself. Usually, the other individual is
crouching (CRO) already. See Figures 31 G, 34 G, J, and van
Lawick-Goodall (1968, p. 277, Figure 39 b).

ROO   rolling over
Losing balance and rolling on the back (on a horizontal substrate).

ROT   rooting
Continuously moving the head from side to side and vice versa
while the mouth is in contact with the mother's body. During every
side to side movement the head may move backwards and forwards
several times. This rooting was only observed in newborns. The
same behavior-unit was described under the name "rooting-reflex"
for human (Prechtl, 1958) as well as for non-human (Hinde, 1974,
p. 166) primate babies. van Lawick-Goodall (1968) used the term
"nuzzling".

RUI   smelling
Putting the nostrils close (within a few centimeters) to another individual or an object.

SAB   mouthing
Taking an object in the mouth and between the lips without biting
on it.

SCH   shove aside
Moving another individual or an object aside with *constant gentle*
speed using the hand or foot.

SCO   scooping
Pushing a baby or infant up onto one's back in a backwards and
upwards movement using the palmar surface of one's hand. At the
start, the baby or infant is either gathered (GAT) or it is already on
the body of the mother in the ventro-ventral position. See van
Lawick-Goodall (1968, p. 227, Figure 19 e): because the infant in
this drawing is older it climbs onto the mother itself; therefore the
orientation of the mother's arm is different.

SCR   scratching
Moving the nails over some substate or the skin of another individual while bending the fingers.

SCS   self-scratching
Moving the nails over the skin of some part of the own body while bending the fingers.

SFI   sniffs finger
Putting the finger-tip with which something has just been touched close to the nostrils. See Figure 32 B.

SHA   shaking
Taking hold of an object or the limb of another individual and pushing and pulling alternately, either in more or less horizontal or in a more or less vertical plane. In the latter case the lower arm is moving around the elbow-joint while the wrist-joint is staying fixed. See Figure 34 F.

SHR   shrugging
Slighly raising one shoulder while lowering the other with the effect that an infant in ventro-dorsal position is shaken off the body. Simultaneously, the mother may reach back and push or pull her infant with one hand.

SIC   sucking in cheeks
Sucking the cheeks inwards, in between the gums. While doing so the face is "relaxed": the lips are closed and the jaws must be parted. See Figure 35 O.

SIT   sitting
The body weight is resting on the buttocks. The torso is in a more or less vertical position, the knees are bent, and the soles of the feet are resting on the substrate. One or two hands may or may not be resting on substrate. See van Lawick-Goodall (1968, p. 201, Figure 14a, c, d, g).

SLA   slapping
Hitting an object or another individual with the palm of the hand(s).

SLS   slapstamping
Slapping (SLA) and stamping (STA) in quick alternation while running quadrupedally. See Figure 34 K.

SNE   sneer
Retracting the upper lip to expose part of the upper teeth. The upper lip may be retracted asymmetrically, sometimes. The nose and the upper lip show horizontal wrinkles. See Figure 34 H.

STA   stamping
Hitting an object, the substrate, or another individual with the sole(s) of the foot (feet). See Figure 34 I and van Lawick-Goodall (1968, p. 277, Figure 39a). Usually, the stamping is done with both feet in quick alternation. See Figure 35 A.

Figure 35.

A = STA	D = SWE	G = WRI	J = TRL	M = UHH
B = STE	E = THO	H = TRA	K = TRL	N = VEN
C = STT	F = WRB	I = TIP	L = EFF	O = SIC

175

STB   standing bipedally
Resting the body weight on the feet while the legs and torso are stretched more or less vertically.

STC   staccato
Rapid series of regular rhythmic uh-grunts (UHH).

STE   rearing
Changing abruptly from a quadrupedal to a bipedal position by raising the torso towards a more vertical position. The upper arms are directed downwards, the lower arms upward and the wrists are bent, stretching the hands forwards. See Figure 35 B.

STQ   standing quadrupedally
Resting the body-weight on hands and feet while the arms and legs are stretched.

STR   struggling over
Making crawling movements over the body of the mother.

STT   startling
Ducking the head and flinging one or both arms across the face, or throwing both hands up into the air. Sometimes, only part of these patterns were seen: e.g., a slight ducking of the head. See Figure 35 C.

SUC   sucking
Having the mother's nipple in the mouth. Actual sucking movements (cheeks moving inward and back) may or may not be seen.

SUM   somersaulting
Turning heels over head in the air and alighting on the back or the shoulders. Because of the speed the individual sits upright or walks again immediately thereafter. See van Lawick-Goodall (1968, p. 181, Figure 7e).

SUP   supporting
Laying the palmar surface of the hand against the back of a ventro-ventrally clinging (CLM, CLN) baby or infant. See van Lawick-Goodall (1968, p. 224, Figure 18).

SWE   swelling
A recurrent (pink) swelling of the ano-genital region of the female correlating with a part of the menstrual cycle. See Figure 35 D. After menstrual bleeding (which occurs when the genital area is not swollen or "negative") there are several more days (varying greatly from individual to individual) before the first signs of sexual swelling occur. Some females reach a period of maximum swelling in 2 or 3 days while others take longer. The period of maximum swelling lasts from 4 to 10 days (or more: long periods of maximum

swelling often occur during pregnancy). From the start of detumescence (when the swelling starts to diminish) there are from 6 to 8 days before menstrual bleeding occurs again. The entire cycle lasts about 35 (in older females) to 40 days (in young females). The period of oestrus occurs at some point during the period of maximum swelling. Copulation is most likely to occur during this period (see Tutin & McGinnis, 1979).

TAK   taking
       Taking hold of an object or another individual.

TAM   taking mother
       Taking hold of the mother.

TAO   taking away object
       Grasping for an object that is in the possession of another individual.

TEM   temper tantrum
       A category covering a variety of behavior-units, some of which are defined elsewhere in this list. Screaming loudly and jumping in the air, flinging one's arms above the head, or hurling oneself to the ground, hugging tree stumps or oneself. All this may be combined with trampling (TRA), beating the ground with the hands (SLA), and rushing off, tumbling over and over. (Mostly observed in an individual who is withheld from some desired object, or action by another individual). I have never observed this behavior in babies and young infants. When a baby or an infant was the target of my observations, it was impossible to observe the behavior of other individuals always in great detail (see Chapter 2). Therefore, this behavior-unit was used for convenience. See also "charging display" (CHD).

THO   throwing
       Flinging an object through an underarm-movement from a bipedal or tripedal position. The object is not aimed specifically and may fly forwards, up into the air, or even backwards. Occasionally it seems that a chimpanzee is aiming deliberately. This, however, may be coincidence. See Figure 35 E.

THU   thrusting
       Making a series of alternating, forward and backward movements with the pelvis.

TIC   tickling
       Putting one or both hands on the body of another individual while making a series of quick, alternative flexing and stretching finger movements. The neck, the belly, and the groin are the favorite body parts to be tickled. See Figure 29 H.

TIL   tilting
Bending the wrist and hooking the fingers of one hand over and under an object or an individual, followed by pulling the hand upwards and slightly towards oneself. The result is that the object (or individual) starts rolling in the direction of the "tilting' individual but falls back into place at the moment when the hand looses contact.

TIP   head-tip
Jerking the head slightly backwards which results in the chin being raised a little. See Figure 35 I.

TOG   tonal grunt
Low pitched, low intense, tonal call.

TOU   touching
Reaching out with a hand (or occassionally with a foot) and contacting an object or another individual with the tips of the fingers (toes) or the palmar surface of the hand.

TRA   trampling
Executing a series of quickly alternated bending and stretching movements of the legs in mid-air (e.g., when dangling (DAN) or lying on the back). See Figure 35 H.

TRL   tree-leaping
A form of exaggerated or embellished locomotion through vegetation above the ground. It includes some motor-patterns which seem "unnecessary" for locomotion: taking rather graceful and rhythmic leaps through the branches of a tree, swinging, and brachiating (BRA), while staying in a more or less upright posture and not progressing in a straight line but remaining more or less "on the spot". See Figures 35 J and K.

TRV   travelling
Locomoting over a distance which is longer than only a few meters. This is usually done on the ground.

UHH   uh-grunt
Explosive grunt. The lips are pushed forward except for the lip-corners. Therefore, no round aperture is visible where the lips part. See Figure 35 M.

UIT   stretching

VAL   falling
Loosing balance and falling down from a height or down a slope (compare with ROO).

VEN   venom-face
Tightening the lips, bulging the upper-lip inwards and not retracting the lip-corners. See Figure 35 N.

VER   resisting
      Taking a firm stand against another individual that is pulling.

VIS   fishing
      Pushing a tool (twig, stem, grass) into a small hole followed by taking this tool out again. Fishing precedes "termite fishing" in the course of development. "Termite fishing" in adults was described by van Lawick-Goodall (1968). Fishing differs from "termite fishing" in that fishing is not well orientated: any hole or even dip is used to fish in, whether or not this is located on a termite mound.

VLP   foot along penis (clitoris)
      Stimulating the erected penis (or clitoris) by stroking it repeatedly, using a foot or the hairs of the lower leg.

WAB   walking bipedally
      Going on feet from place to place. See van Lawick-Goodall (1968, p. 178, Figure 2f).

WAQ   walking quadrupedally
      Going on hands and feet from place to place. See van Lawick-Goodall (1968, p. 178, Figure 2a, b, e). The speed of progression is scored separately on a three-point scale (see HSP and FSP).

WIO   rubbing the eyes
      Rubbing the eyes, using the hands.

WON   bouncing up and down
      Flexing the arms and legs a little, while standing quadrupedally (STQ), followed by straightening them with a rather jerky movement. This causes the individual to loose contact with the substrate. This sequence may be repeated several times.

WRB   wristbending
      Flexing the wrist (often the fingers as well) while holding the back of the hand out towards another individual. See Figure 35 F.

WRI   wristshaking
      Shaking the own hand vigorously with flexible wrist, while extending the arm fully or partly towards another individual. See Figure 35 G.

YAW   yawning
      Opening the mouth widely in such a way that the lower jaw is much depressed and making a prolonged inspiration followed by an expiration.

ZCO   cough
      Single-syllable breathy exhalation with a very sudden onset (see "soft bark" in van Lawick-Goodall, 1968, p. 309).

ZEG   effort-grunt
      Explosive expel of air resulting when breath, after being held while

making some physical effort, is released. May be vocalized. Mouth and lips slightly open.

ZFG   food-grunts
Series of grunts emitted just before or during eating.

ZHO   whimper-ho
Soft, low-pitched single syllable sound. May develop into a whimper and is accompanied by the pout-face (PTF).

ZRG   rough-grunt
Low-intense, low-pitched single syllable sound with dull timbre and acoustical roughness. Duration rather short.

ZRU   rough-uh
Uh-grunt with acoustical roughness.

ZSK   squeak
Very short scream.

ZWH   whimpering
Series of short calls. Each of these is a pure, noiseless vocalization. The pitch and the intensity of these calls rises and lowers during the series. May develop into crying (CRY). Accompanied by pout-face (PTF).

Appendix B

Groups of Behavior Categories

All behavior categories of Appendix A can be divided into 11 groups in such a way that in each group only a part of the body is involved (i.e., the torso, the right arm, the face, etc.). Intra-group categories are mutually exclusive. Categories from different groups may combine. The continuous stream of behavior of the whole organism was described in terms of a sequence of combinations of these categories.

Group I: TORSO ACTIONS

BCO BEN COP CTA HHC LOB MOU OKO PBB PRE ROC
SHR STT UIT VER

Group II: LIMB ACTIONS

AOH ARA ATH BAL BAN BEC BIS BOB BOW BRN BRS
BWH CAR CLM CLN CON CRA CRO CUP DAB DAO DEF
DRA DRU DTG EHD EHU EMF EMH FIM FLP FLL GAT
GRL GRO GRS HAH HAL HAP HAW HEK HIN HNF HNH
HNM HOH HPH HWO INS LEG LIF MAN MHA MON MOV
MRP NES NEU OIN ONP OOH OTB OTP PAT PEU PIN
PLU POF POK PUL PUN PUS PWR RAK REF RHA ROL
SCH SCO SCR SCS SHA SLA SLS STA SUP TAK TAM
TAO THO THU TIC TIL TOU TRA VLP VIS WIO WON
WRB WRI

Group III: HEAD ACTIONS

COB ROT TIP

Group IV: MOUTH ACTIONS

BAT BIP BIT BKI BWM CHE FED GNA LFI LIK OMK
PKI RUI SAB SFI SUC

Group V: EYE ACTIONS

CAL EYC EYO FWE GLI LAF LAR LAT LUP PFC

Group VI: FACIAL EXPRESSIONS

COM EFF FLI GFC GFO GLC HPF MOS PFF PFH PTF
RFA SIC SNE VEN YAW

Group VII: VOCALIZATIONS

CRY DSC GRN GRU HCA IBA ISC ISQ IWA LAC LIP
STC TOG UHH ZCO ZEG ZFG ZHO ZRG ZRU ZSK ZWH

Group VIII: BODY-POSITION AND LOCOMOTION

BAR BRA CLI CRU DAN FRE GAL GAM GOR GYM JUM
LIE LIU PIR PLW RAO ROO SIT STB STE STQ SUM
TRL WAB WAQ

Group IX: DIRECTION

APP AVO FOL LVE

Group X: AUTONOMOUS ONE

PEN SWE

Group XI: AUTONOMOUS TWO

HAI KOT

References

Altmann, S. A. Sociobiology of rhesus monkeys. II: Stochastics of social communication. *Journal of Theoretical Biology,* 1965, *8,* 490–522.

Amsterdam, B. Mirror self image reactions before age two. *Developmental Psychobiology,* 1972, *5,* 297–305.

Andrew, R. J. The information potentially available in mammal displays. In R. A. Hinde (Ed.), *Nonverbal communication.* London: Cambridge University Press, 1972.

Annett, J. *Feedback and human behavior.* Baltimore, MD: Penguin Books, 1969.

Anohkin, P. K. The role of the orienting-exploratory reaction in the formation of the conditioned reflex. In L. G. Voronin, A. M. Leontiev, A. R. Luria, E. N. Sokolov, & O. S. Vinogradova (Eds.), *Orienting reflex and exploratory behavior.* Moscow: Academy of Pedagogical Sciences, 1958.

Baerends, G. P. Fortpflanzungsverhalten und Orientierung der Grabwespe Ammophila campestris jur. *Tijdschrift voor Entomologie,* 1941, *84,* 68–275.

Baerends, G. P. Aufbau des tierischen Verhaltens. In J.-G. Helmcke & G. C. Hirsch (Eds.), *Handbuch der Zoologie* (VIII). Berlin: Walter de Gruyter & Co., 1956.

Baerends, G. P. A model of the functional organization of incubation behavior. *Behaviour Supplement,* 1970, *17,* 263–312.

Baerends, G. P. An evaluation of the conflict hypothesis as an explanatory principle for the evolution of displays. in G. P. Baerends, C. Beer, & A. Manning (Eds.), *Function and evolution in behaviour.* Oxford: Clarendon press, 1975.

Baerends, G. P. The functional organization of behaviour. *Animal Behaviour,* 1976, *24,* 726–738.

Baerends-van Roon, J. M., & Baerends, G. P. *The morphogenesis of the behaviour of the domestic cat.* Amsterdam: North Holland Publishing Company, 1979.

Balzamo, E., Bradley, R. J., Bradley, D. M., Pegram, G. V., & Rhodes, J. M. Sleep ontogeny in the chimpanzee: From birth to two months. *Electroencephalography and Clinical Neurophysiology,* 1972, *33,* 41–46.(a).

Balzamo, E., Bradley, R. J., & Rhodes, J. M. Sleep ontogeny in the chimpanzee: From two months to forty-one months. *Electroencephalography and Clinical Neurophysiology,* 1972, 33, 47–60.(b)

Barrett, P., & Bateson, P. The development of play in cats. *Behaviour,* 1978, *66,* 106–120.

Bastock, M., Morris, D., & Moynihan, M. Some comments on conflict and thwarting in animals. *Behaviour,* 1953, *6,* 56–84.

Bateson, P. P. G., & Hinde, R. A. *Growing points in ethology.* Cambridge: Cambridge University Press, 1976.

Bauer, H. R. Behavioral changes about time of reunion in parties of chimpanzees in the Gombe Stream National Park. In *Contemporary primatology.* Basel, Switzerland: Karger, 1975.

Benedict, H. Early lexical development: Comprehension and production. *Journal of Child Language,* 1979, *6,* 183–200.

Berg, W. K., & Berg, K. M. Psychophysiological development in infancy: State, sensory function, and attention. In J. D. Osofsky (Ed.), *Handbook of infant development.* New York: Wiley, 1979.

Berlyne, D. E. *Conflict, arousal and curiosity.* New York: McGraw-Hill, 1960.

Bingham, H. C. Sex development in apes. *Comparative Psychology Monographs,* 1928, *5,* 1–165.

Blakemore, C. Environmental constraints on development in the visual system. In R. A. Hinde & J. Stevenson-Hinde (Eds.), *Constraints on Learning.* New York: Academic Press, 1973.

Blurton Jones, N. (Ed.) *Ethological studies of child behaviour.* London: Cambridge University Press, 1972.

Blurton Jones, N. Comparative aspects of mother-child contact. In N. Blurton Jones (Ed.), *Ethological studies of child behaviour.* London: Cambridge University Press, 1972.(a)

Bohm, D. Some remarks on the notion of order. In C. H. Waddington (Ed.), *Towards a theoretical biology* (2) *Sketches.* Edinburgh: Edinburgh University Press, 1969.

Bolk, L. *Das Problem der Menschwerdung.* Jena: Verlag von Gustav Fischer, 1926.

Bower, T. G. R. The evolution of sensory systems. In R. B. MacLeod & H. L. Pick (Eds.), *Perception. Essays in honor of James J. Gibson.* Ithaca, NY: Cornell University Press, 1974.

Bower, T. G. R. Concepts of development. *Proceedings of the XXIst international congress of psychology.* Paris: Presses Universitaires de France, 1978.

Bower, T. G. R., & Wishart, J. Towards a unitary theory of development. In E. Thoman (Ed.), *Origins of the infant's social responsiveness.* Hillsdale, NJ: Lawrence Erlbaum Associates, 1979.

Brannigan, C. R., & Humphries, D. A. Human non-verbal behavior, a means of communication. In N. Blurton Jones (Ed.), *Ethological studies of child behaviour.* London: Cambridge University Press, 1972.

Brazelton, T. B. *Neonatal behavioral assessment scale.* London: William Heinemann Medical Books, Ltd., 1973.

Brazelton, T. B., Koslowski, B., & Main, M. The origins of reciprocity in the early infant-mother interaction. In M. Lewis & L. A. Rosenblum (Eds.), *The effect of the infant on its caregiver.* London: Wiley, 1974.

Brazelton, T. B., Tronick, E., Adamson, L., Als, H., & Weise, S. Early mother-infant reciprocity. In R. Porter & M. O'Connor (Eds.), *Parent infant interaction.* (Ciba Foundation Symposium 33). Amsterdam: Elsevier, 1975.

Bronson, G. W. *Fear of the unfamiliar in human infants.* Paper presented at the meeting of CASDS-CIBA, London 1969.

Bronson, G. W. Infants' reactions to unfamiliar persons and novel objects. *Monographs of the Society for Research in Child Development,* 1972, *37,* (Serial number 148).

Bronson, G. W. Aversive reactions to strangers: A dual process interpretation. *Child Development,* 1978, *49,* 495–499.

Bruner, J. The growth and structure of skill. In K. Connolly (Ed.), *Mechanisms of motor skill development.* London: Academic Press, 1970.

Bruner, J. Nature and uses of immaturity. In K. Connolly & J. Bruner (Eds.), *The growth of competence.* London: Academic Press, 1974.

Bruner, J. Foreword. In A. Lock (Ed.), *Action, gesture and symbol: The emergence of language.* London: Academic Press, 1978.

Bullowa, M. *Before speech: The beginning of interpersonal communication.* London: Cambridge University Press, 1979.

Bygott, J. D. *Agnostic behaviour and dominance in wild chimpanzees.* Unpublished doctoral dissertation, University of Cambridge, 1974.

Bygott, J. D. Agnostic behavior, dominance, and social structure in wild chimpanzees of the Gombe National Park. In D. A. Hamburg, & E. R. McCown (Eds.), *The great apes. Perspectives on human evolution.* (Vol. V). Menlo Park, CA: The Benjamin/Cummings Publishing Company, 1979.

Campos, J. J., Emde, R., Gaensbauer, T., & Henderson, C. Cardiac and behavioral interrelationships in the reaction of infants to strangers. *Developmental Psychology,* 1975, *11,* 589-601.

Carter, F. S. Comparisons of baby gorillas with human infants at birth and during the postnatal period. *Annual Report of the Jersey Wildlife Preservation Trust,* 1973, 29-33.

Casaer, P. *Postural behaviour in newborn infants.* London: William Heinemann Medical Books, 1979.

Chevalier-Skolnikoff, S. The ontogeny of communication in the Stumptail Macaque (Macaca arctoides). *Contributions to Primatology,* 1974, *2,* 1-174.

Chevalier-Skolnikoff, S. A Piagetian model for describing and comparing socialization in monkey, ape, and human infants. In S. Chevalier-Skolnikoff & F. E. Poirier (Eds.), *Primate bio-social development: Biological, social, and ecological determinants.* New York: Garland Publishing Inc., 1977.

Chomsky, N. *Aspects of the theory of syntax.* Cambridge: MIT Press, 1965.

Clark, C. B. A preliminary report on weaning among chimpanzees of the Gombe National Park, Tanzania. In S. Chevalier-Skolnikoff & F. E. Poirier (Eds.), *Primate bio-social development: Biological, social and ecological determinants.* New York: Garland Publishing Inc., 1977.

Clutton-Brock, T. H. *Feeding and ranging behaviour of the red colobus monkey.* Unpublished doctoral dissertation, University of Cambridge, 1972.

Clutton-Brock, T. H. Feeding behaviour of Colobus Guereza in East-Africa. *Folia Primatologica,* 1975, *23,* 165-207.

Coghill, G. E. *Anatomy and the problem of behaviour.* London: Cambridge University Press, 1929.

Condon, W. S. A primary phase in the organization of infant responding behaviour. In H. R. Schaffer, (Ed.), *Studies in mother-infant interaction.* London: Academic Press, 1977.

Condon, W. S. Neonatal entrainment and enculturation. In M. Bullowa (Ed.), *Before speech: The beginning of interpersonal communication.* Cambridge: Cambridge University Press, 1979.

Connolly, K. *Mechanisms of motor skill development.* London: Academic Press, 1970.

Connolly, K. Factors influencing the learning of manual skills by young children. In R. A. Hinde & J. Stevenson-Hinde (Eds.), *Constraints on learning.* London: Academic Press, 1973.

Connolly, K., & Bruner, J. *The growth of competence.* London: Academic Press, 1974.

Cools, A. R. Physiological significance of the striatal system: New light on an old concept. In J. Szentagothai, J. Hamori, & M. Palkovits (Eds.), *Proceedings of the international physiological sciences Congress* (Vol. 2). *Regulatory functions of the CNS subsystems.* New York: Pergamon Press, 1981. (a)

Cools, A. R. Aspects and prospects of the concept of neurochemical and cerebral organization of aggression: Introduction of new research strategies in brain and behaviour studies. In D. Benton & P. Brain (Eds.), *Biology of aggression.* The Netherlands: Sythoff & Noordhoff International Publishing, 1981. (b)

Cools, A. R., & Bercken, J. H. L. van den. Cerebral organization of behaviour and the neostriatal function. In A. R. Cools, A. H. M. Lohman, & J. H. L. van den Bercken (Eds.),

Psychobiology of the striatum. Amsterdam: Elsevier North-Holland, 1977.

Davenport, R. K. Some behavioral disturbances of great apes in captivity. In D. A. Hamburg & E. R. McCown (Eds.), *The great apes. Perspectives on human evolution,* (Vol. V). Menlo Park, CA: The Benjamin/Cummings Publishing Company, 1979.

Dawkins, R. Hierarchical organization: A candidate principle for ethology. In P. P. G. Bateson & R. A. Hinde (Eds.), *Growing points in ethology.* Cambridge: Cambridge University Press, 1976.

Dienske, H., & Metz, H. A. J. Mother-infant body contact in macaques. A time interval analysis. *Biology of Behaviour,* 1977, *2,* 3–37.

Duffy, F. H., Snodgrass, S. R., Burchfiel, J. L., & Conway, J. L. Bicuculline reversal of deprivation amblyopia in the cat. *Nature,* 1976, *260,* 256–257.

Egan, P. J. Object-play in cats. In J. S. Bruner, A. Jolly, & K. Sylva (Eds.), *Play—Its role in development and evolution.* New York: Penguin Books, 1976.

Eibl-Eibesfeldt, I. Beitrage zur Biologie der Haus- und der Ahrenmaus nebst einigen Beobachtungen an anderen Nagern. *Zeitschrift für Tierpsychologie,* 1950, *7,* 558–587.

Eibl-Eibesfeldt, I. Beobachtungen zur Fortpflanzungsbiologie und Jugendentwicklung des Eichhörnchens (Sciurus vulgaris L.). *Zeitschrift für Tierpsychologie,* 1951, *8,* 370–400. (a)

Eibl-Eibesfeldt, I. Gefangenschaftsbeobachtungen an der persischen Wüstenmaus (Meriones persicus persicus Blanford): Ein Beitrag zur vergleichenden Ethologie der Nager. *Zeitschrift für Tierpsychologie,* 1951, *8,* 400–423. (b)

Elliott, J., & Connolly, K. Hierarchical structure in skill development. In K. Connolly & J. Brunner (Eds.), *The growth of competence.* London: Academic Press, 1974.

Escalona, S. K. *The roots of individuality.* London: Tavistock Publications, 1968.

Escalona, S. K. The differential impact of environmental conditions as a function of different reaction patterns in infancy. In J. C. Westman (Ed.), *Individual differences in children.* London: Wiley, 1973.

Fagen, R. M., & Goldman, R. N. Behavioural catalogue analysis methods. *Animal Behaviour,* 1977, *25,* 261–274.

Fentress, J. C. Behavioral networks and the simpler systems approach. In J. C. Fentress (Ed.), *Simpler networks and behavior.* Sunderland, MA: Sinauer Associates, Inc., 1976. (a)

Fentress, J. C. System and mechanism in behavioral biology. In J. C. Fentress (Ed.), *Simpler networks and behavior.* Sunderland, MA: Sinauer Associates, Inc., 1976. (b)

Fentress, J. C. How can behavior be studied from a neuro-ethological perspective? In H. M. Pinsker & W. D. Willis, Jr. (Eds.), *Information processing in the nervous system.* New York: Raven Press, 1980.

Fentress, J. C. Ethological models of hierarchy and patterning of species specific behavior. In E. Satinoff & P. Teitelbaum (Eds.), *Handbook of behavioral neurobiology: Volume 6, Motivation.* New York: Plenum Press, 1983.

Fouts, R. S. Acquisition and testing of gestural signs in four young chimpanzees. *Science,* 1973, *180,* 978–980.

Freeman, N. C. G., & Rosenblatt, J. S. The interrelationship between thermal and olfactory stimulation in the development of home orientation in newborn kittens. *Developmental Psychobiology,* 1978, *11,* 437–457.

Gardner, R. A., & Gardner, B. T. Teaching sign language to a chimpanzee. *Science,* 1969, *165,* 664–672.

Gardner, R. A., & Gardner, B. T. Comparative psychology and language acquisition. *Annals of the New York Academy of Sciences,* 1978, *309,* 37–76.

Gauthier-Pilters, H. Einige Beobachtungen zum Droh, Angriffs, und Kampfverhalten des Dromedarhengstes, sowie über Geburt und Verhaltensentwicklung des Jungtieres, in der nordwestlichen Sahara. *Zeitschrift für Tierpsychologie,* 1959, *16,* 593–604.

Geber, M. The psycho-motor development of African children in the first year and the influence of maternal behavior. *Journal of Social Psychology,* 1958, *47,* 185–195.

Gesell, A. *The embryology of behavior.* New York: Harper, 1945.

Golani, I. Homeostatic motor processes in mammalian interactions: A choreography of display. In P. P. G. Bateson & P. H. Klopfer (Eds.), *Perspectives in ethology* (Vol. 2). New York: Plenum Press, 1976.

Golani, I., Wolgin, D. L., & Teitelbaum, Ph. A proposed natural geometry of recovery from akinesia in the lateral hypothalamic rat. *Brain Research,* 1979, *164,* 237–267.

Goldman, P. S. Maturation of the mammalian nervous system and the ontogeny of behavior. In J. S. Rosenblatt, R. A. Hinde, E. Shaw, & C. Beer (Eds.), *Advances in the study of behavior.* New York: Academic Press, 1976.

Gould, S. J. *Ontogeny and phylogeny.* Cambridge, MA: The Belknap Press of Harvard University Press, 1977.

Goy, R. W. Reproductive behavior in mammals. In C. W. Lloyd (Ed.), *Human reproduction and sexual behavior.* Philadelphia, PA: Lea and Febiger, 1964.

Goy, R. W., & Goldfoot, D. A. Experiential and hormonal factors influencing development of sexual behavior in the male rhesus monkey. In *The neurosciences, Third study program.* Cambridge, MA: MIT Press, 1973.

Grant, E. C. An ethological description of non-verbal behaviour during interviews. *British Journal of Medical Psychology,* 1968, *41,* 177–184.

Grau, C., Delgado-Garcia, J. M., Garcia-Austt, E., & Delgado, J. M. R. Short rhythms in monkey behaviour. *I.R.C.S. Medical Science: Neurobiology and Neuropsychology; Physiology; Psychology;* 1975, *3,* 139.

Greenfield, P. M. Structural parallels between language and action in development. In A. Lock (Ed.), *Action, gesture, and symbol: The emergence of language.* New York: Academic Press, 1978.

Griffin, D. R. *The question of animal awareness.* New York: Rockefeller University Press, 1976.

Hailman, J. P. The ontogeny of an instinct. *Behaviour Supplement XV,* 1967.

Hall, W. G., & Rosenblatt, J. S. Suckling behavior and intake control in the developing rat pup. *Journal of Comparative and Physiological Psychology,* 1977, *91,* 1232–1247.

Hanby, J. Sociosexual development in primates. In P. P. G. Bateson & P. H. Klopfer (Eds.), *Perspectives in ethology* (Vol. 2). New York: Plenum Press, 1976.

Hayes, C. *The ape in our house.* New York: Harper, 1951.

Hayes, K. J., & Nissen, C. H. Higher mental functions of a home-raised chimpanzee. In A. M. Schrier & F. Stollnitz (Eds.), *Behavior of non-human primates* (Vol. 4). New York: Academic Press, 1971.

Hebb, D. O. Drives and the C.N.S. (conceptual nervous system). *Psychological Review,* 1955, *62,* 243–254.

Hinde, R. A. Appetitive behaviour, consummatory act, and the hierarchical organization of behaviour—with special reference to the great tit (Parus major). *Behaviour,* 1953, *5,* 189–224.

Hinde, R. A. *Animal behavior.* New York: McGraw-Hill, 1970.

Hinde, R. A. Development of social behavior. In A. Schrier & F. Stollnitz (Eds.), *Behavior of non-human primates* (Vol. 3). New York: Academic Press, 1971.

Hinde, R. A. *Biological bases of human social behavior.* New York: McGraw-Hill, 1974.

Hinde, R. A., & Spencer-Booth, Y. The behaviour of socially living rhesus monkeys in their first two and a half years. *Animal Behaviour,* 1967, *15,* 169–196.

Hinde, R. A., & Stevenson-Hinde, J. *Constraints on learning.* New York: Academic Press, 1973.

Hofer, M. A. Hidden regulatory processes in early social relationships. In P. P. G. Bateson & P. H. Klopfer (Eds.), *Perspectives in ethology* (Vol. 3): *Social behavior.* New York: Plenum Press, 1978.

Holst, E. von, & Mittelstaedt, H. Das Reafferenzprinzip. *Naturwissenschaft,* 1950, *47,* 409–422.

Hooff, J. A. R. A. M. van. Aspecten van het sociale gedrag en de communicatie bij humane en hogere niet-humane primaten. Unpublished doctoral dissertation, University of Utrecht, 1971.

Humphrey, T. Postnatal repetition of prenatal activity sequences with some suggestions of their neuro-anatomical basis. In R. J. Robinson (Ed.), *Brain and early behaviour.* London: Academic Press, 1969.

Hutt, S. J., & Hutt, C. *Direct observation and measurement of behavior.* Springfield, IL: Charles C. Thomas, 1970.

Ingram, D. Sensori-motor intelligence and language development. In A. Lock (Ed.), *Action, gesture, and symbol: The emergence of language.* London: Academic Press, 1978.

Jeddi, E. Contact comfort and behavioral thermoregulation. *Physiology and Behavior,* 1970, *5,* 1487-1493.

Jeddi, E. Thermoregulatory efficiency of neonatal rabbit search for fur comfort contact. *International Journal of Biometeorology,* 1971, *15,* 337-341.

Kagan, J. The growth of the face schema: Theoretical significance and methodological issues. In J. Hellmuth (Ed.), *The exceptional infant* (Vol. 1). Seattle WA: Special Child Publications, 1967.

Kagan, J. Attention and psychological change in the young child. *Science,* 1970, *170,* 826-832.

Kagan, J. Do infants think? *Scientific American,* 1972, *226,* 74-82.

Kagan, J. Discrepancy, temperament, and infant distress. In M. Lewis & L. A. Rosenblum (Eds.), *The origins of fear.* New York: Wiley, 1974.

Kelleher, R. T. Stimulus producing responses in chimpanzees. *Journal for the Experimental Analysis of Behavior,* 1958, *1,* 1.

King, M. C., & Wilson, A. C. Evolution at two levels in humans and chimpanzees. *Science,* 1975, *188,* 107-116.

Klopfer, P. H. *An introduction to animal behavior: Ethology's first century.* Englewood Cliffs, NJ: Prentice-Hall. 1974.

Koffka, K. *The growth of the mind.* New York: Harcourt, Brace, and Co., Inc., 1924.

Konner, M. J. Aspects of the developmental ethology of a foraging people. In N. Blurton Jones (Ed.), *Ethological studies of child behaviour.* London: Cambridge University Press, 1972.

Konner, M. J., & Worthman, C. Nursing frequency, gonadal function, and birth spacing among !Kung hunter-gatherers. *Science,* 1980, *207,* 788-791.

Koopmans-van Beinum, F. J., & Stelt, J. M. van der. Early stages of infant speech development. *Proceedings from the Institute of Phonetic Sciences of the University of Amsterdam,* 1979, *5,* 30-43.

Korner, A. F. Individual differences at birth: Implications for early experience and later development. *American Journal of Orthopsychiatry,* 1971, *41,* 608-619.

Korner, A. F., & Thoman, E. Visual alertness in neonates as evoked by maternal care. *Journal of Experimental Child Psychology,* 1970, *10,* 67-78.

Kortlandt, A. Eine Übersicht der angeborenen Verhaltungsweisen des mittel-europäischen Kormorans (Phalacrocorax carbo sinensis [Shaw & Nodd.]), ihre Funktion, ontogenetische Entwicklung und phylogenetische Herkunft. *Archives Neerlandaises de Zoologie,* 1940, *4,* 401-442. (a)

Kortlandt, A. Wechselwirkung zwischen Instinkten. *Archives Neerlandaises de Zoologie,* 1940, *4,* 443-520. (b)

Kortlandt, A. Aspects and prospects of the concept of instinct (vicissitudes of the hierarchy theory). *Archives Neerlandaises de Zoologie,* 1955, *11,* 155-284.

Kovach, J. K., & Kling, A. Mechanisms of neonate sucking behaviour in the kitten. *Animal Behaviour,* 1967, *15,* 91-101.

Kruijt, J.P. Ontogeny of social behavior in Burmese red junglefowl (Gallus gallus spadiceus). *Behaviour Supplement XII,* 1964.

Laidler, K. Language in the Orang-utan. In A. Lock (Ed.), *Action, gesture, and symbol: The emergence of language.* London: Academic Press, 1978.

Lashley, K. S. The problem of serial order in behavior. In L. A. Jeffres (Ed.), *Cerebral mechanisms in behavior: The Hixon symposium.* New York: Wiley, 1951.

Lawick-Goodall, J. van. *My friends the wild chimpanzees.* Washington, DC: The National Geographic Society, 1967. (a)

Lawick-Goodall, J. van. Mother-offspring relationships in free-ranging chimpanzees. In D. Morris (Ed.), *Primate ethology.* London: Weidenfeld and Nicolson, 1967. (b)

Lawick-Goodall, J. van. The behaviour of free-living chimpanzees in the Gombe Stream Reserve. *Animal Behaviour Monographs,* 1968, *1,* 161–311.

Lawick-Goodall, J. van. *In the shadow of man.* Boston, MA: Houghton Mifflin Company, 1971.

Lawick-Goodall, J. van. Cultural elements in a chimpanzee community. *Symposium of the Fourth International Congress of Primatology,* 1973, *1,* 144–184.

Lempers, J. D., Flavell, E. R., & Flavell, J. H. The development in very young children of tacit knowledge concerning visual perception. *Genetic Psychology Monographs,* 1977, *95,* 3–53.

Lewis, W. C. Coital movements in the first year of life. *International Journal of Psychoanalysis,* 1965, *46,* 372–374.

Lewis, M. Infants' responses to facial stimuli during the first year of life. *Developmental Psychology,* 1969, *1,* 75–86.

Lewis, M., & Brooks, J. Self, other, and fear: Infants' reactions to people. In M. Lewis & L. A. Rosenblum (Eds.), *The origins of fear.* New York: Wiley, 1974.

Lewis, M., & Rosenblum, L. A. *The origins of fear.* New York: Wiley, 1974.

Lewkowicz, D. J., & Turkewitz, G. Intersensory interaction in newborns: Modification of visual preferences following the exposure to sound. *Child Development,* 1981, *52,* 827–832.

Lock, A. *Action, gesture, and symbol: The emergence of language.* London: Academic Press, 1978.

Looft, W. R., & Svoboda, C. P. Structuralism in cognitive developmental psychology: Past, contemporary, and future perspectives. In K. F. Riegel & G. C. Rosenwald (Eds.), *Structure and transformation.* New York: Wiley, 1975.

Marsden, C. D., Merton, P. A., Morton, H. B., & Adam, J. E. R. The role of afferent feedback in the regulation of movement. In D. J. Chivers & J. Herbert (Eds.), *Recent advances in primatology* (Vol. 1): *Behaviour.* London: Academic Press, 1978.

Marshall, J. C., Newcombe, F. G., Battison, R. M., Fromkin, V. A., Heeschen, C. F. E., Pattee, H. H., Ploog, D. W., Plooij, F. X. Weniger, D. & Zaidel, E. The structuring of language by biological and neurological processes, group report 4. In U. Bellugi & M. Studdert-Kennedy (Eds.), *Sign language and spoken language: Biological constraints on linguistic form.* Basel, Switzerland: Verlag Chemie, 1980.

McFarland, D. J. *Feedback mechanisms in animal behaviour.* London: Academic Press, 1971.

McFarlane, J. A. Olfaction in the development of social preferences in the human neonate. In R. Porter & M. O'Connor (Eds.), *Parent-infant interaction* (Ciba Foundation Symposium 33). Amsterdam, Elsevier, 1975.

McCall, R. B., Eichorn, D. H., & Hogarty, P. S. Transitions in early mental development. *Monographs of the Society for Research in Child Development,* *42*(3) (Serial No. 171), 1977.

McGuire, I., & Turkewitz, G. Visually elicited finger-movements in infants. *Child Development,* 1978, *49,* 362–370.

Menzel, E. W., Jr. Patterns of responsiveness in chimpanzees reared through infancy under conditions of environmental restriction. *Psychologische Forschung,* 1964, *27,* 337–365.

Metz, J. A. J. Stochastic models for the temporal fine structure of behaviour sequences. In

D. J. McFarland (Ed.), *Motivational control systems analysis*. London: Academic Press, 1974.

Metz, J. A. J. Modeling animal behaviour by finite Markov systems. *Proceedings of the IFAC symposium on control mechanisms in bio- and ecosystems* (Vol. 5). Leipzig: International Federation of Automatic Control, 1977.

Miller, G., Galanter, E., & Pribram, K. *Plans and the structure of behavior*. New York: Holt, Rinehart, & Winston, 1960.

Morath, M. The four-hour feeding rhythm of the baby as a free running endogenously regulated rhythm. *International Journal of Chrono-biology*, 1974, *2*, 39–45.

Morgan, G. A., & Ricciuti, H. N. Infants responses to strangers during the first year. In B. M. Foss (Ed.), *Determinants of infant behaviour*. London: Methuen, 1969.

Mounoud, P. The development of systems of representation and treatment in the child. In B. Inhelder & H. Chipman (Eds.), *Piaget and his school. A reader in developmental psychology*. Berlin: Springer-Verlag, 1976.

Napier, J. R., & Napier, P. H. *A handbook of living primates*. London: Academic Press, 1967.

Nash, L. T. The development of the mother-infant relationship in wild baboons (Papio anubus). *Animal Behaviour*, 1978, *26*, 746–759.

Nicolson, N. A. A comparison of early behavior development in wild and captive chimpanzees. In S. Chevalier-Skolnikoff & F. E. Poirir, (Eds.), *Primate bio-social development: Biological, social and ecological determinants*. New York: Garland Publishing Inc., 1977.

Oakley, D. A., & Plotkin, H. C. Ontogeny of spontaneous locomotor activity in rabbit, rat and guinea pig. *Journal for Comparative and Physiological Psychology*, 1975, *89*, 267–273.

Oster, H. Facial expression and affect development. In M. Lewis & L. A. Rosenblum (Eds.), *Development of affect*. New York: Plenum Press, 1978.

Oster, H., & Ekman, P. Facial behavior in child development. In A. Collins (Ed.), *Minnesota symposia on child psychology* (Vol. 11). Hillsdale, NJ: Lawrence Erlbaum Associates, 1978.

Paine, R. S. Neurological examinations of infants and children. *Pediatric Clinics of North America*, 1960, *7*, 471.

Papousek, H., & Papousek, M. Mothering and the cognitive head-start: Psychobiological considerations. In H. R. Schaffer (Ed.), *Studies in mother-infant interaction*. London: Academic Press, 1977.

Parker, C. E. Behavioral diversity in ten species of nonhuman primates. *Journal of Comparative and Physiological Psychology*, 1974, *87*, 930–937.

Parmelee, A. H. The ontogeny of sleep patterns and associated periodicities in infants. *Prenatal and Postnatal Development of the Human Brain*, 1973, *13*, 298–311.

Patterson, F. Conversations with a gorilla. *National Geographic*, 1978, *154(4)*, 438–465. (a)

Patterson, F. The gesture of a gorilla: Language acquisition in another pongid. *Brain and Language*, 1978, *5*, 72–97. (b)

Peiper, A. Instinkt und angeborenes Schema beim Säugling. *Zeitschrift fur Tierpsychologie*, 1951, *8*, 449–456.

Peiper, A. *Cerebral function in infancy and childhood*. New York: Consultants Bureau, 1963.

Phoenix, C. D. Sexual behavior of laboratory- and wild-born male rhesus monkeys. *Hormones and Behavior*, 1978, *10*, 178–192.

Piaget, J. *The origins of intelligence in children*. New York: International University Press, 1952.

Piaget, J. *The construction of reality in the child*. New York: Basic Books, 1954.

Piaget, J., & Inhelder, B. *The psychology of the child*. New York: Basic Books, 1969.

Plooij, F. X. Number concept in a chimpanzee. Unpublished manuscript, Universities of Amsterdam and Nijmegen, 1970.

Plooij, F. X. In het voetspoor van de chimpansee. *Vakblad voor Biologen,* 1974, *54(22),* 362–366.

Plooij, F. X. Some basic traits of language in wild chimpanzees. In A. Lock (Ed.), *Action, gesture, and symbol: The emergence of language.* London: Academic Press, 1978. (a)

Plooij, F. X. Ontwikkeling van preverbale communicatie in de moeder-kind interaktie: Methodologische aspekten. In F. J. Mönks & P. G. Heymans (Eds.), *Communicatie en interaktie bij het jonge kind.* Nijmegen: Holland: Dekker en van de Vegt, 1978. (b) (English translation available upon request)

Plooij, F. X. How wild chimpanzee babies trigger the onset of mother-infant play and what the mother makes of it. In M. Bullowa (Ed.), *Before speech: The beginning of interpersonal communication.* London: Cambridge University Press, 1979.

Plooij, F. X. *The behavioural development of free-living chimpanzee babies and infants.* Unpublished doctoral dissertation, Groningen, 1980.

Polit, A., & Bizzi, E. Characteristics of motor programs underlying arm movements in monkeys. *Journal of Neurophysiology,* 1979, *42,* 183–194.

Pond, C. M. The significance of lactation in the evolution of mammals. *Evolution,* 1977, *31,* 177–199.

Powers, W. T. *Behavior: The control of perception.* Chicago, IL: Aldine Publishing Co., 1973.

Prechtl, H. F. R. Die Kletterbewegungen beim Säugling. *Monatschrift für Kinderheilkunde,* 1953, *101*(12), 519–521.

Prechtl, H. F. R. The directed head turning response and allied movements of the human baby. *Behaviour,* 1958, *13,* 212–242.

Prechtl, H. F. R. The behavioral state of the newborn infant (a review). Duivenvoorde lecture. *Brain Research,* 1974, *76,* 185–212.

Prechtl, H. F. R., & Schleidt, W. M. Auslösende und steuernde Mechanismen des Saugaktes. *Zeitschrift für Vergleichende Physiologie,* 1950, *32,* 257–262.

Prechtl, H. F. R., & Schleidt, W. M. Auslösende und steuernde Mechanismen des Saugaktes. *Zeitschrift für Vergleichende Physiologie,* 1951, *33,* 53–62.

Prechtl, H. F. R., & Beintema, D. *The neurological examination of the full-term newborn infant.* London: The Spastics Society Medical Education and Information Unit in association with William Heinemann Medical Books, Ltd., 1964.

Premack, D. On the assessment of language competence in the chimpanzee. In A. M. Schrier & F. Stollnitz (Eds.), *Behaviour of non-human primates* (Vol. 4). London: Academic Press, 1971.

Pribram, K. H. Self-consciousness and intentionality. In G. E. Schwartz & D. Shapiro (Eds.), *Consciousness and self-regulation* (Vol. 1). London: Wiley, 1976.

Pusey, A. Age changes in the mother-offspring association of wild chimpanzees. In D. J. Chivers & J. Herbert (Eds.), *Recent advances in primatology* (Vol. 1). London: Academic Press, 1978.

Pusey, A. E. Inbreeding avoidance in chimpanzees. *Animal Behaviour,* 1980, *28,* 543–552.

Redshaw, M. Cognitive development in human and gorilla infants. *Journal of Human Evolution,* 1978, *7,* 133–141.

Resko, J. A. The relationship between fetal hormones and the differentiation of the central nervous system in primates. In W. Montagna & W. A. Sadler (Eds.), *Reproductive behavior.* New York: Plenum Press, 1973.

Resko, J. A. Sex steroids in the circulation of the fetal and neonatal rhesus monkey: A comparison between male and female fetuses. *Inserm,* 1974, *32,* 195–204.

Rheingold, H. L. General issues in the study of fear, section I. In M. Lewis & L. A. Rosenblum (Eds.), *The origins of fear.* New York: Wiley, 1974.

Riesen, A. H., & Kinder, E. F. *Postural development of infant chimpanzees.* New Haven, CT: Yale University Press, 1952.

Rijt-Plooij, H. H. C. van de. Mother-infant relations in free-living chimpanzees of the Gombe

Stream National Park, Tanzania. Unpublished doctoral dissertation, Cambridge, 1982.

Rosenblatt, J. S. Stages in the early behavioral development of altricial young of selected species of non-primate mammals. In P. P. G. Bateson & R. A. Hinde, (Eds.), *Growing points in ethology*. Cambridge: Cambridge University Press, 1976.

Rumbaugh, D. M., Gill, T. V., & Glaserfield, E. von. Reading and sentence completion by a chimpanzee. *Science*, 1973, *182*, 731–733.

Salapatek, P. Pattern perception in early infancy. In L. B. Cohen & P. Salapatek (Eds.), *Infant perception: From sensation to cognition* (Vol. 1): *Basic visual processes*. New York: Academic Press, 1975.

Sander, L. W. Regulation and organization in the early infant-caretaker system. In R. J. Robinson (Ed.), *Brain and early behaviour*. London: Academic Press, 1969.

Sander, L. W. Infant and caretaking environment. Investigation and conceptualization of adaptive behavior in a system of increasing complexity. In E. J. Anthony (Ed.), *Explorations in child psychiatry*. New York: Plenum Press, 1975.

Sander, L. W. Regulation of exchange in the infant caretaker system: A viewpoint of the ontogeny of "structures". *Downstate Series of Research in Psychiatry and Psychology*, 1977, *1*, 13–34.

Sander, L. W., Julia, H. L., Stechler, G., & Burns, P. Continuous 24-hour interactional monitoring in infants reared in two caretaking environments. *Psychosomatic Medicine*, 1972, *34*, 270–282.

Schaffer, H. R. The onset of fear of strangers and the incongruity hypothesis. *Journal of Child Psychology and Psychiatry*, 1966, *7*, 95–106.

Schaffer, H. R. Cognitive structure and early social behaviour. In H. R. Schaffer (Ed.), *The origins of human social relations*. London: Academic Press, 1971.

Schaffer, H. R. The multivariate approach to early learning. In R. A. Hinde & J. Stevenson-Hinde (Eds.), *Constraints on learning*. New York: Academic Press, 1973.

Schaffer, H. R. Cognitive components of the infant's response to strangeness. In N. Lewis & L. A. Rosenblum (Eds.), *The origins of fear*. New York: Wiley, 1974.

Schaffer, H. R. *Studies in mother-infant interaction*. London: Academic Press, 1977.

Schaffer, H. R., & Emerson, P. E. The development of social attachments in infancy. *Monographs of the Society for Research in Child Development*, 1964, *29*, (Number 3).

Schenkel, R. Zur Ontogenese des Verhaltens bei Gorilla und Mensch. *Zeitschrift für Morphologische Anthropologie*, 1964, *54*, 233–259.

Schneider, K. M. Aus der Jugendentwicklung einer künstlich aufgezogenen Schimpansin III. Vom Verhalten: A. die Bewegungsweisen der ersten 10 Monate. *Zeitschrift für Tierpsychologie*, 1950, *7*, 485–558.

Schneirla, T. C. Levels in the psychological capacities of animals. In R. W. Sellars, V. J. McGill, & M. Farber (Eds.), *Philosophy for the future: The quest of modern materialism*. New York: The Macmillan Company, 1949.

Schneirla, T. C. The concept of levels in the study of social phenomena. In M. Sherif & C. Scherif (Eds.), *Groups in harmony and tension*. New York: Harper and Brothers, 1953.

Schneirla, T. C. Aspects of stimulation and organization in approach-withdrawal processes underlying vertebrate behavioral development. In D. S. Lehrman, R. Hinde, & E. Shaw (Eds.), *Advances in the study of behavior*. New York: Academic Press, 1965.

Schneirla, T. C. Observation and experimentation in the field study of behavior. In L. R. Aronson, E. Tobach, J. S. Rosenblatt, & D. S. Lehrman (Eds.), *Selected writings of T. C. Schneirla*. San Francisco, CA: W. H. Freeman and Co., 1972.

Shafton, A. *Conditions of awareness*. Portland, OR: Riverstone Press, 1976.

Siegel, S. *Nonparametric statistics for the behavioral sciences*. New York: McGraw-Hill, 1956.

Simpson, M. J. A. Social displays and the recognition of individuals. In P. P. G. Bateson & P. H. Klopfer (Eds.), *Perspectives in ethology* (Vol. 1). New York: Plenum Press, 1974.

Simpson, M. J. A. Daytime rest and activity in socially living rhesus monkey infants. *Animal Behaviour,* 1979, *27,* 602–612.

Simpson, M. J. A., & Simpson, A. E. One-zero and scan methods for sampling behaviour. *Animal Behaviour,* 1977, *25,* 726–731.

Sinclair, H. Sensorimotor action patterns as a condition for the acquisition of syntax. In E. Ingram & R. Huxley (Eds.), *Language acquisition: Models and methods.* New York, Academic Press, 1971.

Sokolov, E. N. Neuronal models and the orienting influence. In M. A. B. Brazier (Ed.), *The central nervous system and behavior* (Vol. 3). New York: Josiah Macy, Jr. Foundation, 1960.

Starck, D. The skull of the fetal chimpanzee (chondocranium and development of osteocranium). In G. H. Bourne (Ed.), *The chimpanzee* (Vol. 6). Basel, Switzerland: Karger, 1973.

Steinbacher, G. Geburt und Kindheit eines Schimpansen. *Zeitschrift für Teirpsychologie,* 1941, *4,* 188–203.

Sterman, M. B., & Hoppenbrouwers, T. The development of sleep-waking and rest-activity patterns from fetus to adult in man. In M. B. Sterman, D. J. MacGinty, & A. M. Adinoldi (Eds.), *Brain development and behavior.* New York: Academic Press, 1971.

Stern, E., Parmelee, A. H., & Harris, M. Sleep state periodicity in prematures and young infants. *Developmental Psychobiology,* 1973, *6,* 357–365.

Struhsaker, T. T. Auditory communication among vervet monkeys. In S. A. Altmann (Ed.), *Social communication among primates.* Chicago, IL: University of Chicago Press, 1967.

Struhsaker, T. T. Social behavior of mother and infant vervet monkeys (Cercopithecus aethiops). *Animal Behaviour,* 1971, *19,* 233–250.

Tavolga, W. N. Application of the concept of levels of organization to the study of animal communication. In L. Krames, P. Pliner, & T. Alloway, (Eds.), *Advances in the study of communication and affect* (Vol. 1): *Nonverbal communication.* New York: Plenum Press, 1974.

Tinbergen, N. An objectivistic study of the innate behavior of animals. *Bibliotheca Biotheoretica,* 1942, *1,* 39–98 (Series D).

Tinbergen, N. The hierarchical organization of nervous mechanisms underlying instinctive behavior. *Symposia of the Society for Experimental Biology,* 1950, *4,* 305–312.

Tinbergen, N. *The study of instinct.* New York: Oxford University Press, 1951. (Second printing, 1974).

Tinbergen, N. On aims and methods of ethology. *Zeitschrift für Teirpsychologie,* 1963, *20,* 410–433.

Touwen, B. *Neurological development in infancy* (Clinics in Developmental Medicine No. 58). London: William Heinemann Medical Books, Ltd., 1976.

Touwen, B. Variability and stereotypy in normal and deviant development. In J. Apley (Ed.), *Care of the handicapped child.* London: William Heinemann Medical Books Ltd.

Trevarthen, C. Descriptive analyses of infant communicative behavior. In H. R. Schaffer (Ed.), *Studies in mother-infant interaction.* London: Academic Press, 1977.

Trevarthen, C., & Hubley, P. Secondary intersubjectivity: Confidence, confiding and acts of meaning in the first year. In A. Lock (Ed.), *Action, gesture, and symbol: The emergence of language.* London: Academic Press, 1978.

Turkewitz, G., Moreau, T., Birch, H. G., & Davis, L. Relationships among responses in the human newborn: The non-association and non-equivalence among different indicators of responsiveness. *Psychophysiology,* 1971, *7,* 233–247.

Turney, T. H. Human neonatal and infant behavioral assessment scales being applied to chimpanzees. *Laboratory Primate Newsletter,* 1978, *17*(3), 14–15.

Tutin, C. E. G. *Mating patterns in a community of wild chimpanzees.* Unpublished doctoral dissertation, University of Edinburgh, 1975.

Tutin, C. E. G., & McGinnis, P. R. Sexual behavior of chimpanzees in the wild. In C. E. Graham (Ed.), *Reproductive biology of the great apes: Comparative and biomedical aspects.* New York: Academic Press, 1979.

Wallen, K., Bielert, C., & Slimp, J. Foot clasp mounting in the prepubertal rhesus monkey: Social and hormonal influences. In S. Chevalier-Skolnikoff & F. E. Poirier (Eds.), *Primate bio-social development: Biological, social and ecological determinants.* New York: Garland Publishing Inc., 1977.

Waters, E., Matas, L., & Sroufe, L. A. Infants' reactions to an approaching stranger: Description, validation and functional significance of wariness. *Child Development,* 1975, *46,* 348–356.

Watzlawick, P., Beavin, J. H., & Jackson, D. D. *Pragmatics of human communication.* New York: W. W. Norton and Co., 1967.

Weiss, P. Self-differentiation of the basic patterns of coordination. *Comparative Psychology Monographs,* 1941, *17,* 1–96.

Welker, W. I. Factors influencing aggregation of neonatal puppies. *Journal for Comparative and Physiological Psychology,* 1959, *52,* 376–380.

Welker, W. I. Ontogeny of play and exploratory behaviors: A definition of problems and a search for new conceptual solutions. In H. Moltz (Ed.), *The ontogeny of vertebrate behavior.* New York: Academic Press, 1971.

Werner, H. *Comparative psychology of mental development.* Chicago, IL: Follett, 1948.

Werner, H. *Einführung in die Entwicklungpsychologie.* Munich: Johann Ambrosius Barth, 1959

Whiten, A., Whiten, S., & Ibeh, A. Human infancy in Britain and Nigeria. *The Nigerian Field,* 1980, *45*(1), 21–26.

Wiener, N. *Cybernetics.* New York: Wiley, 1948.

Wood, S., Moriarty, K. M., Gardner, B. T., & Gardner, R. A. Object permanence in child and chimpanzee. *Animal Learning and Behavior,* 1980, *8,* 3–9.

Wrangham, R. W. Artificial feeding of chimpanzees and baboons in their natural habitat. *Animal Behaviour,* 1974, *22,* 83–93.

Wrangham, R. W. *The behavioural ecology of chimpanzees in Gombe National Park.* Unpublished doctoral dissertation, University of Cambridge, 1975.

Yerkes, R. M., & Tomilin, M. I. Mother-infant relations in chimpanzees. *Journal of Comparative Psychology,* 1935, *20,* 321–360.

Young, M., & Ziman, J. Cycles in social behaviour. *Nature,* 1971, *229,* 91–95.

Zegans, S., & Zegans, L. Fear of strangers in children and the orienting reaction. *Behavioral Science,* 1972, *17,* 407–419.

Zelazo, P. R., Zelazo, N. A., & Kolb, S. "Walking" in the newborn. *Science,* 1972, *176,* 314–315.

Zihlman, A. L., Cronin, J. E., Cramer, D. L., & Sarich, V. M. Pygmy chimpanzee as a possible prototype for the common ancestor of humans, chimpanzees, and gorillas. *Nature,* 1978, *275,* 744–746.

Author Index

Subject Index